THE END OF CHAR KWAY TEOW

AND OTHER HAWKER MYSTERIES

ieat · ishoot · ipost

THE END OF
CHAR KWAY TEOW
AND OTHER HAWKER MYSTERIES

DR. LESLIE TAY

WINNER OF ASIA PACIFIC'S BEST FOOD BLOG

EPIGRAM BOOKS / SINGAPORE

First edition
Copyright © Epigram Pte Ltd, 2010

Published by
Epigram Books
1008 Toa Payoh North #03-08
Singapore 318996
Tel: (65) 6292 4456
Fax: (65) 6292 4414
enquiry@epigram.com.sg
www.epigram.com.sg

10 9 8 7 6 5 4 3 2 1

Distributed by
MarketAsia Distributors
601 Sims Drive #04-05 Pan-I Complex
Singapore 387382
Tel: (65) 6744 8483
Fax: (65) 6744 8486
jl@marketasia.com.sg

Edited by Ruth Wan
Cover design by Stefany

Photography © Dr. Leslie Tay
Photograph of author by Nicholas Leong

Living Gallery picture (p6 and p11) courtesy of the
National Museum of Singapore

This book is supported under the National Heritage Board's
Heritage Industry Incentive Programme (Hi²P).

National Library Board, Singapore
Cataloguing-In-Publication Data
Tay, Leslie, 1969-
The End of Char Kway Teow and
Other Hawker Mysteries/
Leslie Tay, Ruth Wan.
Singapore: Epigram Books, 2010.
p. cm.
Includes index.
ISBN-13 : 978-981-08-6515-3 (pbk.)

1. Peddlers – Singapore – Guidebooks.
2. Singapore – Guidebooks. I. Tay, Leslie, 1969- II. Title.

TX907.5
647.955957 – dc22   OCN650751459

Printed in Singapore.

TO MY COLLEGE SWEETHEART,
WIFE AND
BEST FRIEND LISA.

CONTENTS

AN AMAZING LABOUR OF LOVE

I landed at Paya Lebar Airport from freezing Berlin in February 1978. As the door swung open, I hit a wall – 32°C and what appeared to be 100 percent humidity. I had finally arrived in Asia.

After clearing customs and immigration, I was off in a cab, which of course was not air-conditioned. A swift 15-minute ride later, there I was, entering a five-star hotel along Orchard Road. Peering outside, I saw the city, busy and bustling, and the locals munching away.

The next day, I was welcomed by a gleaming executive chef, who exclaimed, "Very busy, go up and eat first then we speak later." So, off I went to Hin's Heavenly Cookhouse. Of course, food was pre-ordered and arrived swiftly. It was an exotic feast – clear soup with quail eggs, jumbo prawns with the shells on, fried rice and of all nightmares, there was no fork and knife. I looked at a pair of chopsticks and a Chinese spoon. Observing all the diners around me, I tried to figure out how to eat with them. As I struggled, the diner next to me quietly moved out of shooting range.

A week later, I took a trip up north where I was introduced to chicken feet ("Can one really eat this?") and Chinese fondue, or steamboat as I later found out. And what is that prickly expensive fruit? Didn't anyone bother to close the lavatory? Nasi what? Lemak or alamak? And the sambal, wow. I fell in love, and till today that love story has never ended. In fact, it has flourished.

Fast forward, 32 years later. My prosperous frame is the best testimony of having fallen hopelessly in love with that ever present mistress of foods – "hawker food". Available in all shapes and sizes and at all costs, from 50 cents to $50, (yes, this version actually exists) and at all locations, from swanky Orchard Road to sweaty Sembawang Shipyard.

The search never stopped. Then recently, I took notice of Dr. Leslie Tay, who runs this blog on local food. Upon a chance meeting, I realised he was a genuine doctor, philanthropist, family man and a foodie who spends his free time researching local dishes. Leslie has done this for years and his collection of locations, dishes and their descriptions is an amazing labour of love.

Singapore is all about hawker food. It has always been a part of our DNA. But the age of mass production has arrived. This means shortcuts like ready-made pastes which make the food taste almost identical. It is a sad new world order but it is the reality. Yet, if we don't share and preserve one of the most famous traditions, born out of need and developed into a true craft, then what will happen in the future?

Therefore, I am a wholehearted supporter of Professor Tommy Koh, who recently tabled the idea of a culinary school for hawkers. Yes, this must be done, especially in this fast moving world before one of the great culinary heritages of the world is lost.

Keep the Singapore chicken rice alive as it is the equivalent of a national monument, a dish comparable to the national anthem. Have you ever met anyone that didn't enjoy this succulent dish? As far as I'm concerned, whether it's $5 (my portion size) of chicken rice or a $150 *poularde de bresse* with truffles, as long as the food is perfectly prepared, both have an equal standing. With one small exception – the former I can and am enjoying rather regularly.

This book makes an important contribution to Singapore's food heritage, not least for being a guide to the best of the best hawker stalls.

Bon appétit, or as we say here, selamat makan!

Peter A Knipp
Publisher, *Cuisine & Wine Asia* magazine and organiser, World Gourmet Summit

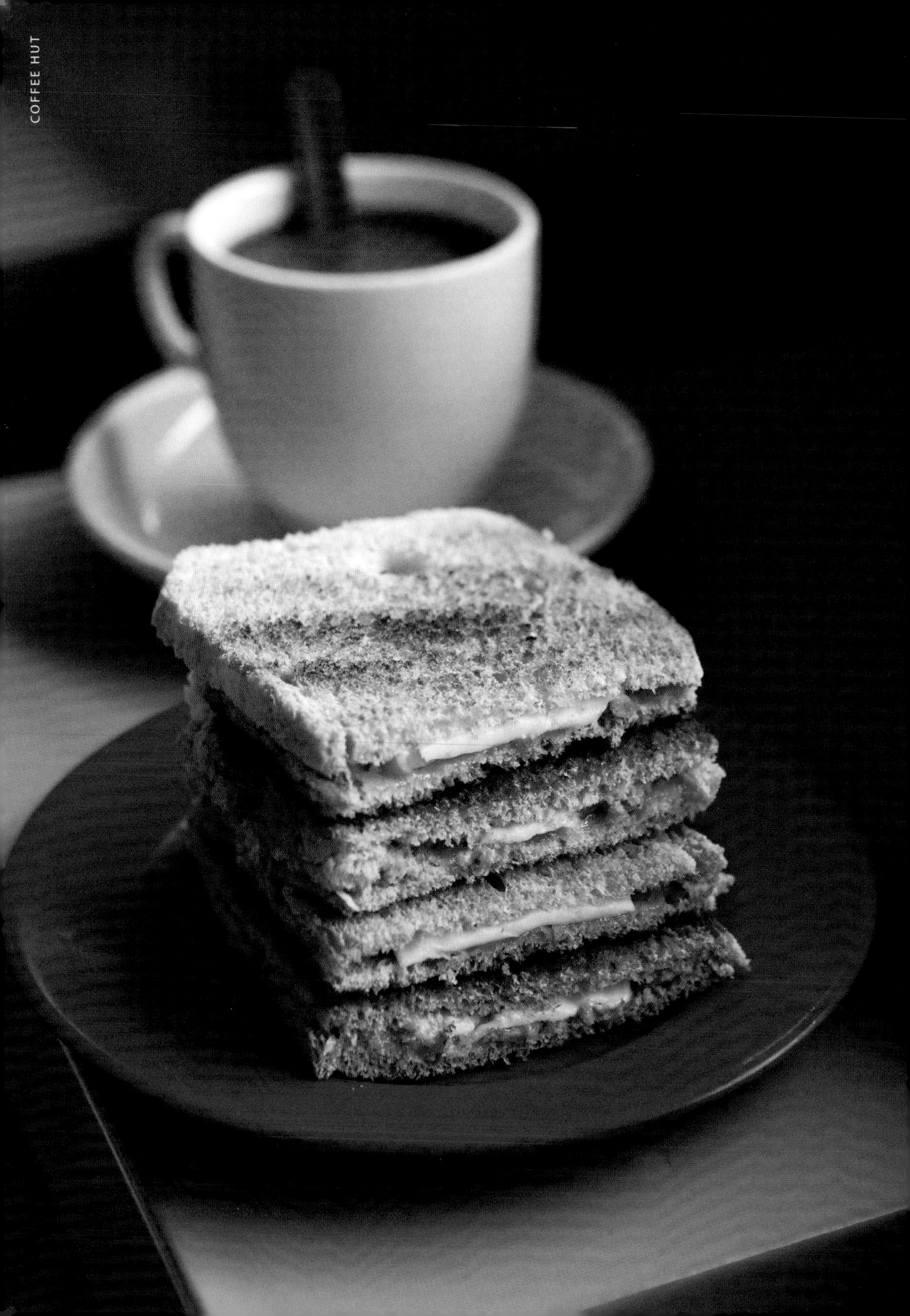

INTRODUCTION

I am a doctor and yes, I love food. For some reason, a lot of people think that doctors are people who only eat healthy food. OK, I do watch my diet, but when I see a plate of Hokkien mee with its glistening noodles and slightly charred bee hoon that has been infused with rich prawn stock, I succumb to its lure just like any other mortal. After all, I was a foodie before I became a doctor. So, if you prick me, will I not bleed? If you tickle me, will I not laugh? And if you give me a plate of Hokkien mee, will I not eat?

This is a book that I never planned to write. What I wrote over the last four years was a blog, an online diary of a few hundred of the best hawker stalls across our island where I went to eat, shoot photographs and post my thoughts online. Hence the blog's name: ieat, ishoot, ipost. Along the way, I spoke to hundreds of hawkers and recorded the oral histories of our hawker dishes. I asked them questions like why chwee kueh (water cake) is called chwee kueh, which part of the pig makes the best char siew (barbe-cued meat), and whether tariking (pulling) the tea makes it taste better. Their answers fascinated me and I recorded them down in the blog. What you have here, is all the interesting bits collected over four years, distilled into a book. Each chapter will deal with one particular hawker dish and end with a list of the best hawker stalls where you too can have your hawker food epiphany.

As I spoke with the hawkers, it became apparent to me that a lot of the dishes that we often take for granted are truly, uniquely Singaporean. Take Hokkien mee for example. This is a dish you will not find anywhere else in the world. Even the humble chwee kueh (water cake), which has its roots in Swatow, China, has evolved into a dish that is unrecognisable in its place of origin. As I listen to the personal stories of these hawkers, I am slowly weaving together a fabric of our society that has played a pivotal role in forging our nation's culture. Much of this information still exists only as oral histories, and I feel privileged to be able to document them.

Hawker food is no ordinary food. It is food that has fed our forefathers and provided simple sustenance for a developing nation. Hawker food is cheap, blue-collar food sold along the streets. It was cooked by migrants for migrants, each looking for a way to make a living in a foreign land. Our hawker food is neither elegant nor classy, but it embodies the essence of being Singaporean. Ask any Singaporean what he or she misses most about home and invariably, the answer would be laksa, prata, chicken rice or char kway teow.

Food has been my passion since I was weaned. I must have inherited it from my mother, who is an excellent cook. She earned her diploma as a Masterchef in Australia at the age of 50, graduating at the top of her class, which comprised mainly chefs half her age. I remember spending my child-hood in the kitchen observing her as she went through different obsessions – from pandan chiffon cakes to Black Forest cakes, bak changs (Chinese dumplings) to curry puffs, she made them all. That was how I first became fascinated with food and the art of cooking.

Growing up, one thing we never did much of was eat at hawker centres. At least, we never went all out to find the best hawker stalls Singapore had to offer. But when I settled back in Singapore after living overseas, I decided that I should try to find the best hawker stalls around. Finding such information online was difficult, and it frustrated me to look at mouth-watering hawker food on the Internet, but not have information about where to eat the best version of it. To counter this, my plan was to make sure each of my blog posts had a nice photo, a proper write-up, a rating, and the address and opening times of the hawker stall. And I made sure everything was catalogued properly for easy reference.

As an avid photographer, I decided that my photographs should aspire to induce drool, and drive the reader to develop an irresistible craving. I thought that if my write-up and photographs could get someone to go halfway across the island to eat something, I would have succeeded. Food photography has since taken off in a big way and it is not uncommon to see food bloggers lugging around DSLRs at hawker centres. My food photography workshops, which are sponsored by Canon, are always packed as more and more enthusiasts endeavour to join us.

ieatishootipost has evolved from being a personal blog to a community of foodies. We now have a burgeoning Facebook fan page of over 10,000 fans, an active forum, Twitter-kakis and over 6,500 readers logging in daily to check out the latest blog posts. We hold regular "makan sessions" where readers are invited to descend upon an appointed place to feast together. These "makan sessions" are where readers get to meet each other in person and befriend other foodies.

These friendships are what I will treasure long after I stop writing the blog. I got to know all of the *ieat* team members through the blog and quite a few have been supporting me since the very early days. Our makankakis have even gone on overseas trips together and I am looking forward to the day when *ieatishootipost* can claim to be a matchmaker for our very first foodie wedding!

Another group of people who have become my good friends are the hawkers themselves, many of whom have seen queues outside their stalls after being featured on the blog. This phenomenon has come to be known as the *"ieat* effect". One particular hawker Auntie was so happy that she even came to my clinic with New Year goodies to express her gratitude. I am really happy that I can help these hawkers and have such an impact on their lives.

I have always felt that as a community, we can make a difference in the lives of those who are less fortunate than ourselves. Each year, the *ieat* team organises events to raise support for various charities. This year, I travelled to Sandakan, Malaysia to see the plight of the displaced children who have no access to education or healthcare and returned with the resolve to help these children. With the support of our community, we are now looking at ways of raising awareness and support for these kids through the blog.

This book is my attempt to find the best of the best hawker food, and along the way discover Singapore's fascinating food culture. I hope it will become your companion in seeking out the best stalls to eat around Singapore.

Life is short and health is precious, so remember: never waste your calories on yucky food!

Dr. Leslie Tay

CHYE KEE CHWEE KUEH

THE SINGAPORE HAWKER SCENE

Nostalgia is a precious commodity in Singapore. In our fast-paced society where land is scarce, most places have a limited life span. So, you are not likely to find the old oak tree where Grandpa was supposed to meet Grandma and run away together. Many significant spots that my wife and I fondly remember from our dating days have either been renovated or demolished. Even Senior Minister Goh Chok Tong's old dating hotspot, the National Library at Stamford Road, is no more.

The hawker scene in Singapore has, likewise, undergone significant changes, much like the rest of our society. You can catch a glimpse of the past at the "Singapore Living Galleries: Food", a permanent exhibit at the National Museum of Singapore *(see pg 10)*. The exhibit takes you back to a time when hawkers hawked their food along the streets – balancing a pot of satay gravy on one end of a pole and a charcoal grill on the other end, shouting "Satay! Satay!" to get people's attention. I had always assumed that the word 'satay' is Malay in origin, but recently learnt that it actually derived from the Tamil word "sathai" which means "flesh", and it was the South Indian Muslims who brought the dish to South East Asia!

Over at the "Tok Tok mee" exhibit, I saw how the "Tok Tok mee" hawkers used to ply the streets of Singapore in their three wheel wooden carts. Their assistants would announce their presence by knocking on bamboo slabs and also help to take orders for the noodles. Once the noodles are cooked, they would deliver the piping hot bowls of noodles directly to the customer's doorstep! Yes, home delivery was alive and well in the good old days!

Hawkers have since been evacuated off the streets and relocated into hawker centres. But that was just the first phase. Now, we are seeing a second phase, where hawker centres are being upgraded into spanking clean, well-ventilated facilities, with clean restrooms to boot.

If you want to eat great food, you have to look for hawkers who are passionate and proud of their heritage and cooking. There are a few types of hawkers nowadays. You have those in food courts who are hired by a boss to run a stall. These hawkers won't know anything about the food they are serving. Then, you have the hawkers who merely buy factory-made stuff to sell – like most beancurd and ngoh hiang (fried pork rolls) hawkers. They are more like food traders rather than hawkers. But, most of the highly rated hawkers belong to a third category – they know their dish inside out, insist on having the best ingredients, and most of the time, this means that they prepare most of the food from scratch. These are the Uncles and Aunties who have been serving up fantastic meals at ridiculously affordable prices day in and day out, most of them work with a smile and a good sense of humour. Yet, as Singaporeans evolve and expectations rise, will we become hard pressed to find hawkers who passionately cook dishes passed down through generations?

I have made it my personal mission to support hawkers who are passionate about providing us with better quality hawker food. I just love the old Uncles at Bukit Merah View Food Centre who still insist on making their carrot cake from scratch, starting by grinding their own flour at the back of their stall. I also love the Teochew Ah Chiks and Ah Sohs at Lao Zhong Zhong who continue to make their ngoh hiang (fried pork rolls) fresh every day, despite the mass availability of factory-made ones. And how about the Uncle who sells the preeminent prawn mee at Pek Kio Market and Food Centre, blending six seafood ingredients to create a prawn soup that can hardly be found anywhere else, even in restaurants?

Another encouraging and exciting segment of the hawker community is also emerging. These are the young-and-upcoming hawkers. A new generation of hawkers who are energetic, innovative and creative with their food. It is always interesting when bankers turned hawkers, like Tina Tan from Hock Lam Street Beef Kway Teow at China Street, or Ho Kuen Loon from Funan Weng Ipoh Hor Fun, take their family's recipe and give it a new twist to keep up with the trends. Then there are what I call the Hawker Hunks, like the young muscular man who sells epok epok (Malay curry puffs) at Eunos Central. Such individuals provide eye candy while dishing out delicious food – what more could women want?

Finally, there are the hawkers who are willing to try out new dishes or flavours, sometimes at the suggestion of hungry and greedy customers, like myself! These hawkers span the generations. I have encountered enterprising young hawkers as well as passionate elderly hawkers who take on new risks and score success, like pork belly satay and Godzilla da pau (big pau).

We Singaporeans are an honest bunch. We know our faults and we openly admit them. Impatient, rude, unforgiving and downright kiasu (afraid of losing), we sigh in frustration when we experience graciousness in other societies and lament that we can't be the same. But hey, all is not lost. There is still a lot of goodness out there, and it is as close as the hawker that you buy your food from every day! If you want to see more graciousness in our society, it starts from yourself. And one of the first people I think we should start being more gracious to, is our humble hawker who works so hard everyday to feed us but often doesn't get the credit he or she deserves.

Before the 1960s, hawker centres were far and few between. Back then hawkers hawked their food out on the streets.

The scenario is recreated at the National Museum of Singapore under a permanent exhibition called Singapore Living Galleries. Here you can find food-related artefacts and sound installations that take you back to a time when satay and Hokkien mee were sold out of pushcarts, when the streets were filled with the sound of clanging woks and ladles, and hawkers called out to passers-by at the top of their voices from their makeshift stalls.

Among other things, the exhibition also showcases a wide variety of Chinese, Indian, Malay and Peranakan spices and includes an installation that allows you to sniff at their enticing aromas.

A must-see for those that are curious about the history of hawker food and how Singapore's street food culture reflects the nation's ethnic diversity.

National Museum of Singapore

93 Stamford Road, Singapore 178897

www.nationalmuseum.sg

Singapore History Gallery: 10am to 6pm daily

Singapore Living Galleries: 10am to 8pm daily

Access to the Singapore History Gallery and all Living Galleries:
adults $10.00, children (aged between 7 and 18) $5.00,
free admission for senior citizens (aged 60 and above),
students and full-time National Servicemen (NSFs).
Terms and conditions apply. The Living Galleries are also free
to all between 6pm and 8pm daily.

Wooden Peranakan Chinese
biscuit mould
1940s
XX-10593

Wooden Peranakan Chinese
cake mould
1940s
XX-0586

Wooden heng kueh mould
1940s
XX-0586

Wooden ang ku kueh mould
1940s
XX-0738

These are moulds for making different types of cakes and biscuits.

Peranakan Chinese biscuit mould
This is carved with overlapping Chinese coins, symbolic of prosperity and good luck.

Heng kueh (Tee bew glutinous rice cake with mung bean filling) mould
The paisley design symbolises long life and prosperity. The incised turtle motif represents
longevity. It is believed that if one eats the tail or head portions of the kueh, one will give
birth to a boy or girl respectively.

Peranakan Chinese cake mould
This is carved with decorative floral motifs.

Ang ku kueh / red turtle, glutinous rice flour cake with mung bean filling) mould
This is carved with a depiction of a turtle. Symbolic of longevity and a baby boy, it is used to
make cakes, devoted for prosperity, to celebrate special occasions such as infants reaching
their first month (full month celebration).

mbolic of
Chinese

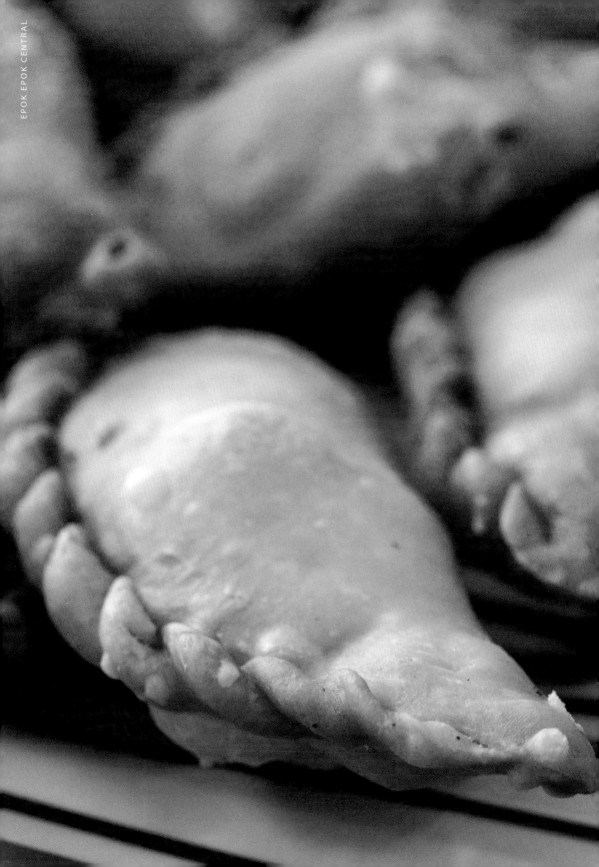

LOCAL LINGO

WHAT I SAY WHEN THE FOOD IS EXTREMELY TASTY AND REALLY HITS THE SPOT

phwaa say I say!

phwaa sayah I say ah!

sedap tasty

shiok really hits the spot

shiokadelicious shiok + delicious

shiokadoo shiok + yabba dabba doo

shiokadoodle doo figure it out yourself

TERMS OF ENDEARMENT USED ON PEOPLE, USUALLY HAWKERS

Ah Beng young Chinese man

Ah Chik Chinese uncle

Ah Hia Chinese older brother

Ah Mah Chinese grandma

Ah Peh Chinese old uncle

Ah Soh Chinese auntie

ang moh literally means "red hair", denotes a westerner

Auntie mature Chinese lady who probably has kids of her own

Food Nazi someone whose food is so good that he can afford to be nasty to everyone

Lao Ban Niang lady boss

Mak Cik Malay auntie

makankaki a portmanteau of makan (food) and kaki (friend) – a friend who you meet to eat with

Pak Cik Malay uncle

Uncle mature male, 40 and above or at least looks it

OTHER FOOD-RELATED TERMS

cze cha literally means, "cook fry", refers to a stall that sells cooked food of different styles

jerlak what you feel when you have overeaten

MSG stands for monosodium glutamate, the stuff that hawkers use as a shortcut to make their food tasty

umami a Japanese word for the fifth taste, which gives food its savoury, full-bodied flavour. MSG makes food umami

wok hei means "breath of wok", that unique smoky flavour when food is fried on a superheated wok

TYPES OF NOODLES

bee hoon thin rice vermicelli

kway teow flat rice sheet noodles

mee kia thin egg noodles

mee poh/mee pok flat egg noodles

BAK
CHOR
MEE

The End of Char Kway Teow

If we have friends from overseas coming to Singapore, how many of us would think of bringing them to eat bak chor mee? No, it is either chilli crab or chicken rice — but bak chor mee is a dish close to Singaporeans' hearts. Simple. Delicious. Underrated.

Whenever I meet Teochew stallholders, our conversation will invariably be in Teochew, and when asked why they are so popular, the standard answer is, "Chngee (fresh) ah, everything is chngee." The Teochew fussiness about freshness is a well-worn cultural trait – Teochews live near the river in Guangdong Province, so, unlike, for example, Szechuan cuisine, where the emphasis is on spices, Teochew cuisine is quite bland in comparison, emphasising on the freshness of ingredients.

One characteristic of good bak chor mee is of course, freshness. Teochew hawkers who pride themselves in making the best bak chor mee have always told me in typical Teochew hao lian (proud) fashion that they use the freshest black prawns, the freshest pork, the freshest everything.

And it does make a difference. Despite being, at its core, just a basic dish of noodles, pork and vinegar, bak chor mee is the third most favourite dish among Singaporeans, after Hokkien mee (#1) and chicken rice (#2), according to the polls done on my blog. If we have friends from overseas coming to Singapore, how many of us would think of bringing them to eat bak chor mee? No, it is either chilli crab or chicken rice – but bak chor mee is a dish close to Singaporeans' hearts. Simple. Delicious. Underrated. And above all, chngee (fresh). Very chngee.

Today, bak chor mee is still as good as it was in the past. People are always saying how good chicken rice, char kway teow or Hokkien mee was in the past. But for bak chor mee, I haven't heard many people complain that it was so much better in the past. Apart from freshness, bak chor mee is really about the noodles. So, you need to start with a good quality egg noodle. With each mouthful, you should be able to enjoy the aroma of the noodles that has been lightly flavoured by pork lard, with the vinegar just cutting through the oil and getting the salivary glands working. I prefer my noodles QQ (al dente), with a firm bite and sufficient curl to give you that serrated feel as you slurp it up. The balance of chilli and vinegar has to be just right, and the combination of pork and sauce really shiok.

There has been much discussion on the difference between mee poh tar, Teochew kway teow mee and bak chor mee and there will be people who would stick out their necks to define 10 different subcategories of mee poh, which is also commonly called mee pok. The way I see it, Teochew mee poh tar – "tar" meaning dry – is a spectrum of different varieties. On one end, you have mee poh tar, which strictly speaking is just blanched mee poh tossed in chilli and oil with some fishballs and maybe fish cakes thrown in. And at the other end of the spectrum, you have bak chor mee, which, strictly speaking, should only include minced pork, but the lines of demarcation have been blurred and that is why you often get freshly sliced pork, liver and fishballs in your bak chor mee. Some hawkers also add fresh prawns, keow (fried wantons), and pork ribs!

. . . . .

Ask anyone where the best bak chor mee in Singapore is and invariably **Hill Street Tai Hwa Pork Noodle** will pop up. The noodles here are really QQ (al dente), the chilli shiok, the lard fresh and the black vinegar just gets your salivary glands working overtime. I really love the soup here. My usual fare is a big bowl of wanton soup with sliced pork, minced pork and pork balls.

. . . . .

Seng Kee Mushroom Minced Pork Noodles has been in business for over 20 years. It was at Eunos before moving to Upper Changi Road. Mr Lee's trademark is the way he makes lots of clanging noises when he is cooking. His bak chor mee is one that you really must try. The noodles are the thin, flat type, with excellent eggy flavour. Being QQ (al dente), they have a very good bite. The ribs are stewed until the tendons become gelatinised, so you can eat the whole thing without leaving any soft bones behind. The sambal chilli is also really shiok, very flavourful and not just plain hot. Mr Lee explained that in order to create a unique sauce that goes into his bak chor mee, he slices up the mushrooms and leaves them overnight to extract the juices before combining them with his secret blend of herbs and spices. I really like the sauce!

The other star of this stall is the fish maw soup. I have never tasted soup this good that goes with bak chor mee. It is chock-a-block full of fish maw, minced pork, pork slices, black fungus and liver. The soup is so full of pork protein precipitates that even if you feel like you need an extreme umami boost (like after having spent a week eating hospital food), I can guarantee that a bowl of this soup will actually be "too much" for you. A very, very shiok and satisfying bowl of soup! The secret ingredients of the soup base are the specially imported dried scallops, grade A fish maw (threadfin no less), old mother hen, tipoh (dried sole fish) and others! By the way, Seng Kee also sells fantastic crab bee hoon *(see chapter on crab)*.

· · · · ·

Also in the East is the Uncle at **132 Mee Poh Kway Teow Mee**. He is the original mee poh man of East Coast, having first started his business at the old Siglap Market almost 40 years ago. When I asked him just what makes his stall so special (it was voted the best mee pok in the East Coast area by *The Straits Times*), he opened up a big bag of medium-sized prawns and told me in typical Teochew hao lian (proud) fashion that he uses the freshest black prawns available in the market. Everything from the pork to the prawns is very, very fresh. And because he insists on using the freshest ingredients and on doing everything the same way he has been doing it for the past four decades, people are willing to illegally park their BMWs, sit around and eat popiah while they queue for 40 minutes, just to satisfy their mee poh craving.

My impression is that Uncle's mee poh tastes very lively and fresh. The first mouthful of that piping hot and fantastically QQ (al dente) flat noodles and you know you are savouring freshly fried pork lard with the combined flavours of freshly blanched prawns, pork and fishballs. It is rumoured that the

chilli here has got buah keluak (Indonesian black nut) in it which gives it that special smoky, savoury flavour. The soup is done the traditional way, using only pork leg bones to prepare the stock. Uncle frowns upon the use of scallops, old mother hen and other less traditional stuff to "sweeten" the soup.

· · · · ·

If tradition is not your thing, and you are more keen to savour New Generation mee poh tar, then head over to **Ah Guan Mee Pok** at Syed Alwi Road. Eric is one enterprising hawker who has brought Japanese ramen concepts into the preparation of our humble mee poh tar, hence taking it to a whole new level. Eric's mee poh is outsourced, but made to Ah Guan's exacting recipe. The mee poh, also known as mee pok, is portioned by weight, then squeezed tight to make it curly. During the cooking process, a timer is used to make sure that each portion of noodles is cooked for exactly 36 seconds.

At Ah Guan, you can only order mee poh as Eric feels that his recipe does not work well with mee kia. This is exactly the kind of thinking that the Japanese apply to their ramen. For the Japanese, each bowl of ramen is designed to perfectly pair a certain type of noodle to a certain sauce, and this cannot be changed by the customer as it would affect the intended flavour. Another thing that cannot be requested is tomato sauce, as Eric feels this will spoil the taste of the noodles. Instead, the noodles are flavoured with a special sauce and vinegar, and you have a choice of whether you want chilli or not. What I like about Ah Guan is that you have the option of adding really good stuff, like scallops, crayfish and fish slices, to your mee poh. For just a few more dollars, this New Generation mee poh tar can be packed with extra goodies that make it all the more delicious!

· · · · ·

The one characteristic of good bak chor mee is freshness of the ingredients, and the bowl of piping hot bak chor mee at **Ah Kow Mushroom Minced Pork Mee** stall tastes really fresh. Those who like their bak chor mee with a bit more vinegar will appreciate the unbridled use of black vinegar here, which is reportedly a special brand of traditional black vinegar from China. The noodles were QQ (al dente) and were complemented very well by the sauce. They were generous with the crispy tipoh (dried sole fish), which was a bonus because I simply love the stuff.

· · · · ·

However, the best value, most elaborate and freshly made bak chor mee I have ever come across is **Teochew Street Mushroom Minced Meat Noodle** in Chinatown. It is really frustrating that there never seems to be a time where the queue takes less than 15 minutes! But then again, I guess everybody knows a good deal when they see one. Each bowl of mee poh tar here is prepared on the spot. Uncle will turn aside to make some dumplings, while waiting for the noodles to cook, then turn back to toss his noodles a few times before turning to his chopping board to slice a few pieces of meat. I also noticed that he would pinch the noodles every time he cooked a batch, in order to see if they were cooked perfectly. All these procedures really slow down the process of producing one bowl of noodles, which definitely contributes to the length of the queue.

There is no doubt that his ingredients are fresh and you really do get quite a few goodies. In each bowl, there is one medium-sized peeled prawn, which tastes like it is a sua lor (sea prawn), rather than a farmed one, several slivers of crispy tipoh (dried sole fish), one dumpling, one pork ball, slices of lean meat, minced meat, braised mushrooms and, something that is unique to this stall, a piece of braised pork skin. All the ingredients are excellent but I can't give this stall top marks because I feel the noodles and sauce lack a bit of flavour.

THE BEDOK BATTLE
OF THE
BAK CHOR MEES

When we talk about bak chor mee, most people refer to the dry version with vinegar, chilli and whether they want liver or not. But, somehow when they talk about the bak chor mee at Fengshan Food Centre in Bedok, everyone seems to know we are referring to the soup version of the dish. It almost seems as if this is the only place that serves bak chor mee soup!

Many people know about these two bak chor mee stalls at Bedok's Fengshan Food Centre. They stand side by side, but which one is better? Both stalls have got their fair share of accolades, but the inner stall, **Xing Ji Rou Cuo Mian** (no. 7), seems to have a longer queue of people than the outer stall, **Seng Hiang Food Stall** (no. 8). So, is this a case where people are simply following the crowd, or is no. 7's bak chor mee really significantly better than no. 8's? I decided to settle the issue once and for all.

Just by looking at the two bowls of bak chor mees, one will notice that no. 8's bowl is bigger. However, the contents look quite similar. Perhaps no. 8's has just slightly more minced pork than no. 7's. Tastewise, the noodles of both stalls are similar. I wouldn't be surprised if they shared the same supplier! The soup of no. 7 is just slightly more tasty than no. 8's but the difference is so small that unless you ate them side by side, I doubt you would be able to tell the difference.

So there you have it. The herd mentality works! The stall with the longer queue – no. 7 – does have the better bowl of noodles. However, if you ask me, I would just order from whichever stall has the shorter queue.

If you are craving bak chor mee in the middle of the night, head down to **Seng Huat Eating House** at Bugis for your foodie fix. This 24-hour stall serves very nice handmade fishballs. The hawker said that handmade fishballs are smoother in texture and have better bounce, compared to the factory-made ones. He was right!

I have never been impressed with bak chor mee stalls that substitute tomato sauce for chilli when you order a bowl of bak chor mee mai hiam (no chilli). To me, a good bak chor mee should taste good even without chilli, as long as they use a good mushroom sauce and a dash of good quality black vinegar. The mushroom sauce at Seng Huat is what makes the dish so good – mushrooms are rich in natural glutamates which give food that savoury umami flavour. This stall uses both tomato sauce and mushroom sauce to flavour their noodles. They use such a small amount of tomato sauce that the taste does not dominate the bowl of noodles. Instead, it adds a complementary tang and sweetness that makes the noodles very well-balanced.

· · · · ·

Finally, one must not forget about **Joo Heng Mushroom Minced Pork Mee**, which makankaki Damien told me is quite legendary and is still drawing the crowds. This is indeed a fine bowl of bak chor mee. The flavours are nicely balanced and you can whiff the eggy aroma of good quality egg noodles with that first mouthful. The texture of the noodles are nice and QQ (al dente). However, although it is as great as the other mee pohs around, it does not really stand one head above the rest.

· · · · ·

Hill Street Tai Hwa Pork Noodle
4.5/5

The noodles are really QQ (al dente), the chilli shiok, the lard fresh and the black vinegar just gets your salivary glands working overtime.

466 Crawford Lane #01-12 S190466, 9.30am to 9pm, closed on 1st and 3rd Mondays of the month

Seng Kee Mushroom Minced Pork Noodles
4.75/5 for fish maw soup
4.5/5 for bak chor mee

The fish maw soup is chock-a-block full of fish maw, minced pork, pork slices, black fungus and liver.

316 Changi Road S419792, 8am to 4.30pm, open everyday

132 Mee Poh Kway Teow Mee
4.5/5

Everything from the pork to the prawns is very, very fresh. Voted the best mee pok in the East Coast area by *The Straits Times*.

MP 59 Food House, 59 Marine Terrace #01-05 S440059, 7am to 3.30pm, closed on Mondays and 1st and 3rd Sundays of the month

Ah Guan Mee Pok
4.5/5

If tradition is not your thing, try this new generation mee poh tar, based on Japanese ramen concepts.

69 Syed Alwi Road S207648, 7am to 9pm, open everyday

Ah Kow Mushroom Minced Pork Mee
4.5/5

They are generous with the crispy tipoh (dried sole fish), which is a bonus.

Hong Lim Complex Temporary Market and Food Centre, 10 Upper Pickering Street #01-17 S058285, 9am to 7pm

Teochew Street Mushroom Minced Meat Noodle
4.25/5

The best value, most elaborate and freshly made bak chor mee. The queue is never less than 15 minutes.

Chinatown Complex Market, 335 Smith Street #02-23 S050335, 12.30pm to 9pm, closed on Mondays and Tuesdays

Seng Huat Eating House
4.25/5

Handmade fishballs that are smoother in texture and have better bounce, compared to the factory-made ones.

492 North Bridge Road (opposite Parco Bugis Junction) S188737, open 24 hours everyday

Joo Heng Mushroom Minced Pork Mee
4.25/5

Eggy aroma of good quality egg noodles you can whiff with that first mouthful.

Ang Mo Kio Market and Food Centre, 628 Ang Mo Kio Avenue 4 Street 61 #01-86 S569163, 7am to 2pm

Xing Ji Rou Cuo Mian (inner stall)
4.5/5

Seems to have a longer queue of people than its close competitor stall no. 8. The soup is just slightly more tasty.

Fengshan Food Centre, 85 Bedok North Street 4, Stall 7 S460085, 5pm to 1am, closed on Mondays

Seng Hiang Food Stall (outer stall),
4.25/5

Has just slightly more minced pork than stall no. 7. Tastewise, the noodles of both stalls are similar.

Fengshan Food Centre, 85 Bedok North Street 4, Stall 8 S460085, 5pm to 12.30am, open everyday

BAK
KUT
TEH

The best time to enjoy bak kut teh is in the morning. This is what the coolies used to do because the dish was considered the "Red Bull" of those times.

When you talk about foods that are uniquely Singaporean, most people will say, "chilli crab," and probably have difficulty naming the rest. This is perhaps because we tend to assume that Chinese food or Malay food are either from China, Malaysia or Indonesia. But when you delve into the history of Singapore food, you will realise the rich heritage we actually have! Indian rojak, chicken rice, Hokkien mee, laksa and chwee kueh (water cake), just to name a few. Yes, all these were invented right here in Singapore.

And then there is bak kut teh. According to Frankie Gwee of the Outram Park Ya Hua Bak Kut Teh stall at Keppel Road, bak kut teh emerged from the Clarke Quay and River Valley area back in the post-war years. Back then, the Chinese coolies used to offload sacks of rice and other goods from the sampans to the godowns, which was back-breaking work. The two rival clans at that time were the Teochews and the Hokkiens, who would compete each other for work. The men needed to eat stuff that would boost their energy, so one enterprising Teochew started selling soup made from boiling pork bones with garlic and pepper. Thus, bak kut teh was born. And yes, you heard me – it was a Teochew invention. Of course, the Hokkiens did not want to lose out, so they also came up with their own version of bak kut teh, which was darker and contained other herbs. Incidentally, there is a very good reason why the Teochew version is so peppery – in the 1800s, the pepper trade in Singapore was predominantly controlled by the Teochews.

Bak kut teh historian, Ah Peng, also the owner of the Ah Peng Bak Koot Teh stall, which closed down in 2008 when he retired, told me that when he was growing up in the 1950s, bak kut teh was sold primarily in two markets – the Teochew enclave of Zhu Zai Chang (New Market) and the Hokkien enclave of Tie Ba Sar in Beach Road. He corrected my misconception that in those days, bak kut teh was food for the poor. It was, then, as it is now, a premium hawker dish. What really surprised me was that coolies in those days were better paid than office workers. As they needed a nutritious source of energy to work, they happily paid 70 cents for a hearty bowl of bak kut teh, 10 cents for a cup of tea and 10 cents for a bowl of rice. On top of that, some even splurged on a cup of rice wine after the whole meal, and smacked their lips loudly as they finished the cup to show the world that they had indeed "arrived".

Another piece of the bak kut teh puzzle was solved when I met up with tea merchant Kenry Poh. His grandfather migrated to Singapore in the 1920s and even at that time, pork bone soup was being served by the Teochews around Clarke Quay, and the Hokkiens around Hokkien Street. It was his grandfather who founded Pek Sin Choon, an established tea

merchant company that is still one of the main suppliers of tea to the bak kut teh stalls in Singapore.

Of course, Malaysians may argue that bak kut teh was invented in Klang Valley. But let's reason it out this way. First and foremost, neither Malaysia nor Singapore invented the concept of boiling pork bone soup. This concept is quite generic, and it must have been around since pigs were first domesticated in China more than 5,000 years ago.

When our forefathers came to Singapore and Malaysia, they brought with them the concept but changed the recipe to suit their needs. Also, what Singapore did invent was eating pork bone soup together with a pot of kung fu tea. In the early days, they used to brew cheap tea in a large kettle and serve it together with the pork bone soup. Later on, the Teochew style of brewing kung fu tea was introduced and more and more people took to drinking tea with their soup. So, gradually, this dish that was originally imported from China as pork bone soup, became known as pork bone and tea, or "bak kut teh".

The Cantonese like to use herbs in their soup, so the Klang version features much more herbs than the Teochew version (in Singapore) which uses only pepper and garlic. As for who started boiling bak kut teh first, we have evidence to show that by the 1920s, the practice of eating pork rib soup with tea was already quite established in Singapore, as attested by our tea merchant, Kenry Poh. We also know that Clarke Quay was established by the British in the second half of the 19th century. So, I think we can narrow down the invention of bak kut teh to the period between 1860 and 1920. We also know that Port Klang was known as Port Swettenham in the colonial days and was only established in 1901. So by virtue of this, it would seem more reasonable to say that bak kut teh was eaten in Clarke Quay way before it was eaten in Port Klang, don't you think? (By the way, this is my own theory, not from any history books!)

Contrary to what is being practiced nowadays, the best time to enjoy bak kut teh is actually in the morning. This is what the coolies used to do because the dish was considered the "Red Bull" of those times. If you don't believe me, try having bak kut teh for breakfast – it actually tastes better at that time of the day. First, order a cup of kung fu tea to cleanse the palate. Then, have a sip of the soup before soaking a piece of you char kway (fried dough fritter) into it. Then, pick up the prime rib, dip it into the dark soya sauce with cut chilli, and savour. The meat should be tender but retain some bite, and have a nice bounce. Drink another cup of tea to wash it all down. Ahhhh!

· · · · ·

For a taste of bak kut teh at the dockyards, go to **Outram Park Ya Hua Rou Gu Char** at Tanjong Pagar. The soup is very good – robust, but not overly peppery. It has a sweet savoury taste that comes from boiling the pork bones until they are almost crumbly. That's when all the rich stuff from the marrow gets released into the soup. When I tasted it, the ribs were cooked until very nice and tender too. I must also make special mention of their fantastic service. Frankie Gwee was extremely hospitable and showed us the right way to drink tea. Great bak kut teh with great service to boot! What more could you ask for?

· · · · ·

Over at Balestier, **Tiong Bee Bah Kut Teh** has been dishing out straightforward no-nonsense bak kut teh, with a well-balanced soup and meat that is wonderfully tender, for years. While there are many famous bak kut teh joints around, nothing beats a boutique bak kut teh stall – Auntie is over 70 years old and only cooks three pots of soup a day. When they are sold out, she goes home. That means that the pork ribs have been simmering in the

pot long enough to ensure that the meat is excellently tender, and in fact, just like how my mother used to make it at home. The soup is very well-balanced, and has that oomph without being overly peppery. Unlike other stalls that try to differentiate themselves by having foot-long ribs or extra ingredients, there are no such gimmicks at this stall. They just serve good ol' bak kut teh, at its best. By the way, this stall also sells fantastic pig's trotters and steamed fish.

. . . . .

The bak kut teh at **Ng Ah Sio Pork Ribs Soup Eating House** is so special that two politicians risked public embarrassment just to try it! Donald Tsang, Chief Executive of Hong Kong, was the first "victim" – the stall turned down his request for a bowl of their soup! The second "victim" was Thaksin Shina-watra, former Prime Minister of Thailand, whose money could buy him lots of stuff, but could not buy him a seat here! Unlike Donald Tsang, Thaksin came during opening hours, but made the mistake of arguing with the owner over a bowl of innards and apparently got himself kicked out of the restaurant! OK, two famous politicians down… Next!

The bak kut teh here was a peppery blast, typical of the Teochew style. Robust and spicy, it is guaranteed to clear your sinuses. (If it doesn't, please see your doctor!) The garlic and pepper residue in the soup is evidence of how long the ingredients have been boiling for. Unfortu-nately, I did not manage to order the prime ribs that day and ended up having off-cuts, so the meat was a bit dry. I think the prime ribs would have been better.

. . . . .

The real beauty of **Rong Chen Bak Kut Teh** is that they do not use soya sauce to flavour the soup, so you can better taste the original flavour of the pork. The soup is sweet and aromatic. They have a good supply of prime ribs and they cut it in pieces that can be eaten by hand. According to the rosy-cheeked owner, he was the first one to introduce the white version of bak kut teh 30 years ago and since then, many other stalls have copied his style to serve lighter coloured bak kut teh. I would have given higher marks for the soup, but the meat was not tender enough to be enjoyed by people with dentures.

· · · · ·

The pork ribs at **Founder Bak Kut Teh Restaurant** are done very well. When I tasted them, they were so tender that they fell off the bone. The soup was very sweet, peppery, light and refreshing. However the side dishes were nothing to be excited about.

Uncle's family used to be pig farmers in Punggol back in the days, before all the pig farms disappeared in Singapore. He loved bak kut teh, so he started experimenting on his own. Since he never learnt how to cook the dish from a bak kut teh master, he called his stall "Founder". As he was a pig farmer, he knows his pork very well and sources only the best pork for his soup. As with most people in the know, Uncle will tell you that Indonesian pork is still the best – Australian and Canadian pork, according to him, have a porky smell, because their pigs are not castrated.

· · · · ·

If you are hankering for bak kut teh in the middle of the night, head over to Joo Chiat where **Sin Heng Claypot Bak Koot Teh** is open 24 hours a day! The restaurant sells both Hokkien and Teochew versions of bak kut teh, so you can have the best of both provinces in one place! The Teochew version's soup here is sweet and peppery, and a tad darker than the typical Teochew bak kut teh being served nowadays. The Hokkien version is reminiscent of

the bak kut teh we find in Malaysia, but I found the taste of the herbs a bit too mild, such that there was not enough kick.

One good thing about this stall is that it serves yam rice. The rice is flavoured with dried shrimp and yam, and is really nice even if eaten on its own. Another good thing is that the restaurant still serves you a pot of kung fu tea to complement the bak kut teh. The side dishes are also very good. I tried their pork spare parts with ginger and shallots, and they were excellent.

. . . . .

If it is Malaysian style bak kut teh you are looking for, then head for **Leong Kee (Klang) Bak Kut Teh**. The soup was a bit bitter rather than sweet the day we tried it. It also lacked the oomph we would expect in a good bak kut teh. But the pork ribs were very nice and tender.

This place also serves really good pig's trotters. Soft, sticky, sweet and savoury, the fat and tendons melt in your mouth and I could feel them going directly into my coronary arteries. Phwa, very shiok, but not something you will want to admit to your cardiologist on your follow-up visit after coronary bypass surgery.

. . . . .

A final doctor's note: although soup dishes may sound healthy, bak kut teh is not that healthy because it is so rich in cholesterol. That is why it helps to take the dish with a cup of tea. The tea's astringent and antioxidant properties help to cut through the fats and cholesterol that come from the pork fat and bone marrow.

. . . . .

LESLIE'S TOP PICKS FOR BAK KUT TEH

Outram Park Ya Hua Rou Gu Char
4.5/5

The soup has a sweet savoury taste that comes from boiling the pork bones until all the rich stuff from the marrow gets released into the soup.

Tanjong Pagar Complex (PSA),
7 Keppel Road #01-05/07 S089053,
7am to 3pm, closed on Mondays

Tiong Bee Bah Kut Teh
4.5/5

Auntie is over 70 years old and only cooks three pots of soup a day. When it is sold out, she goes home.

588F Jalan Datoh (off Balestier Road) S329899,
7am to 3pm, closed on alternate Mondays

Ng Ah Sio Pork Ribs Soup Eating House
4.25/5

It is so special that two politicians risked public embarrassment just to try it! The bak kut teh is robust and spicy, guaranteed to clear your sinuses.

208 Rangoon Road S218453,
6am to 2pm, closed on Mondays

Rong Chen Bak Kut Teh
4.25/5

They do not use soya sauce to flavour the soup, so you taste more of the original flavour of the pork.

Eng Ho Hup Coffeeshop,
22 Sin Ming Road S570022, 7am to 4pm

Founder Bak Kut Teh Restaurant
4.25/5

Uncle was a pig farmer so he knows his pork very well and sources only the best pork for his stall.

347 Balestier Road (New Orchid Hotel)
S329777, 12pm to 2pm and 6pm to 2am,
closed on Tuesdays

Sin Heng Claypot Bak Koot Teh
4.5/5 for Hokkien version
4.25/5 for Teochew version
4.25/5 for pork spare parts with ginger and shallots

The yam rice is flavoured with dried shrimp and yam, and is really nice even if eaten on its own. The restaurant still serves you kung fu tea to complement the bak kut teh.

439 Joo Chiat Road S427652,
open 24 hours, closed on Mondays

Leong Kee (Klang) Bak Kut Teh
4.25/5 for pig's trotters
3.75/5 for bak kut teh

This place has really good pig's trotters. Soft, sticky, sweet and savoury, the fat and tendons melt in your mouth.

321 Beach Road (Jalan Sultan Gate and
Beach Road) S199557,
11am to 9pm, closed on Wednesdays

BEANCURD

The End of Char Kway Teow

With more and more stalls starting to make their own beancurd, factory-made beancurd has, for me at least, become what Kong Guan pau is to handmade pau.

As any beancurd afficionado will know, the texture of beancurd, locally known as tau huay, is what determines whether it is any good. It must be super smooth, soft and silky. At the same time, the taste cannot be sacrificed for texture – I like beancurd that retains the taste of the soya beans. It should not be too watered down. But some hawkers heavily dilute the soya bean milk, in order to achieve a smooth texture.

Beancurd that is freshly made at the stall is always better than the factory-made version. With more and more stalls starting to make their beancurd on the premises, factory-made beancurd has, for me at least, become what Kong Guan pau is to handmade pau. The texture of freshly made beancurd is finer and smoother because the factory-made ones are made to be able to withstand the trauma of transporting the beancurd from the factory to the stall. The ones made on the premises are moved very little once the beancurd has set and each vat of freshly made beancurd can optimally last only a few hours, so it has to be eaten fresh. If you want to taste what beancurd used to taste like before hawkers started procuring factory-made ones, look out for a machine making soya milk at the stall.

· · · · ·

I really admire the Uncle at **No Name Tau Huay** stall at Whampoa for holding on to tradition. His tau huay is still made with shi gao (gypsum) rather than lactone, which is used in many places, especially franchised stalls in shopping centres. Unlike shi gao, lactone is very forgiving and gives consistent results. Making tau huay using shi gao, on the other hand, is an art form that requires the skills of an experienced tau huay maker. After making tau huay for more than 40 years, this Uncle still has days when his tau huay does not set properly. However, when it does, traditional or artisanal tau huay made with shi gao is softer and silkier than the modern lactone tau huay.

The day I tried Uncle's tau huay, it had the perfect texture. Unlike the lactone version that often chisels like jelly, this tau huay disintegrated in the mouth with the slightest pressure. We don't usually expect good service at hawker stalls, but this particular stall is manned by Uncle's young China-born wife, who is the most hardworking and cheerful hawker I have ever met. Every time I see her, she is as busy as a hummingbird with her hands flying all over the stall, but always with a perpetual smile on her face! If you are down and depressed, get a bowl of tau huay there and soak in her energy.

· · · · ·

The beancurd at **Tan Soon Mui Beancurd** at Serangoon Gardens was such an unexpected and delightful find. I could tell you about how the stall is three generations old, founded by the grandpa in 1966. I could also tell you about how they remove the skin from the soya beans to make sure you do not get that waxy taste in your mouth. And I could tell you about how they use four ingredients to make the sugar syrup. But I don't need to. All I have to say is that this is the best bowl of beancurd I have eaten in a long while and it is only half the price of the other famous ones I have tried. The soya bean taste is evident and the texture sublime. It is excellent and ironically, one of the cheapest bowls of beancurd around.

Those of you who have heard of Tan Soon Mui will probably know them as a manufacturer of chin chow (grass jelly drink). While they have a factory that sells chin chow to hawkers, their special chin chow is sold only at their stall. The special characteristic of this chin chow is the texture, though I thought it was lacking in any special chin chow taste. Still it was quite a refreshing bowl of dessert to have on a hot Singapore day.

· · · · ·

Finally, any chapter on beancurd would not be complete without an investigation into the famous Rochor Beancurd Dynasty, which has spawned many different beancurd stalls in Singapore. Here's how the story goes: once upon a time, a beancurd seller had four children. They worked as a happy family, until some dispute over the shares of the company arose, and the four children split up to run their own businesses. The second and fourth brothers used to operate the Rochor Original stall at Short Street and spawned a branch at Sims Avenue. The eldest brother left to start Rochor Beancurd House, with the same logo, over at Geylang. The fourth brother then had a dispute with the second brother and left to open Beancurd City, first at Jalan Besar and then another stall just next to Rochor Original. He subsequently gave up his stall that was next to Rochor Original, and it was taken over by the third sister (who used to be helping the fourth brother), who renamed the stall Eryimin. So, which one has the best beancurd? I went to find out!

Common knowledge has it that the **Rochor Original Beancurd**, the most famous beancurd stall in Singapore, has the best beancurd around. After all, Anthony Bourdain was taken to this stall to taste the best of what Singapore had to offer. I found the beancurd very good, but certainly not the best a beancurd could be. Even though it was silky smooth, it tasted too diluted for me.

Surprisingly, **Eryimin**'s beancurd was slightly smoother than the Rochor Original stall right next to it, but the taste was slightly more diluted. The sugar had a bit more colouring in it. But, the truth of the matter is, when I blindfolded my wife and her parents and asked them to guess which was which, they got it wrong 50 per cent of the time. This just proves that both stalls' beancurds are very similar in taste and texture.

My personal favourite is the beancurd from **Beancurd City** – the texture was soft and silky, but they still managed to retain the taste of the soya beans. A very enjoyable bowl of beancurd.

Conclusion: between Rochor Original and Eryimin, go for the stall with the shorter queue! But in my opinion, Beancurd City is better than both Rochor Original and Eryimin!

· · · · ·

LESLIE'S TOP PICKS FOR BEANCURD

No Name Tau Huay
4.6/5

The beancurd is still made with shi gao (gypsum) rather than lactone. It is softer and silkier than the modern lactone variety.

Whampoa Drive Makan Place (Whampoa Food Centre) 90 Whampoa Drive #01-57 S320090, 6.30am to 4.30pm, closed on Mondays

Tan Soon Mui Beancurd
4.5/5 for beancurd
4/5 for chin chow (grass jelly drink)

The best beancurd I have eaten in a long while and it is only half the price of the other famous ones I have tried.

Serangoon Garden Market and Food Centre, 49A Serangoon Garden Way Stall 41 S555945, 8am to 8pm, closed on Mondays

Rochor Original Beancurd
4.25/5

Commonly known as the most famous beancurd stall in Singapore. Even though the beancurd is silky smooth, it tastes too diluted for me.

2 Short Street S188211, noon to midnight, open everyday

Eryimin
4.25/5

The beancurd is very similar in taste and texture to that of Rochor Original Beancurd, the stall right next to it. Go for the one with the shorter queue!

4 Short Street S188212, noon to midnight, open everyday

Beancurd City
4.5/5

The beancurd is soft and silky, and still manages to retain the taste of the beans.

133 Jalan Besar (after Desker Road) S208851, 11.30am to midnight, open everyday

BEEF KWAY TEOW

The End of Char Kway Teow

Very few places still make their own beef balls, but when they do, you can definitely taste the difference.

Have you ever wondered why beef kway teow is called "kway teow", even though most of the time, you eat it with thick bee hoon? Well, there are really two types of beef kway teow in the market – the one with the thick bee hoon and sticky gravy is Hainanese style. The other is the Teochew style beef kway teow that uses kway teow and the dry version is served with just a dash of sesame oil, soya sauce and chilli. According to Tina Tan of the Hock Lam Beef Kway Teow stall at China Street, the traditional Teochew version also comes with salted vegetables and plenty of groundnuts, without the familiar chinchaluk (shrimp sauce).

When given a choice, I always choose the dry version of beef kway teow, since I can still get soup on the side. Plus, the dry version just has more kick! I love my beef slices tender and slightly pink, and the soup should be robust and filled with bovine goodness. As for the meatballs, very few places still make their own beef balls, but when they do, you can definitely taste the difference. Incidentally, did you know that in order to make the balls springy, the meat is not minced, but actually beaten? In the good old days, hawkers used two rectangular metal batons to pound the meat. Pounding it straightens out the protein strands, causing the meat to be springy in texture. The same method is used to make springy fishballs.

· · · · ·

The beef balls at **Bugis (Longhouse) Lim Kee Beef Noodles** are the world's second best (the best has yet to be found!) They make their beef balls from scratch and you can definitely taste the difference. The balls are springy, and not adulterated with flour, so you get 100 per cent beef protein. There are lots of air bubbles trapped in each ball, such that its texture is like a cross between a fishball and a soufflé. I could eat a whole bowl of these while watching TV!

The Hainanese style beef noodles at this stall are also very good, so much so that I could not stop thinking about them even after I got home! The dry version's thick gravy contained enough bovine essence to make you want to moo, and that's no bull. I have never tasted a better gravy – so savoury, so beefy, so tasty, so shiokadoodle doo! The meat was really soft and tender, and they didn't overcook it, so it was still pink when served.

· · · · ·

Hai Nan Xing Zhou Beef Noodles has been selling Hainanese style beef kway teow for over 40 years. Uncle's stall is still remembered as the beef kway teow stall from Cuppage Centre. The soup version of the dish was wonderfully robust and sweet. Definitely one of the best I've tasted! As for the dry version, I was undoubtedly impressed by the stewed beef tendons, which were so soft, they melted in your mouth, coating your buccal cavity with soft and gooey goodness. The beef slices were tender but the beef balls were outsourced, so they were not that special. The sauce was good, but maybe because my expectations were too high as makankaki Damien had said that this stall sells the best beef kway teow in Singapore, I felt it did not have maximum oomph.

· · · · ·

Don't let the simple, unadorned frontage of the **Changi Beef Kway Teow Noodle** stall fool you. Within this unassuming stall lies a pot of gravy so good, I guarantee you can taste the flavour by just looking at it! Seriously, the gravy of the dry version was to die for. It was the best gravy I have ever seen and tasted! Savoury and full of bovine goodness! The beef strands floating in the gravy is a preview to what is going to happen when you scoop a spoonful and put it in your mouth. Think of it as sharks' fin soup, but with beef instead of crabmeat! In addition, the soup version was also pretty good – sweet and robust, with the meat tender and flavoursome. One of the better beef soups around!

· · · · ·

My beef kway teow list would be incomplete without the inclusion of the famous **Hock Lam Street Beef Kway Teow** stall that has been around for almost a century. The fourth generation owner of this stall, Tina Tan, gave up her high paying bank job to take over the family business! She was adamant to preserve the recipe in its original form, so the noodles here only come with salted vegetables and plenty of groundnuts, without the familiar chin-chaluk (shrimp sauce). The sliced beef was nice and very tender – Tina said it was still sliced by hand and no tenderiser was used. The stewed beef and tripe are both very good. The beef balls are nice, but are no longer made in the stall. The sauce could be more shiok, but because Teochew food empha-sises more on the freshness of the ingredients, so Teochew sauces tend to be a little more bland as compared to the sauces of other dialect groups.

In my journey to find the best beef kway teow, I also discovered two other types of beef kway teow in Singapore. They are the less well-known Seremban beef kway teow and Hakka style beef kway teow.

· · · · ·

Mr Wong's Seremban Beef Noodle is possibly the only stall in Singapore that sells Seremban beef noodles. The dry version is sweeter than the local version, with the sweetness coming from the sweet black sauce and other condiments added to the bee hoon before the beef sauce is draped over. I found it quite nice, as I like my food a little on the sweet side. I also liked the peanuts and sesame seeds that you can help yourself to. It is certainly very different from the other beef noodles I have eaten. The soup version was also good, and sweeter than our local version as well, with the extra sweetness coming from the carrots and radishes. The beefy aroma was very strong and I found it to be, overall, a satisfying bowl of soup. Generally, this dish is good for those who like things sweeter, but if you are looking for that beefy umami rush, you might be disappointed.

· · · · ·

The Beef House sells Hakka style beef noodles that comes with ping pong ball sized beef balls in a clear soup, accompanied by thin bee hoon, kway teow or mee kia. The beef balls were super bouncy, and you get a serious temporomandibular joint workout when you bite into them. I suspect that if I did drop one by mistake, it would have just bounced back up onto the table! They were juicy and had a nice beef flavour – the beef balls are still made in-house so it is no surprise that I have never tasted anything quite like it anywhere else. The mee kia I had that day was one of the best I have ever tasted – QQ (al dente), yet soft enough to absorb all the subtle flavours of the minced pork.

· · · · ·

The End of Char Kway Teow

LESLIE'S TOP PICKS FOR BEEF KWAY TEOW

Bugis (Longhouse) Lim Kee Beef Noodles
4.5/5

They make their beef balls from scratch and you can definitely taste the difference. The balls are springy, not adulterated with flour, so you get 100 per cent beef protein.

Golden Mile Food Centre, 505 Beach Road #B1-27 S199583, 11am to 9pm, open everyday

Hai Nan Xing Zhou Beef Noodles
4.5/5 for dry version
4.25/5 for soup version

The soup version of the dish is wonderfully robust and sweet. Definitely one of the best I have tasted!

Kim Keat Palm Market and Food Centre, 22 Toa Payoh Lorong 7 #01-06 S310022, 8am to 7pm, closed on Mondays

Changi Beef Kway Teow Noodle
4.5/5 for soup version
4/5 for dry version

Seriously, the gravy of the dry version is to die for. It is the best gravy I have ever seen and tasted! Savoury and full of bovine goodness!

Changi Village Market and Food Centre, 2 Changi Village Road #01-19 S500002, 11am to 11pm, open everyday

Hock Lam Street Beef Kway Teow
4/5

This stall has been around for almost a century. The sliced beef is nice and very tender – the stall owner says it is still sliced by hand and no tenderiser is used.

Far East Square, 22 China Street #01-01 S048761, 9.30am to 8pm from Mondays to Fridays, 10.30am to 5pm on Saturdays, Sundays and public holidays

Mr Wong's Seremban Beef Noodle
4/5

Possibly the only stall in Singapore that sells Seremban beef noodles. Overall, good for those who like things sweeter.

Marine Parade Central Market and Food Centre, 84 Marine Parade Central #01-184 S440084, 11am to 8.30pm, open everyday

The Beef House
4.5/5 for mee kia
4/5 for beef balls

The beef balls are super bouncy, and you get a serious temporomandibular joint workout when you bite into them.

Gar Lok Eating House, 217 Syed Alwi Road S207776, 9am to 6pm, closed on Fridays

BIRYANI

One way to test for true basmati rice is to drop a handful of cooked rice on the floor — it is supposed to separate like grains of sand.

In Singapore, *biryani* is often called nasi *briyani*. Being an Indian dish, the Malay word "nasi" which means rice should not even be there. But this shows how biryani has evolved to become a Singaporean dish which incorporates local Malay influence.

In recent years, some hawkers have tried to differentiate their biryani by calling it dum biryani – the word "dum" means that the biryani is cooked by baking the rice with the meat and spices in a sealed large pot. Actually, the word "dum" is redundant because all biryani is supposed to be cooked this way, though many hawkers take shortcuts by cooking the rice and meat separately before combining them together in a big pot.

The secret to a great biryani lies in the basmati rice, arguably one of the world's most expensive rice. As such, many attempt to use other types of rice and pass them off as basmati. (You can't really blame the hawkers as they have to sell a plate of biryani for only $3!) The most obvious characteristic of basmati is its ability to elongate to at least twice its length when cooked. However, it is not just the lengthening of the rice during cooking that makes basmati rice special. The other key characteristic is the alluring fragrance it gives off when cooked. In fact, the Hindi word "basmati" means "the fragrant one" and the rice owes its fragrance to an aromatic compound that is also found in pandan leaves. As basmati is low in starch, it is light, fluffy, but not sticky when cooked. (You will never be able to make sushi with this rice!) One way to test for true basmati rice is to drop a handful of cooked rice on the floor – it is supposed to separate like grains of sand. Being low in starch also means that basmati has a low glycemic index, making it more suitable for diabetics.

Good basmati rice needs to be aged for two years in order for the rice to dry properly. When dry, the rice should be opaque – a transluscent grain means the rice is still young (and "wet"). You need to age the rice properly because a dry grain is the key to a great biryani as it readily absorbs all the flavours of the spices. If you are wondering why I know so much about biryani, it is not because I am an expert, but because I have been talking to a passionate and dedicated biryani expert, the owner of Bismillah Biryani Restaurant, Arif, who has so much to share with me every time I visit him.

People look for different things in a biryani. For me, the rice is of prime importance, then the meat and the curry. I also like the cucumber achar (pickles) to be nice and sweet, so as to contrast with the savoury flavours of the curry. I love my basmati rice light and fluffy, with each grain separate, unbroken, fragrant and aromatic, yet firm to the bite, and not mushy. The springy texture of good biryani rice makes it delicious enough to eat it on its own, without any gravy. As for the meat, I love it when the mutton is super tender, aromatic, and seasoned just right such that there is no strong mutton smell.

· · · · ·

When it comes to the best biryani rice in Singapore, my pick is **Bismillah Biryani Restaurant** at Dunlop Street. The owner and chef there, Arif, had me at, "Our basmati rice is half an inch long." He has been running the restaurant for five years and he is the best kind of chef-cum-owner you can get – having retired early, he claims that he is running his stall to show Singaporeans what real biryani is all about, rather than to make money. I always say that there is only one ingredient needed to make great food: passion. It is passion that drives Arif to purchase a professional spice grinder to grind his own spices, and to procure a whole sheep so that every pot of biryani that he cooks contains meat from the same animal. It also takes a lot of confidence to not use any butter or ghee to flavour the rice, but to depend solely on good quality spices.

Both makankakis Liverpool and Cactuskit, who are biryani afficionados, agree that this is the best biryani they have ever eaten. The rice has so absorbed the fragrant spices that they linger in the mouth for quite a while. I found the mutton excellent – it was tender, fragrant and did not have a gamey flavour because the meat had been blanched in hot water before being marinated. Amazingly, the rice was quite light, since no oil or ghee was used in the cooking, so you can eat a whole portion without feeling too guilty.

Arif claims that he is the only person who actually cooks the rice and meat in the pot over a charcoal fire, with charcoal on top of the pot as well. This, according to him, is how biryani should be made.

· · · · ·

When I first tasted **Geylang (Hamid's) Briyani Stall**, I got so enamoured, I just had to keep going back because I couldn't get enough of it. This is one of the tastiest hawker meals you can buy in Singapore! You will certainly derive a lot of pleasure per dollar from this dish. The texture of the rice was near perfect. The grains were fluffy, separate and firm to the bite, and you could taste the buttery ghee and spices. (I say near perfect because Hamid does not use top grade basmati rice here. For $3, what do you expect?) The mutton was so tender you could separate it with a fork and it would literally dissolve in your mouth. The chicken masala gravy was the real killer – the combination of the gravy with the rice will give you 100 per cent satisfaction. Hamid also told us that sometimes on Wednesdays, he will make a very special fish biryani using top grade basmati rice, and this dish is supposed to be even more shiok. Amazing!

· · · · ·

The **Briyani Bistro** (formerly known as House of Biryani) sells Afghan, Iranian and Turkish dum biryani. The rice is beautiful with every grain perfectly steamed, fragrant, aromatic and firm to the bite. The curry lamb was fantastic – they used the back of the lamb (t-bone) to cook the curry so the meat was very tender. The thing to die for was the tomato sambal, which was sweet, not overly spicy and had large pieces of well-caramelised onions in it. The rice we had was the Afghan version, which was not oily and most similar to our local biryani. The Turkish dum biryani was a tad oily and had raisins and nuts in it, while the Iranian biryani tasted too much like normal boiled rice.

· · · · ·

As part of my biryani pilgrimage, I visited the **Thohirah Restaurant** which was recommended by some of the readers of my blog. They served rice that was nicely done. I loved eating the rice just by itself, without the gravy. Every grain was separate and unbroken. The springy texture was satisfying to bite, and the cucumber achar (pickles) was also very good.

· · · · ·

Another famous biryani stall which everyone talks about is **Allauddin's Briyani** at Buffalo Road. The fame of this stall is undisputed, having been in business for over 40 years. Many who have grown up eating the biryani here would defend it with their lives. So I was not surprised that out of all the biryani stalls in the vicinity, this was the only one with a long queue. But, sad to say, Allauddin's fell short of my expectations. The rice was monochrome in colour, and a little overcooked such that some of the grains were mushy and broken. However, the taste of the biryani was excellent, and the dhalchat (lentil curry) and chicken curry complemented the rice really well.

· · · · ·

Finally, I must also pay homage to the Grand Daddy of biryani – the **Famous Islamic Beryani Shop**, which has been around since 1911. Once again, although many people had raved about this restaurant to me, overall, the taste of the biryani here did not measure up to my expectations. Like Allauddin's, the rice was monochrome in colour and although the grains were separate and unbroken, they did not have good bite. I did, however, like the lemon drink that was served with the biryani – with such a unique, refreshing flavour, it's definitely worth trying!

· · · · ·

LESLIE'S TOP PICKS FOR BIRYANI

Bismillah Biryani Restaurant
4.75/5

Amazingly, the rice is quite light, since not much oil or ghee is used in the cooking, so you can eat a whole portion without feeling too guilty.

50 Dunlop Street S209379, 11am to 10.30pm, open everyday

Geylang (Hamid's) Briyani Stall
4.75/5

The texture of the rice is near perfect. The grains are fluffy, separate and firm to the bite, and you can taste the buttery ghee and spices.

Geylang Serai Market and Food Centre, 1 Geylang Serai #02-146 S402001, 9am to 5pm, closed on Mondays

Briyani Bistro
(formerly known as House of Biryani)
4.5/5

The thing to die for is the tomato sambal, which is sweet, not overly spicy and has large pieces of well-caramelised onions in it.

742 North Bridge Road (corner of North Bridge Road and Kandahar Street) S198710, 11am to 7pm, closed on Sundays, Mondays and public holidays

Thohirah Restaurant
4.25/5

I love eating the rice just by itself. Every grain is separate and unbroken. The springy texture is satisfying to the bite, and the cucumber achar (pickles) is also very good.

258 Jalan Kayu (next to the car park) S799487, open 24 hours everyday

Allauddin's Briyani
4/5

The fame of this stall is undisputed, having been in business for over 40 years. The biryani is excellent, and the dhalchat (lentil curry) and chicken curry complement the rice really well.

Tekka Market and Food Centre, 665 Buffalo Road #01-297 S210665, 8am to 3pm, open everyday

Famous Islamic Beryani Shop
3.75/5

This stall has been around since 1911. However, the taste of the biryani here did not measure up to my expectations.

754 North Bridge Road (corner of North Bridge Road and Klapa Road) S198772, 10.30am to 9.30pm, closed 1pm to 2pm on Fridays

BRAISED
DUCK

LIAN KEE DUCK RICE

The End of Char Kway Teow

As duck is a potentially tough meat, it matters who slices your duck. It could make the difference between tough, dry meat and succulent, tender meat.

I should really love braised duck since it is a Teochew dish and I am 100 per cent unadulterated Teochew. However, for me, braised duck does not make my mouth water as much as char siew (barbecued meat). I think that braised duck can only attain a certain level of shiok-ness which will never surpass something like say, a bowl of laksa. I have yet to eat a version of braised duck that I can really go shiokadoodledoo to.

There are two types of braised duck – the Teochew version is more savoury, with braising sauce the consistency of water, while the Hokkien version is sweeter, with thick and gooey braising sauce. When I eat braised duck rice, I don't go for the duck meat, as I would with chicken when I eat chicken rice. Instead, I go for the tau pok (fried beancurd) and the lor (braising sauce). If they have braised peanuts, it's a bonus.

· · · · ·

One of the most famous braised duck stalls in Singapore is **Lim Seng Lee Duck Rice** at South Buona Vista. The duck meat here is moist and tender, and the unique sweet vinegar chilli is the perfect accompaniment. Shiok! But just one problem – a small plate of thinly sliced duck meat costs $5 and during peak periods, the wait can be pretty long. Still, this Teochew braised duck was good enough to make me think about travelling all the way to the West to eat it. But it is still not good enough to make me pay a premium and suffer a long queue for.

· · · · ·

Ah Seng Braised Duck Rice is a popular stall selling a nice Teochew version of braised duck. The braising sauce is nice and the duck tender. Lots of people rave about it, and I thought it was good enough to be included in my list of top picks, but nothing in particular to rave about.

· · · · ·

East Coast Lagoon Food Village seems hardly the place to go for braised duck. To me the beach means satay, rojak, Hokkien mee and roti john. Braised duck seems too melancholic for the beach. But the braised duck at **Cheok Kee Duck Rice** was very good. The lor (braising sauce) was Hokkien style – thick and sticky – and it was a little sweet, but the herbs were not overpowering. Overall, a good braised duck rice, but not something I would drive all the way from Jurong to eat, especially since they have branches elsewhere.

· · · · ·

The braised duck at **Lian Kee Duck Rice** was good, but I am not sure if this is as good as braised duck gets. The braised duck man here is a second generation Teochew hawker who has been working since he was a kid when the stall first opened in 1976. He claims that his braising sauce is made from 13 herbs and spices and the recipe has not changed for the last 35 years.

Everything about his braised duck revolves around the cauldron of braising sauce, which is used to flavour everything from the duck to the porridge and even the beancurd. So in a sense, the sauce is the deciding factor when eating braised duck.

• • • • •

Finally, the last of my top picks would be **Ah Xiao Teochew Braised Duck** at Aljunied. This Teochew braised duck was highly recommended by makankaki Smart, who claimed that it was one of the best in Singapore. I had really high hopes when the dish came but surprisingly, my first impression was that the meat was a little tough and a tad dry. Tastewise, the braising sauce was not as sweet as the Hokkien version, but was quite pang (fragrant). I sat there giving my muscles of mastication a good workout, wondering why Smart would even recommend such a place.

That's when Lao Ban Niang spotted me taking pictures of the plate of duck and popped over with the usual, "Are you a reporter?" question. When I complained that the duck was a bit tough, she immediately explained that her worker was not as adept at slicing the meat as she was, and offered to demonstrate how it should be done. When I was presented with the second plate of braised duck, I must say it looked quite different from the first plate. This time, it was sliced thinner and each slice was more tender and juicy. So, there you have it – a very important tip: as duck is a potentially tough meat, it matters who slices your duck. It could make the difference between tough, dry meat and succulent, tender meat, even if the meat all came from the same part of the same duck to start with!

So, if you are patronising this stall, make sure you ask the Lao Ban Niang to slice the braised duck for you!

• • • •

LESLIE'S TOP PICKS FOR BRAISED DUCK

Lim Seng Lee Duck Rice

4.5/5

The duck meat here is moist and tender, and the unique sweet vinegar chilli is the perfect accompaniment. Shiok!

38 South Buona Vista Road S118164,
10.30am to 8.30pm, closed on Sundays

Ah Seng Braised Duck Rice

4/5

This is a popular stall selling a nice Teochew version of braised duck. The braising sauce is nice and the duck tender.

Serangoon Garden Market and Food Centre,
49A Serangoon Garden Way Stall 44 S555945,
11am to 9pm, open Mondays to Saturdays

Cheok Kee Duck Rice

4/5

The braised duck here is very good – the lor (braising sauce) is Hokkien style – thick and sticky – and it is a little sweet, but the herbs are not overpowering.

East Coast Lagoon Food Village,
1220 East Coast Parkway, Stall 29 S468960,
11am to 10pm, open everyday

Lian Kee Duck Rice

4.25/5

The braised duck man here claims that his braising sauce is made from 13 herbs and spices and the recipe has not changed for the last 35 years.

Hin Hollywood Canteen,
57 Tanjong Katong Road S436952,
10am to 8.30pm, open everyday

Ah Xiao Teochew Braised Duck

4/5

If you are patronising this stall, make sure you ask the Lao Ban Niang to slice the braised duck for you!

Aljunied Market and Food Centre,
117 Aljunied Avenue 2 #01-18 S380117,
11.30am to 7.30pm, closed on Mondays

CARROT
CAKE

How does that Michael Jackson song go again — *"It doesn't matter if you're black or white"*? I beg to differ. When it comes to carrot cake, there are three types of people in the world. Those who love the BLACK one. Those who love the WHITE one. And those who think that carrot cake is supposed to have cream cheese icing.

My taste for carrot cake has undergone some evolution. As a kid, I used to like black carrot cake, which is cut up into small little pieces and fried with an extra shot of black sauce. Now, I find myself moving away from the dark side to embrace white carrot cake. While both types of carrot cake, also known as chye tau kway, have their merits, the reason why I am leaning towards the white version is because it is a little more sophisticated than the black version.

With the black version, most of the taste comes from the sweet black sauce, and texture is not really an issue. But with the white version, the flavour profile is more complex. You have the taste of the chye poh (preserved radish), the carrot cake itself and the eggs, each with its own distinctive flavour. Then you have the contrast in texture between the crispy eggs and the soft carrot cake. How does that Michael Jackson song go again – *"It doesn't matter if you're black or white"*? I beg to differ. When it comes to carrot cake, there are three types of people in the world. Those who love the BLACK one. Those who love the WHITE one. And those who think that carrot cake is supposed to have cream cheese icing.

I had always assumed that the white carrot cake came first before someone decided to add sweet black sauce to turn it into the black version. But it turns out that the original carrot cake that was brought over here by our migrant forefathers from China was the black version, and it was Singaporeans who turned it from black to white!

I also noticed that a stall either does black or white carrot cake very well, but rarely both. In either case, I have always thought that the best carrot cakes come from hawkers who make and steam their own carrot cake, instead of outsourcing to a supplier. Somehow, it gives the stall a feeling of authenticity – food that is freshly made by hand, on site, is always better than mass-produced food.

· · · · ·

And when it comes to freshly handmade carrot cake, it does not get any better than **Bukit Merah View Carrot Cake**. Yes, some hawkers make their carrot cake from rice flour, but how many hawkers go one step further and actually mill the rice grains themselves? This stall does! This stall is 60 years old, and is probably the last of its kind in Singapore. In the good old days, stone mills were a common sight at hawker stalls – they

were used for milling all types of grain, from soya beans (to make soya bean milk) to peanuts (to make peanut paste) and of course, broken rice (to make carrot cake).

Three brothers run this stall – one takes the morning shift, one takes the evening and the youngest makes the carrot cake. They mill the broken rice into a watery solution. Then, hot water is added, which cooks the starch, and turns it into a paste. Finally, radishes are added, and the mixture is poured into a round tray and steamed for four hours! This is quite a lot of work, and I am amazed that the brothers are still doing it! The youngest brother is proud of the fact that his carrot cake retains its texture even when left overnight, unlike the factory-made ones.

So, what is this carrot cake like? The texture is very good – soft, but not mushy. I must admit though that tastewise, it is almost the same as some of the other carrot cake stalls I have tried, since the taste mainly comes from the fish sauce, eggs and chye poh (preserved radish) anyway. Their style of carrot cake is crispy and chunky. Both the white and black versions are excellent, but if I had to choose, I would go for their black version, which is just slightly better than their white version. I salute the brothers for their passion in keeping the carrot cake tradition alive!

· · · · ·

A skilful hawker will be able to make his carrot cake nice and crisp on the outside, and soft and flavourful on the inside. And this is the texture **Chey Sua Carrot Cake** manages to get, every time. This stall has a loyal following, and its reputation is almost legendary. The contrast in texture is what Chey Sua does very well – and they do this by basically frying one side to a crisp while leaving the other side only lightly fried. Like many other good carrot cake stalls, Chey Sua still makes its own carrot cake. In particular, they steam their carrot cake in small aluminium bowls which the stall owner claims are 40 years old. The stall was first started by the owner's mother, who passed on the skills of making carrot cake to her daughter. According to the owner, the dish is still being fried the same way that her mother used to do it. Unfortunately, I felt that the flavour of the carrot cake lacked a bit of oomph the day I tried it.

· · · · ·

The **Carrot Cake** stall at Chomp Chomp in Serangoon Gardens has been around for quite a while. It is one of those heritage hawker stalls where business has been passed down from father to son. The father used to peddle his carrot cake around Philip Street in Serangoon and settled at Chomp Chomp in 1976. He is still around, but his son has well and truly taken over.

The white version of carrot cake at this stall is better than the black version. It is fried till crispy, and the nice, savoury flavour comes from the secret fish sauce which has gone through some tweaking by the owner, plus the addition of prawns.

· · · · ·

Guan Kee at Changi steams its own carrot cake and you should be able to taste the difference with the white version since the flavour is not masked by black sauce. But, I must honestly tell you that the white version is not that great, which is a bit of a disappointment. However, the black version is well worth wasting a few calories over. The Uncle fries it till it has all those wonderfully caramelised charred bits that are oh-so-heavenly!

· · · · ·

I also found really good carrot cake in the most surprising of locations – Newton Food Centre, the place with Singapore's greatest concentration

A NEW GENERATION
CARROT CAKE
HAWKER

Have a look at the next evolution in carrot cake, courtesy of the Gen X-ers from **Seng Kee Carrot Cake**, who are coming up with innovative ways of updating age-old favourites. Let me take you through the process of making next genera-tion carrot cake. First, you buck the trend of taking the easy way out and invest in a really cool machine that can steam trays of homemade carrot cake! You may be able to just make out the bits of radish in this carrot cake.

Next, innovate the method of frying the carrot cake. First, fry the chye poh (preserved radish) in the middle of the pan until fragrant. Then, when they are really nice and almost crispy, mix the chye poh with the carrot cake and add the eggs, making sure that it is about 2cm thick. Fry until crispy on the outside and just cooked on the inside. This whole process takes almost 10 minutes!

Wallah! Next generation carrot cake – crispy on the outside, yummy on the inside, 2cm thick and not so oily!

of BBQ seafood stalls and a place more well known for tourists, as well as hawkers who are out to make a quick buck from tourists. However, I must say that the carrot cake at **Heng Carrot Cake** turned out to be better than expected. The stall has been there since Newton Food Centre was first built in 1971 and the hawkers are still steaming their own carrot cake because they insist that homemade carrot cake tastes better. Their efforts are quite evident in the white version – the texture of the carrot cake was just nice. It was softer and more "wobbly" than the commercial version and you could even make out the strips of radish in it. It was fried till crispy on the outside, but moist and soft on the inside. Very tasty. The black version was also very good and they managed to fry it till it was nice and caramelised. This may be one of the rare stalls where I find that both white and black versions are just as good.

· · · · ·

The End of Char Kway Teow

LESLIE'S TOP PICKS FOR CARROT CAKE

Bukit Merah View Carrot Cake
4.6/5 for black carrot cake
4.5/5 for white carrot cake

Some hawkers make their carrot cake from rice flour at their stall, but how many hawkers go one step further and actually mill the rice grains themselves? This stall does!

Bukit Merah View Food Centre,
115 Bukit Merah View #01-279 S151115,
7am to 2pm, 6pm to 1am, open everyday

Chey Sua Carrot Cake
4.25/5

The contrast in texture is what Chey Sua does very well – and they do this by basically frying one side to a crisp while leaving the other side only lightly fried.

Toa Payoh West Market and Food Court,
127 Toa Payoh Lorong 1 #02-30 S310127,
6am to 1pm, closed on Mondays

Carrot Cake
4.25/5

The white version of carrot cake at this stall is better than the black version.

Chomp Chomp Food Centre,
20 Kensington Park Road, Stall 36 S557269,
5.30pm to midnight, closed on alternate Tuesdays

Guan Kee
4.25/5

The black version is well worth wasting a few calories over. The Uncle fries it till it has all those wonderful caramelised charred bits that are oh-so-heavenly!

Changi Village Market and Food Centre,
2 Changi Village Road #01-02 S500002,
11am to 11pm, closed on Mondays

Heng Carrot Cake
4.25/5

The carrot cake here is softer and more "wobbly" than the commercial version and you can even make out the strips of radish in it.

Newton Food Centre,
500 Clemenceau Avenue North #01-28 S229495,
open in the evenings everyday

Seng Kee Carrot Cake
4/5

Try the next generation carrot cake here!

Bukit Timah Food Centre and Market,
116 Upper Bukit Timah Road #02-182 S588172,
7.30am to 11pm, closed on Thursdays

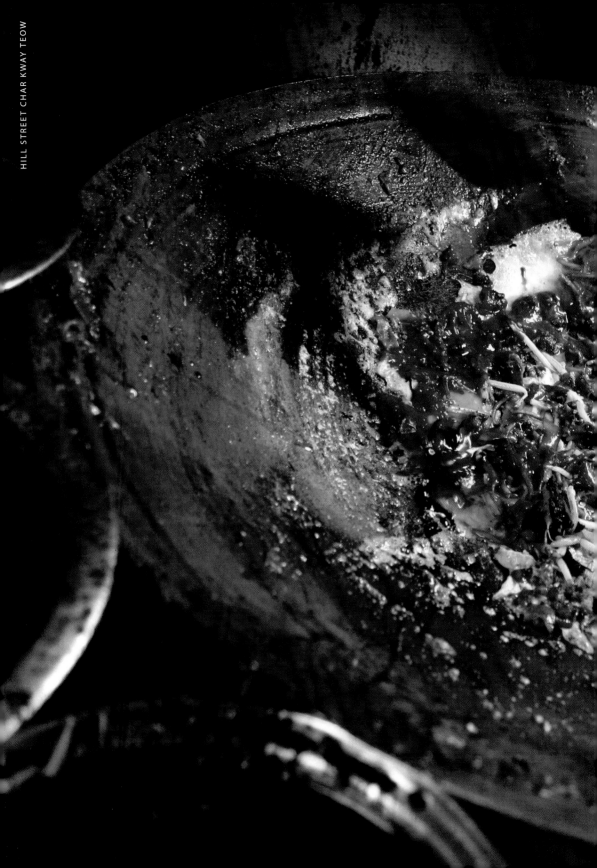

CHAR
KWAY
TEOW

The End of Char Kway Teow

Frying a plate of char kway teow seems to be a dying art in Singapore. Of all the hawker dishes, char kway teow is the most artisanal because the essence of a plate of char kway teow lies almost solely in the hands of the hawker.

C har kway teow has such a bad reputation. Ask anyone to name you the most unhealthy hawker food they can think of, and char kway teow will probably be one of the dishes mentioned. After all, it is nothing more than starch fried in pork lard, and flavoured with fish sauce and sweet black sauce. And then, the fear of contracting Hepatitis A from eating partially cooked cockles puts another nail in the coffin. A healthy char kway teow? Sounds like an incontrovertible oxymoron.

As a result, the popularity of char kway teow has waned over the years and now, you can hardly name 10 good char kway teow stalls in Singapore. That is a real shame, because when fried well, char kway teow really hits the spot. So, the thing with char kway teow is to make sure you never waste precious calories on a mediocre plate. Make sure you hantam (whack) the best versions of this dish – one that is fried with good lard: crispy, crunchy and oh-so-savoury, to get that knockout punch. The hawker must control his fire well and the timing of the stir-fry must be just right – this will ensure that the char kway teow comes out with the right texture every time. Unfortunately, frying a plate of char kway teow seems to be a dying art in Singapore. Of all the hawker dishes, char kway teow is the most artisanal because the essence of a plate of char kway teow lies almost solely in the hands of the hawker. The other ingredients – like kway teow, eggs, sweet sauce and cockles, are pretty generic. (The only "special ingredient" might be the chilli.) Unlike Hokkien mee, everything is pretty much laid bare, so there is no way to hide your poor frying skills.

The way I see it, the future of char kway teow looks pretty bleak. Of the most famous char kway teows in town, only a few next generation hawkers are stepping up to take over the ladle of the char kway teow masters. I think there are many reasons for this – firstly, you do not earn much from selling char kway teow. Secondly, it is not a dish that can be easily translated and franchised since there are no secret ingredients involved. Sure, you could set up a stall in a food court and employ someone to fry char kway teow, but unlike chicken rice, there is nothing you can really control from a central kitchen. Thirdly, unlike dishes like prawn mee and Hokkien mee, where you can increase the price by adding sexier ingredients, like bigger prawns or even crabs, there aren't really higher grade cockles you can add to char kway teow. And even if you are able to find a new generation hawker who doesn't mind the heat and hard work of frying char kway teow, as well as the limited rewards and little prospect of expansion, you will still have to deal with the pressure from the Health Promotion Board, which warns people that pork lard and eggs are really bad for health, and we should eat less of it!

My personal test for a good char kway teow is whether I can actually finish the whole plate. I hardly do this nowadays (because of health reasons), but if I do, then the char kway teow must be really shiok! I guess the most important aspect of a good char kway teow, apart from taste (which comes from the lard, the wok fire and the timing of the stir-fry), is the texture and fluidity of the noodles. The noodles have got to be lively and smooth when you slurp them up, rather than limp.

· · · · ·

I think that any self-confessed char kway teow fan will need to try the char kway teow at **Hill Street Char Kway Teow** at least once in his lifetime. After reviewing several other char kway teow stalls, I still haven't found any other stall that could surpass this old man's plate. This char kway teow is the real deal.

The texture and taste of the kway teow here is absolutely fabulous. Plus the owner, Mr Ng, uses a liberal amount of crunchy sweet towgay (beansprouts) and koo chai (chives) which culminates in an explosion of taste and texture in your mouth. Mr Ng also told me that his sweet black sauce has undergone a bit of modification. Oh yes, a bit of pandan leaves, a bit of this and a bit of that goes into the secret black sauce of unrevealed origins. You should look at how Uncle swirls his kway teow around the wok with a ladle in the right hand and chopsticks in the left! He's still enjoying his job, nay, his passion after 48 years. Unfortunately, his sons do not want to take over the business, so it is only a matter of time before this great hawker legend becomes just a distant memory. Is this as good as char kway teow gets? So far, for me at least, it sure is.

· · · · ·

Hai Kee Teochew Char Kway Teow stall, now at Telok Blangah, is famous for its long queue which used to start at 4.30pm even though it was open for business only at 5pm, when it was still at Commonwealth Food Centre.

The End of Char Kway Teow

The Teochew Ah Chik here has been frying char kway teow for over 30 years, and has built his reputation as the char kway teow stall that is generous with cockles. Day in, day out. "Mai hiam! Mai haam! See you joi! Mai mee, mai ter lah!" (No chilli, no cockles, more black sauce, no noodles or pork lard.) Talk about repetitive stress disorder! But this man always seems to be enjoying himself quite a bit.

The taste of the char kway teow here is just right. It's got that nice savoury flavour mixed with a tinge of sweetness, and just the right amount of fish sauce. Definitely good enough to spend some precious calories and cholesterol points on!

· · · · ·

Good char kway teow is indeed hard to find. But I have found **Meng Kee Char Kway Teow** to be another stall worth spending some of your calories on. This stall is manned by a father and daughter team. From what I hear, unlike a lot of other stalls where the "old hand" is still the champion, the father has been quite successful in imparting his skills to his daughter. I haven't eaten the father's version, but I'm told that his version is more oily while the daughter's is more wet.

I found myself finishing off the whole plate of this char kway teow. This is certainly one stall that has a high Satisfaction per Calorie (S/C) rating!

· · · · ·

If you want to taste something with a bit of vintage, check out **No. 18 Zion Road Fried Kway Teow**. The hawker at this stall has been around since the days when John Travolta had a really cool hairstyle and a prominent chin. I prefer char kway teow with lots of towgay (beansprouts) and koo chai (chives) as it gives that special crunchy sweetness and balances out the rich savoury flavours of the lup cheong (waxed Chinese sausages), lard and noodles. So, when this plate of char kway teow came, I was pretty excited. It was one good looking, dare I say, sexy plate of noodles!

The kway teow was slippery and lively, and has that "this wok has been used to fry the kway teow since before you were born" taste. However, my seasoned makankakis, HolyC and Smart, both insisted that it used to be even better once upon a time. For me, a dash more black sauce would have made the dish more shiok.

· · · · ·

I was most impressed with the hawker at **Guan Kee Char Kway Teow**. He is part of that generation of Singaporeans that continues to exemplify the spirit of our founding fathers – that of hard work and dedication to even the most menial of tasks. In the two hours I spent at Ghim Moh Market and Food Centre that day, there was a perpetual queue of at least 15 people waiting in line for this stall's char kway teow. This Uncle was totally focused on frying his noodles. His forehand and backhand strokes, which he has perfected over the last 41 years, have become so ingrained that I believe each new plate of char kway teow gets exactly the same number of swirls as the one before!

Uncle doesn't talk much. He doesn't even waste energy smiling. He has just one goal in mind – to fry your char kway teow. Such is the dedication to his craft that his wife proudly proclaimed that the plate of char kway teow I was about to enjoy is exactly the same as what he was serving 41 years ago. After all that, I wish I could honestly tell you that this was the best plate of char kway teow in the world. But I can't. All I can say is that my tastebuds might be different from the thousands of people who frequent his shop weekly. I thought the texture of the kway teow was excellent – the noodles were slippery and lively, something that is made possible by the generous use of freshly prepared pork lard. Auntie tells

A 20-YEAR-OLD HEALTHY CHAR KWAY TEOW!

To counter the bad reputation char kway teow has for being unhealthy, an increasing number of char kway teow stalls are putting more vegetables on top of their noodles, so as to disguise the artery-clogging properties of what is essentially rice noodles in a lard-based sauce.

But if you think that the drive towards a healthier char kway teow is a recent trend, you'll be surprised to hear that the hawker at **Heng Huat Fried Kway Teow** has been frying his char kway teow this way for over 20 years, from the time he took over his father's stall at Spottiswoode Park. He started adding vegetables not because of health reasons, but because he felt it actually tasted better that way. He claims that he was the first one to fry char kway teow this way, and that other people, especially the famous stall at Golden Mile Food Centre, copied him.

I actually like this char kway teow better than the more famous one at Golden Mile. Uncle adds chye poh (preserved radish) to the char kway teow and that gives it a bit of kick. Still, I am a firm believer that char kway teow requires lard and without lard, it is impossible for char kway teow to reach its full potential. That said, this char kway teow is actually enjoyable although there is no lard, and the vegetables will definitely soothe your conscience.

me that the rest of the condiments, from the soya sauce to the chilli and sweet sauce, come straight from the bottle. To me, the char kway teow lacked the smoky flavour of caramelised soya sauce, which is what makes char kway teow so utterly tasty, but it was still good enough to be on my list of top picks.

．．．．．

If you want to try a different kind of char kway teow, head over to **Dong Ji Fried Kway Teow** at Old Airport Road Food Centre. I am sure that the first thing you will say when you see the char kway teow there will be, "Ay? How come this plate of char kway teow got prawns one?" Ah, how very observant. Not only are there prawns in the char kway teow, there is squid, and of course, the obligatory cockles.

The char kway teow here seems to be more like a fusion between the Penang and Singapore styles. Uncle fries the prawns first to infuse the lard with crustacean flavour before adding in the kway teow, just like how the Penang hawkers do it. And after frying the kway teow, Uncle will add cockle juice to bring the flavour back towards Singapore. So, the real beauty of Dong Ji's version is that you get the best of both worlds in this one plate of char kway teow.

One of the big differences between Penang char kway teow and Singapore char kway teow is the level of sweetness. Our style is usually sweeter because of the liberal use of sweet black sauce, while the Penang style is more savoury. This stall is somewhere in between and honestly, I thought the plate of char kway teow was pretty good. The kway teow was lively and I liked the way it sort of stuck momentarily to the lips as it leapt off the chopsticks into the mouth.

．．．．．

LESLIE'S TOP PICKS FOR CHAR KWAY TEOW

Hill Street Char Kway Teow
4.75/5

Mr Ng uses a liberal amount of crunchy sweet towgay (beansprouts) and koo chai (chives) which culminates in an explosion of taste and texture in your mouth.

Bedok South Market and Food Centre, 16 Bedok South Road #01-187 S460016, open for lunch till 4pm, then 6pm onwards till he runs out of food, closed on Mondays

Hai Kee Teochew Char Kway Teow
4.5/5

The taste of the char kway teow here is just right. It has got that nice savoury flavour mixed with a tinge of sweetness, and just the right amount of fish sauce.

Telok Blangah Crescent Market and Food Centre, 11 Telok Blangah Crescent #01-102 S090011, 5pm to 10pm, closed on Sundays

Meng Kee Char Kway Teow
4.5/5

I find myself finishing off the whole plate of this char kway teow. This is certainly one stall that has a high Satisfaction per Calorie (S/C) rating!

Wei Xuan Eating House, 22 Havelock Road, #01-669 S160022, 10.30am to 7pm from Mondays to Saturdays, 10.30am to 4pm on Sundays

No. 18 Zion Road Fried Kway Teow
4.25/5

The hawker at this stall has been around since the days when John Travolta had a really cool hairstyle and a prominent chin.

Zion Road Riverside Food Centre, 70 Zion Road, Stall 17 S247792, 12pm to 3pm and 6pm to 11pm, open everyday

Guan Kee Char Kway Teow
4/5

The texture of the kway teow is excellent – it is slippery and lively, something that is made possible, I am told, by the generous use of freshly prepared pork lard.

Ghim Moh Market and Food Centre, 20 Ghim Moh Road #01-12 S270020, 9.30am to 2.30pm, closed on Mondays and Fridays

Dong Ji Fried Kway Teow
4.25/5

The char kway teow here seems to be more like a fusion between Penang (more savoury) and Singapore (sweeter) styles.

Old Airport Road Food Centre, 51 Old Airport Road #01-138 S390051, 8am to 2pm, open everyday

Heng Huat Fried Kway Teow
4/5

This char kway teow is actually enjoyable although there is no lard, and the vegetables will definitely soothe your conscience.

Pasir Panjang Food Centre, 121 Pasir Panjang Road #01-36 S118543, 11am to 9.30pm, closed on Sundays and public holidays

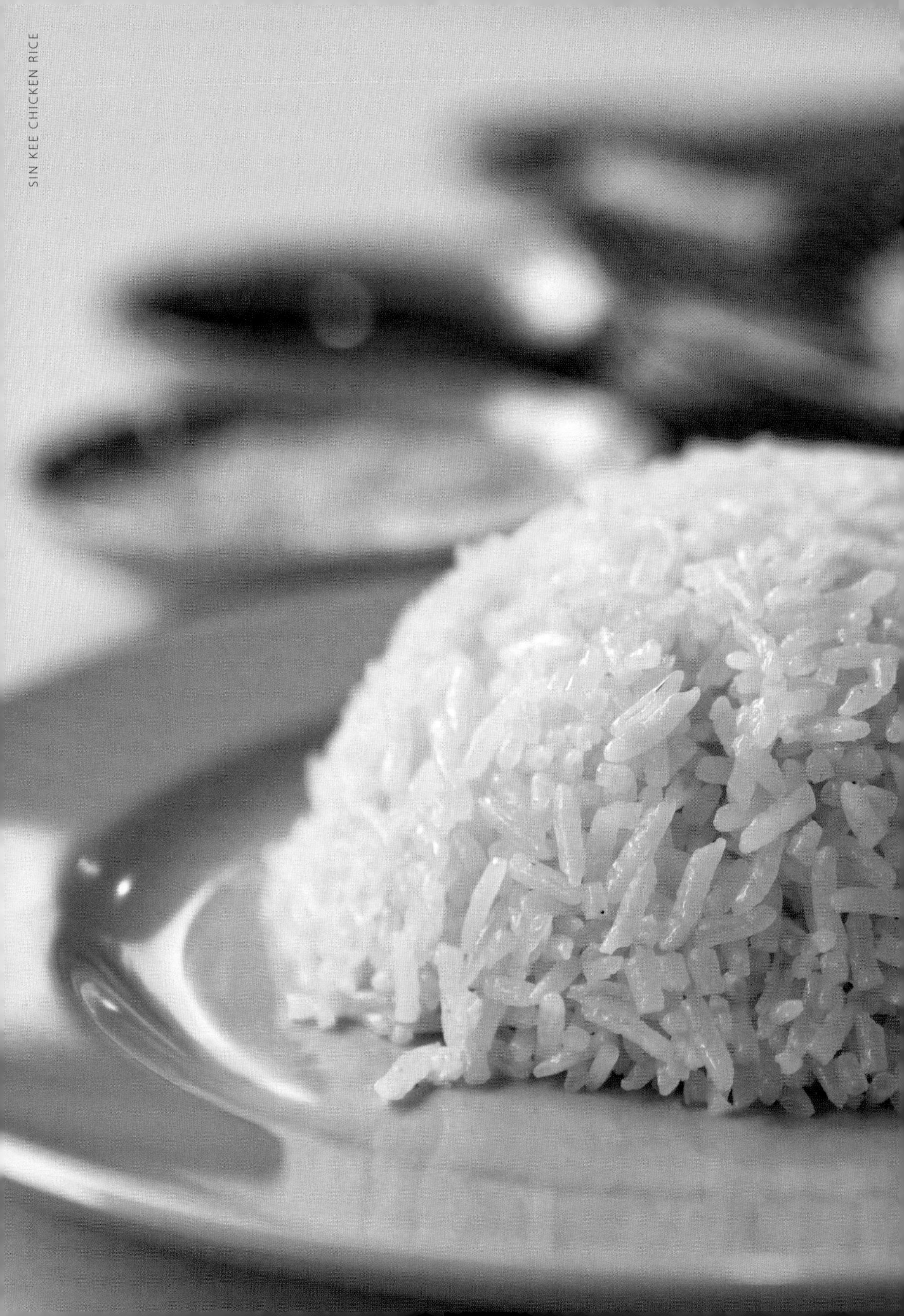

CHICKEN
RICE

Heaven is a piece of thigh meat with chilli, ginger and thick soya sauce. Put the whole thing in your mouth and POW! Cool tender flesh, crunchy skin, smooth gelatin, tangy, spicy, savoury, and gingery flavours all combine to give that SHIOK feeling!

I will be the first to admit that I am not a chicken rice purist. According to chicken rice purists, authentic Hainanese chicken is never put into cold water after cooking, and never hung because it will drain out all the precious juices. The chicken must be an old mother hen, which has laid two eggs (not one, not three, exactly two!) and it must be served plain, without drizzling sauce of any kind. To not follow any one of the above rules would be violating the Hainanese Chicken Rice Code.

But for the heathens among us, like me – the pariah of chicken rice eaters, I actually like my chicken with the yummy savoury sauce that some hawkers drizzle over it. The addition of sauce is one of the biggest differences between traditional chicken rice and modern-day chicken rice. Perhaps this soya based sauce is necessary because chickens nowadays do not taste as "chicken-y" as the free-range chickens in the past, so some sauce is necessary to give it a bit more flavour. Some call it the Cantonese style chicken rice in Singapore, and this style is now widely accepted. In fact, while people say there are three key ingredients in chicken rice – the chicken, the rice and the chilli – I propose that there are four. The fourth being the drizzling sauce. There are many good chicken rice places in Singapore, as the technique of making good chicken rice is quite well known in the public domain. Even the generic food court chicken rice is often better than anything you can find overseas! Yet, it is difficult to find chicken rice that comes up tops in all four categories of chicken, rice, chilli and drizzling sauce. Somehow, hawkers tend to excel in only one or two categories.

To me, the best chicken rice needs a winning combination of (1) soft, white voluptuous, succulent chicken meat, the type you can really sink your teeth into, and smooth, silky skin with a lovely gelatinous layer underneath; (2) fragrant rice, each grain coated with savoury chicken broth or chicken oil, and it must not be mushy, but full of texture and flavour; (3) chilli sauce with "kick" – not too sweet, and lime juice should be used instead of vinegar; and (4) fragrant drizzling sauce, usually a mix of sesame oil and soya sauce. Heaven is a piece of thigh meat with chilli, ginger and thick soya sauce. Put the whole thing in your mouth and POW! Cool tender flesh, crunchy skin, smooth gelatin, tangy, spicy, savoury, and gingery flavours all combine to give that SHIOK feeling!

Chicken rice connoisseurs would all agree that the Golden Age of chicken rice ended when the legendary Swee Kee closed its doors over 20 years ago. Back then, there was no competition. If you wanted to showcase the best that Singapore had to offer a tourist, you would bring him or her to Swee Kee.

Today, there are many types of chicken rice to choose from – kampung chicken rice, boneless chicken rice, traditional Hainanese chicken rice vs Cantonese style chicken rice, and even Sakura chicken rice, which comprises chicken farmed in Malaysia using Japanese technology – these chickens are not given any hormones and are allowed to roam around in an open, air-conditioned enclosure, hence making them "happier", or so people say.

Then, there is also "high-class" chicken rice, the ones served in air-conditioned restaurants. The most famous is the chicken rice at Chatterbox, located at the Meritus Mandarin Hotel. As part of my involvement in the TV programme *Buzzing Cashier*, I actually got a chance to meet Chef Han, who has been executive sous chef of the Meritus Mandarin for the past 36 years. This is where we need to set some of Singapore's hawker history straight – Chef Han has been the man in charge of Chatterbox's chicken rice since its inception and he really is the one who is responsible for its fame. However, the general public's perception is that Chatterbox's chicken rice chef left years ago to open his own stall in Pasir Ris. This is only half true. Actually, the chef who left was the chef in charge of making the chicken rice. But the real person in charge, and more importantly, the one who taught the chicken rice chef, is still helming Chatterbox. So let's set the record straight once and for all!

To find the best of the best, I ate my way through over 30 chicken rice stalls and even conducted a poll among my readers. The poll revealed the top 10 chicken rice stalls in Singapore are:

(1)   Tian Tian Hainanese Chicken Rice

(2)   Boon Tong Kee

(3)   Wee Nam Kee Hainanese Chicken Rice

(4)   Pow Sing Restaurant

(5)   Heng Ji Chicken Rice

(6)   Five Stars Kampung Chicken Rice

(7)   Tong Fong Fatt

(8)   Sin Kee/Xin Ji Famous Chicken Rice

(9)   Nan Xiang Chicken Rice

(10) Hainanese Delicacy (Far East Centre)

· · · · ·

Indeed, there is no dispute that **Tian Tian Hainanese Chicken Rice** is a very famous and well-established chicken rice stall in Singapore. It is so famous that the name, Tian Tian, is synonymous with Maxwell Road Food Centre, and this stall was the only chicken rice that Anthony Bourdain tasted when he was in town. I did feel some trepidation when we taste-tested the chicken rice at Tian Tian, given such high expectations, but the chicken rice passed with flying colours! Again, when Tian Tian expanded from its humble hawker stall at Maxwell to open a full-fledged restaurant in Joo Chiat, I paid them a visit to taste-test the food. And once again, I was not disappointed.

The thing I was most impressed with at Tian Tian was their perfectly cooked chicken – they managed to get that wonderful layer of gelatin just under the skin, even though the chicken was cooked through to the bones, with the flesh still wonderfully tender. It really is one of the best chickens around. The rice was beautifully presented, with each grain coated with savoury chicken broth. It was not too oily, and the texture and flavour were excellent. When I tried the rice at the Joo Chiat restaurant, it did not taste as flavourful and oily as the Maxwell Road Food Centre version. Madam Foo told me that they did cut down on oil because of health reasons. However, it was still very good. The chilli sauce was quite shiok and very different from other stalls. The secret was the use of lime juice instead of vinegar!

When I visited the Joo Chiat restaurant, I had the great opportunity to speak with Tian Tian's chicken supplier who happened to drop by.

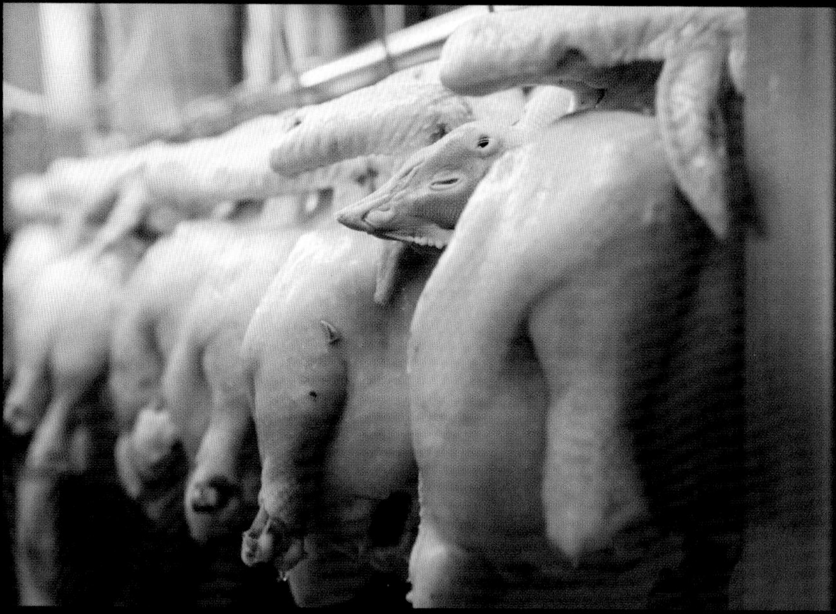

Tian Tian procures the highest grade of chicken from the supplier – each chicken weighs at least 2kg. These chickens come from Batu Pahat. Good chicken rice sellers usually choose the large chickens because the meat is tastier. The taste of the meat also depends very much on the type of feed the supplier uses. Chickens like the ones at Tian Tian have been fed quality grains like corn, resulting in chicken with richer and better tasting meat.

The expansion of Tian Tian into a restaurant means we are going to be able to enjoy Tian Tian for at least another generation. Now, we can all eat Tian Tian chicken rice in air-conditioned comfort with several side dishes to choose from, rather than having to sweat it out at Maxwell Road Food Centre. It is also a great place to bring overseas guests to showcase one of Singapore's iconic hawker dishes!

. . . . .

I think it is just human nature to side with the underdog. So when it comes to chicken rice, not many people would support the big players like **Boon Tong Kee**, saying that they are too commercial and lack the personal touch. However, makankaki Holydrummer swears by the Boon Tong Kee chicken rice in Katong, and so I gave it a try – the overall experience was surprisingly good. From rice to chicken to chilli sauce, I thought that even though not one item stood out, they were all competent and worked well in harmony. I really appreciated the pickles that came with the chicken. Though not traditional, they added a little bit of zing to the whole experience. The other item I liked was the minced ginger they provided – it was a little on the sweet side and very fragrant. One of the best ginger sauces I have come across.

. . . . .

Over at Whampoa, **Nan Xiang** is one of the few stalls that still fries its rice before cooking. A lot of chicken rice stalls have stopped this practice because it is too labour intensive, especially when you have to cook bucket loads of rice. So when you eat the rice here, you can appreciate the extra fragrance and texture that sets it apart from other stalls. Apart from the rice, I really liked the ginger here. It was different from the ginger served at other places. It had a nice saltiness that went well with the chicken, but the owner was mum about what goes into it. If you love hot chilli, you will love the chilli sauce here, which is made from chilli padi and lime juice. That extra touch of lime juice rather than vinegar is also another indication that the owner is passionate about his food. The chicken is good, but much the same as any other good chicken rice stall around. But overall, this chicken rice gets high marks from me, because of the rice and condiments.

· · · · ·

Tong Fong Fatt is a bit like Boon Tong Kee as it is also a brand name. The original Tong Fong Fatt was at Chong Pang village and started off selling sugarcane juice! Then, Augustine Koh took over his father's business in the 1990s, and decided to sell chicken rice with his brother-in-law at ABC Brickworks Food Centre. Augustine told me he wanted to make chicken rice that would appeal to the younger generation – meaning, chicken that is really tender and slippery, and with a sauce that is really special.

I found the chicken rice at Tong Fong Fatt delicious! The texture was very good, the meat was tender, and the skin as slippery and smooth as Ipoh hor fun! And as the piece de resistance, the secret sauce really sets Tong Fong Fatt apart from the rest. I was told that 12 ingredients go into making the sauce and it was a recipe Augustine came up with through trial and error. Mind you, Augustine is not even Hainanese. He's Teochew, and like most Teochews, myself included, we tend to like our food on the sweet side. When I tasted the rice, there was that nice sweet aftertaste, which I discovered was because the rice was cooked with a small amount of rock sugar. The texture of the rice was also excellent, as was the ginger. It was not raw ginger, but a nicely simmered concoction of ginger in chicken oil. On the other hand, the chilli lacked character and did not have that citrus lime zesty fragrance.

· · · · ·

Another great stall that everyone talks about is **Heng Ji Chicken Rice** in Chinatown. It is quite amazing that even with the number of chicken rice stalls at Smith Street Food Centre, this stall still stands out for many foodies. I guess it has something to do with the stall's long history at the food centre and of course, the standard of the chicken rice. The lady boss told me that her chickens are special. Just how special, she did not say. She just said to try it first to see if I felt it was special too. And indeed it was. The chicken was not exceptionally large, perhaps around 1.6kg, but I felt the meat had a very nice savoury flavour which was missing in many of the chicken rice sold at food courts. The rice that day was a bit of a disappointment. It certainly looked great, with that light tea colour and slightly broken grains, but the flavour was only so-so. Makankaki Holydrummer commented that they used a lot of fried shallots, which might explain the brown colour of the rice. The chilli sauce was a bit surprising and unique in that it was exceptionally sweet. Very unlike any chicken rice chilli I know and I am sure some people might not even consider it to be chicken rice chilli.

· · · · ·

Although **Sin Kee/Xin Ji Famous Chicken Rice** is a well-known chicken rice stall, I think it is seriously underrated. This is the famous stall that used to be on the second level of the Margaret Drive Food Centre, which has now

KAMPUNG
CHICKEN RICE

I am an unabashed lover of plump white chicken. To me, eating kampung chicken is like eating peanuts one at a time when what I really want is to scoop up a whole handful and stuff it in my mouth. For the uninitiated, kampung chicken is really a misnomer. The chickens are not really raised in a kampung. What makes them different is that they are a different breed of chicken brought in from France. Our local battery hens have white feathers and take about 60 days to grow to eating size. They spend their whole life in a cage with limited movement, pecking away at chicken feed (which is why if you sit on a sofa and munch on potato chips, you too will grow nice and fat)! The kampung chicken has orange feathers and a black head, and spends about 80 days in an enclosed space where it can exercise its muscles. That's why the chicken always reminds me more of a rock climber than a sumo wrestler.

As kampung chickens go, **Five Stars Kampung Chicken Rice** is one of the best I have tasted. The chicken is tasty and the wonderful thing is Five Stars always manages to get that layer of jelly under the skin, which makes up for the lack of fats. What I was really impressed with was the sauce they poured over the chicken – the boss, Mr Li, told me that the secret of the sauce is that they brew it themselves from soya sauce, with added soya beans and rock sugar. The sauce had a wonderful floral aroma and synergised perfectly with the chicken. Tasted great, but as I already said, I felt like I was eating peanuts one at a time!

The rice here is very good even though Mr Li admitted he did not fry the rice in oil before cooking it. The interesting thing is that because kampung chicken has got more flavour than your average local battery hen, a lot of the flavour of the rice comes from the chicken broth rather than the chicken fat. I was skeptical at first, but my group of makankakis agreed that the rice was flavourful and not too oily. The texture was also perfect, with each grain easily separated and whole.

Despite my preference for voluptuous succulent chicken meat, I was pleasantly surprised with my kampung chicken meal. All my other makankakis actually prefer this to the fat white chicken because this kampung chicken had more "chicken-y" taste. For me, I think I would only be totally happy if they could serve me a kampung chicken that is morbidly obese!

moved to a coffeeshop down the road. The thing that really got me was the fragrance of the special sauce they drizzle over the meat. There is just something so fragrant, so umami, so special about it. Perhaps the age of the stall and its premises have something to do with it? How else can you explain why old stalls tend to produce food that tastes better than air-conditioned food places?

The chicken here is how chicken should taste like – plump, voluptuous, juicy and tender, so that when you bite into the flesh, you don't get chewy bits stuck in your teeth. The rice was also very enjoyable. Take it plain, and as you swallow, smell the aroma and let the sweet taste of carbohydrates linger at the back of your palate for an extra instant. Not too oily or garlicky, this rice is one of the best I have tried.

• • • • •

Wee Nam Kee Hainanese Chicken Rice is a heritage hawker stall that has been located at Novena for the longest time. I liked the rice there, as it tasted quite rustic and had enough flavour without being too oily. However, seasoned makankaki Smart felt the rice tasted a bit bland. Although Wee Nam Kee uses the tender non-kampung type of chicken, they are not battery hens that need to be concerned about going on a diet. Although tender and juicy, the chickens here are nowhere as voluptuous as the ones from Sin Kee. Still, it is good for those who enjoy tender chicken but are concerned about the increasing convexity of their waistlines.

• • • • •

LESLIE'S TOP PICKS FOR CHICKEN RICE

Tian Tian Hainanese Chicken Rice
4.6/5 for chicken
4.5/5 for chilli sauce
4.25/5 for rice

They manage to get that wonderful layer of gelatin just under the skin, even though the chicken is cooked through to the bones, with the flesh still wonderfully tender.

Maxwell Road Food Centre,
1 Kadayanallur Street #01-10 S069184,
11am to 8pm, closed on Mondays

443 Joo Chiat Road S427656,
10.30am to 10.30pm, open everyday

Boon Tong Kee (Katong)
4.5/5

Though not traditional, the pickles that come with the chicken add a little bit of zing to the whole experience.

199 East Coast Road (opposite Holy Family Church) S428902, 11am to 10pm, open everyday

Nan Xiang Chicken Rice
4.5/5

This is one of the few stalls that still fries its rice before cooking. You can appreciate the extra fragrance and texture that sets it apart from other stalls.

Whampoa Drive Makan Place (Whampoa Food Centre), 90 Whampoa Drive #01-21 S320090, 11am to 10pm, open everyday

Tong Fong Fatt (Ghim Moh)
4.5/5 for chicken
4.25/5 for rice

The secret sauce here really sets it apart from the rest – I was told that 12 ingredients go into making the sauce.

Ghim Moh Market and Food Centre,
20 Ghim Moh Road #01-49 S270020,
10am to 9pm, open everyday

Heng Ji Chicken Rice
4.5/5 for chicken
4/5 for rice
3.5/5 for chilli sauce

The chilli sauce is a bit surprising and unique in that it is exceptionally sweet, which is unlike any other stall's chicken rice chilli.

Chinatown Complex Market,
335 Smith Street #02-131 S050335,
3pm to 9pm, open everyday

Sin Kee/Xin Ji Famous Chicken Rice
4.25/5

The thing that really gets me is the fragrance of the special sauce they drizzle over the meat. There is just something so fragrant and so umami about it.

Mei Chin Food Centre, 159 Mei Chin Road #02-22 S140159, 11am to 8pm, closed on Mondays

Wee Nam Kee Hainanese Chicken Rice
4.25/5

The chicken meat here is tender and juicy but is nowhere as voluptuous as the ones from Sin Kee.

Novena Ville (opposite Novena Church),
275 Thomson Road #01-05 S307645,
10am to 2am, open everyday

Five Stars Kampung Chicken Rice
4.5/5 for rice
4.25/5 for chicken

The chicken is tasty and the wonderful thing is Five Stars always manages to get that layer of jelly under the skin, which makes up for the lack of fats.

191/193 East Coast Road S428897,
9am to 3am, open everyday

CHINESE
ROJAK

There are several things I look for in a great rojak. Topping the list is great hae kor (fermented prawn paste).

I f you had to describe the ingredients of rojak to a westerner, I am sure he would not want to eat it. Seriously, does fruit salad dressed with a sauce made from fermented prawns sound delectable? Not only that, you get to eat it with a blackened duck egg that smells of urine. But to Singaporeans, rojak is yummy. It might not look good, but if you get rojak with freshly toasted you char kway (fried dough fritter), really flavoursome prawn paste and freshly roasted ground peanuts, it is just heavenly! To westerners, it is the stuff they see in *Fear Factor*!

There are several things I look for in a great rojak. Topping the list is great hae kor (fermented prawn paste). This is one ingredient that sets a good rojak apart from the rest. It might seem improbable for a paste made from decomposing prawns to be considered appropriate for a salad, but somehow it seems to work. Hae kor is made from belachan, which is essentially made of shrimps that have been left out to rot. The rotting process degrades the protein and releases lots of glutamates, making the paste such an excellent ingredient for many dishes. It essentially does what parmesan cheese does – it gives dishes a boost of naturally occurring gluta-mates (the natural form of MSG). There is only one undisputed source of good hae kor, and that is Penang.

The second thing I look for in a great rojak is torch ginger flower (bungah kantan). This ingredient gives rojak its typical fragrance, yet hawkers often omit it these days. The best rojak stalls also include jellyfish in the mix, and this is also another ingredient that is often omitted in run-of-the-mill rojak stalls. Lastly, and for me most importantly, the peanuts must be freshly ground. Commercially ground peanuts are widely available these days, but they lack the wonderful fragrance and moisture that freshly pounded peanuts have. For me, rojak is all about a well-balanced, sweet, savoury, tangy, spicy sauce with crumbly moist ground peanuts coating you char kway (fried dough fritter) that has been freshly toasted or grilled over charcoal.

· · · · ·

Passion. That is what separates the good from the great. And passion is what makes the hawker at **Lau Hong Ser Rojak** fry and grind his own peanuts while other hawkers get theirs from a factory. Passion makes him insist on using only the best hae kor (fermented prawn paste) from Penang and a chilli that he makes himself. It makes him continue toasting his you char kway (fried dough fritter) slowly over a small charcoal fire, even though there is a long queue of people waiting to eat his rojak. Passion makes him continue to treat each plate of rojak as if it were his last. Oh yes, I love passionate people.

Now people with passion can sometimes be perceived as eccentric. The difference between someone who is eccentric and someone who is a downright obnoxious fusspot is that we admire what the eccentric does. So when this hawker insists on opening his stall from 4.38pm to 1.38am, we forgive him because he is a genius. It takes a real hao lian (proud) Teochew Ah Hia (and I mean "proud" in a good sense) to be able to pull off a stunt like this and still have people calling up an hour ahead to place their orders.

The rojak at this stall is freshly made and served with a thick, fragrant peanut sauce by the side. The sauce is as good as rojak sauce can get. The you char kway (fried dough fritter) and tau pok (fried beancurd) are well toasted and crispy. What else can one ask for in a plate of rojak, except for a shorter waiting time?

· · · · ·

Not many people know about this one but over at East Coast Lagoon Food Village, **Kampong Rojak** serves up a really mean you char kway (fried dough fritter) rojak. The you char kway is grilled fresh over charcoal till it is just slightly charred. It is nice and crispy on the outside, but fluffy and chewy on the inside. After grilling, the you char kway is cut up and tossed in the sauce. They use very good quality Penang hae kor (fermented prawn paste) and are really generous with the roasted peanuts which they grind themselves.

The rojak here is addictive. I usually finish up all the you char kway (fried dough fritter), and then sit there picking up the peanuts bit by bit until I clean up the entire plate. The coarsely ground peanuts are a bit oily and really pang (fragrant).

· · · · ·

Hoover Rojak is one of those heritage hawkers who has spanned the generations. They have a special machine that mixes the Penang hae kor (fermented prawn paste) with their special blend of ingredients, and their sauce is perfect. The other good thing is that they also have jellyfish, and their century eggs are really good. So good that you can actually buy them by the boxes!

However, I cannot give them top marks because the you char kway (fried dough fritter) is not grilled, and to my horror, they use dry and tasteless commercially ground peanuts! Still, their hae kor (fermented prawn paste) and century eggs do make up for these shortcomings.

· · · · ·

I was a bit apprehensive when I saw the lady at **Soon Heng Silver Stream Rojak** toasting the you char kway (fried dough fritter) in an ovenette and using commercially procured ground peanuts. Still, I did find the rojak here very nice. The balance between sweet and sour was perfect, and the hae kor (fermented prawn praste) was very good. But I found the peanuts a little dry. Though they were generous with them, they just did not match the type of peanuts that are fried and ground daily by hawkers themselves. Nevertheless, I am giving this rojak high marks as the servings are generous and they include cuttlefish.

· · · · ·

Toa Payoh Rojak stall, which ironically is located in Old Airport Road Food Centre, is so popular that it has a numbering system like those found in clinics. The reason why the dish takes so long to prepare is because the hawker insists on charcoal-grilling the you char kway (fried dough fritter) before cutting them up and mixing them with the rojak sauce. I really enjoyed the tau pok (fried beancurd) and you char kway here as they were super crispy. The Penang hae kor (fermented prawn paste) rojak sauce was excellent. The only setback was the peanuts, which were not

ground at the stall, but procured from a special supplier. But after they were mixed in with the sauce, they tasted alright. Good news – the old man has an heir apparent in line, so we will get to savour this rojak for another generation.

· · · · ·

Finally, I also checked out **Clementi Brothers Rojak** at Zion Riverside Food Centre. This stall proudly shows off its Penang hae kor (fermented prawn paste) with the words "best quality" on it to assure you that you are getting the best fermented prawns there are. The rojak sauce here was indeed good, but I did not like the peanuts which were commercially bought and thus, too dry. The you char kway (fried dough fritter) was toasted and allowed to cool for too long, so they were not crispy. Overall, this is a better-than-average rojak that is worth eating when you are at this food centre.

My sources tell me that the original Clementi Brothers Rojak, situated at Clementi, is much better. This stall at the Zion Riverside Food Centre is called a "branch", but actually, what happened was that the father of the original stall was very generous and gave his recipe to a relative and even gave her permission to call the stall a branch of his famous stall.

· · · · ·

LESLIE'S TOP PICKS FOR CHINESE ROJAK

Lau Hong Ser Rojak
4.75/5

The rojak at this stall is freshly toasted and served with a thick, fragrant peanut sauce by the side. The sauce is as good as rojak sauce can be.

Dunman Road Food Centre,
271 Onan Road #02-14 S424768,
4.38pm to 1.38am, closed on Sundays

Kampong Rojak
4.5/5

The rojak here is addictive. I usually finish all the you char kway (fried dough fritter), and then sit there picking up the peanuts bit by bit until I clean up the entire plate.

East Coast Lagoon Food Village,
1220 East Coast Parkway, Stall 9 S468960,
dinner till 11pm, open everyday

Hoover Rojak
4.25/5

Their jellyfish and century eggs are really good! So good, that you can actually buy them by the boxes!

Whampoa Drive Makan Place (Whampoa Food Centre), 90 Whampoa Drive #01-06 S320090, 10.30am to 9.30pm on Mondays and Wednesdays to Sundays, 10.30am to 6pm on Tuesdays

Soon Heng Silver Stream Rojak
4.25/5

The balance between sweet and sour is perfect and the hae kor (fermented prawn paste) is very good.

HDB Hub, 480 Toa Payoh Lorong 6 #B1-23, S310480, 11am to 8pm, open everyday

Toa Payoh Rojak
4.25/5

This stall is so popular that it has a numbering system like those found in clinics. The hawker insists on charcoal-grilling every you char kway (fried dough fritter).

Old Airport Road Food Centre,
51 Old Airport Road #01-108 S390051,
12pm to 8pm, closed on Sundays

Clementi Brothers Rojak (branch)
4/5

This stall proudly shows off its Penang hae kor (fermented prawn paste) with the words "best quality" on it to assure you that you are getting the best fermented prawns there are.

Zion Riverside Food Centre,
70 Zion Road, Stall 21 S247792,
12pm to 10pm, closed on Mondays

CHWEE
KUEH

Chwee kueh is called chwee kueh because of the little dimple in the middle, where water collects after steaming.

I f you want to eat truly authentic and freshly made chwee kueh (water cake) in Singapore, you have to check out **Chye Kee Chwee Kueh** at Macpherson. This is such a unique stall. Not only does Uncle make his chwee kueh from rice flour, he goes one step further and freshly mills rice flour from broken rice grains, right in his stall! Amazing dedication and passion.

Uncle tells me he used to work in a factory that produces chwee kueh, before setting up his stall. His chwee kueh is made purely from milled rice, whereas the ones he used to make at the factory had tapioca flour in them. The process is pretty straightforward – water is added to the broken rice, fed into a machine and the milky solution comes out, which is then passed through the machine a second time. Hot water is added to the solution to thicken it, and then it is poured into moulds and steamed.

I really enjoyed Uncle's chwee kueh. It tasted like rice, but with a smooth and pasty texture. The chye poh (preserved radish) topping was a little different from the usual ones – it was less oily and had a very dry and chewy texture. While some of my makankakis complained that the chye poh was too dry, I actually really liked it.

. . . . .

I have always wondered why chwee kueh is called chwee kueh. Meaning "water cakes" in Teochew, I assumed it had something to do with the high proportion of water in the ingredient mix. Just mix lots of water with rice flour, and steam. That's it! Top it with fried chye poh (preserved radish) and chilli, and serve!

I only recently discovered that chwee kueh is called chwee kueh because of the little dimple in the middle, where water collects after steaming. I learnt this fascinating fact from the Uncle who runs **Ghim Moh Chwee Kueh** at Ghim Moh Market and Food Centre. There are many chwee kueh stalls in Singapore, and most of them sell chwee kueh that has been made by a machine in the factory, but this passionate Uncle makes his chwee kueh by hand. He pointed out that the version of chwee kueh we have is uniquely Singaporean. Chwee kueh is a Teochew dish that our forefathers modified when they arrived in Singapore. You can find chwee kueh in Swatow today, but it is topped with fried shallot oil and not chye poh (preserved radish). In Malaysia, they have their own unique version – a dessert plate-sized chwee kueh, compared to our sauce plate-sized version.

In the good old days, when hawkers made chwee kueh in clay moulds and milled their own rice, chwee kueh was so transparent you could see the bottom of the mould from the top of the kueh. There was a lot of skills involved in making the chwee kueh – the experienced chwee kueh hawker would always source for old rice to make chwee kueh, as it had greater ability to absorb water and was more fragrant. The amount of water added to the flour would also depend on the weather, as humidity was a factor in determining the outcome.

The familiar aluminium moulds were introduced in the 1970s when the National Environment Agency deemed clay moulds to be unsanitary, as they may have cracks which could serve as hiding places for bacteria. However, the Uncle from Ghim Moh Chwee Kueh stall, whose mother started selling chwee kueh from a pushcart in 1959, insists that the clay moulds made the chwee kueh more fragrant. But he is grateful for the switch to aluminium moulds since he used to experience clay mould break-ages almost everyday. He, together with a handful of other hawkers I found, continues to hand make chwee kueh everyday at his stall. Just take one bite and you'll taste the difference in this very pang (fragrant) snack that I bet you can't just eat one of!

Uncle and his wife still wake up early every morning to pour rice flour mixture into 1,500 aluminium moulds. The chwee kueh here is a glimpse of what chwee kueh was like in the past, and the long line of people queuing to buy this delectable snack every day is a testament to how handmade chwee kueh beats factory-made ones hands down. The topping for the chwee kueh here is different from the toppings I have eaten elsewhere. According to Uncle, this is a traditional recipe for chwee kueh topping – garlic, pork lard and chye poh (preserved radish). He does not add sesame seeds or sugar, so this chwee kueh is kiam pang (salty and savoury), not sweet and savoury, which is the more common taste of chwee kueh.

· · · · ·

Over in the East, anyone who frequents Bedok Interchange Food Centre will know about the famous **Bedok Chwee Kueh** stall. The texture of the kueh is very smooth and the chye poh (preserved radish) is sweet and savoury, and very yummy. This chwee kueh has expanded to many stalls islandwide, which is great as good chwee kueh is now available to more people!

· · · · ·

The old Tiong Bahru Market was famous for all the great eats, and the chwee kueh at **Jian Bo Shui Kweh** was one of them. I really like the texture of this chwee kueh. It is soft to the bite, so much so that you can basically eat it even after you remove both upper and lower dentures. The texture sets it apart from all the other chwee kueh I have eaten, and the reason for this is that they still mill their own rice flour!

The second great thing about this chwee kueh is the tasty fried chye poh (preserved radish). If you look closely, you will also notice the generous use of sesame seeds. Very pang (fragrant) indeed!

· · · · ·

LESLIE'S TOP PICKS FOR CHWEE KUEH

Chye Kee Chwee Kueh
4.5/5

Uncle makes his chwee kueh from his own rice flour, freshly milled from broken rice grains, right in his stall!

89 Circuit Road #01-129 S370089,
6.30am to 3pm, open everyday

Ghim Moh Chwee Kueh
4/5

The chwee kueh here is a glimpse of what chwee kueh was like in the past. The topping for the chwee kueh here is different from the toppings I have eaten elsewhere. This chwee kueh is kiam pang (salty and savoury), not sweet and savoury.

Ghim Moh Market and Food Centre,
20 Ghim Moh Road #01-31 S270020,
6.15am to 7pm, open everyday

Bedok Chwee Kueh
4.25/5

This chwee kueh has expanded to many stalls islandwide, which is great as good chwee kueh is now available to more people!

Bedok Interchange Food Centre
(New Upper Changi Road Food Centre),
207 New Upper Changi Road #01-53 S460207,
7am to 11pm, open everyday

Jian Bo Shui Kweh
4/5

I really like the texture of this chwee kueh – it is soft to the bite, so much so that you can basically eat it after you remove both upper and lower dentures.

Tiong Bahru Market and Food Centre,
30 Seng Poh Road #02-05 S168898,
6.30am to 11pm, open everyday

CRAB

The End of Char Kway Teow

My personal favourite is crab bee hoon. Bee hoon is an excellent medium for absorbing all the flavours of crab and other ingredients. And when crab roe is mixed in with the noodles, the gravy has this extra oomph that is just so shiok!

When I got my very first paycheck, half of it went towards paying for a Tasmanian King crab dinner for my parents and in-laws. Indeed, crabs, especially good crabs, do not come cheap, not even the crabs sold in hawker centres and cze cha restaurants.

Still, there is no denying that with the huge variety of crabs available in Singapore, and everything being relatively fresh, it is difficult to avoid being really ngian (hard up) for crabs and having irresistible cravings, once in a while. And that is why the *ieat* Crab Fest which I organised in 2009 at Chin Huat Live Seafood Restaurant was so popular. During the Crab Fest we feasted on a global array of crabs – Tasmanian King crab, Dungeness crab, Red Alaskan King crab, Cromer crab, Snow crab, even the locally-found Swimmer crab, and of course, the ever-popular Sri Lankan crab and Indonesian crab. Phwaa sayah!

So what is Singapore's favourite crab dish? With recent crab fads like crab bee hoon and salted egg crab, I had half-suspected that the Singapore classic, chilli crab, might be ousted from its preeminent position of popularity. But according to the polls conducted on my blog, chilli crab still came out tops, with 49.6 per cent voting it as their favourite dish, followed by black pepper crab (30.2 per cent) and salted egg crab (20.2 per cent).

My current personal favourite, though, is crab bee hoon. Bee hoon is an excellent medium for absorbing all the flavours of crab and other ingredients. And when crab roe is mixed in with the noodles, the gravy has this extra oomph that is just so shiok! There are generally two types of crab bee hoon in Singapore – the soup version and the dry version, but I prefer the dry version.

· · · · ·

The top place for crab bee hoon in Singapore is undoubtedly **Sin Huat Seafood Restaurant** at Geylang. I first heard of this restaurant a few years back when Anthony Bourdain featured it in his TV programme. But because of the exorbitant prices, I resisted checking it out. I also heard that Danny, the owner and chef, is a bit of a Food Nazi, and that further prevented me from eating there.

But, how can any self-professed foodie not visit this infamous restaurant at least once in his liftime? So, how was the crab bee hoon? The verdict: shiok. The best crab bee hoon I have ever tasted! Aside from one of the claws being slightly atrophied, the rest of the crab was solid. The bee hoon was neither too dry nor too wet, and had wonderfully soaked in the flavours of the crab, ginger and a mysterious stock. It was excellent, though I suppose I was expecting it to be more mind-blowing, given all the hype.

I was also lucky enough to talk to Danny – turns out our Food Nazi started off as a pig farmer and was forced to open a restaurant when the government shut down the last of the pig farms in Punggol in the early 1990s. Out of desperation, Danny learnt how to cook the usual cze cha stuff and was soon attracting a good following. Then, one day, a patron told him that he did not want to order a crab dish and a hor fun separately, and asked if Danny could just combine the two together – I think you can guess the rest. Our humble pig farmer perfected his recipe for crab bee hoon and submitted it for the Asia Food Competition in 1997. The rest is history!

· · · · ·

One of my favourite places to eat crabs is **Chin Huat Live Seafood Restaurant**. My personal favourites here are the golden sauce Sri Lankan crabs, Alaskan King crabs steamed in egg white and Snow crab bee hoon in superior broth. Situated at Sunset Way beneath a block of HDB flats, Chin Huat represents the new generation of cze cha stalls which have upgraded into comfortable air-conditioned eating places, while maintaining heartland prices.

· · · · ·

But now let's turn our attention to Singapore's favourite crab dish – chilli crab. Some time back in October 2009, the Malaysian Tourism Minister created a mini furore when she claimed that chilli crab was a Malaysian dish that had been hijacked by Singapore. Her glib comment invited a slew of media articles all affirming that chilli crab originated in Singapore. I took the opportunity to visit Madam Cher Yam Tian, who is the creator of chilli crab, to get her story.

Those of us who were around in the 1970s might remember the days when Changi was the end of the world and a trip to Changi Beach was as much an adventure as a trip to Bintan is nowadays. To get to Changi, you had to pass by Upper East Coast Road and it was here, in the kampungs, among attap houses, that the story of chilli crab began.

Madam Cher and her husband lived in one of those attap houses. Her husband, Mr Lim, who was a policeman, would catch crabs from the beach and bring them home for dinner. Being Teochew, she would simply steam the crabs and eat them plain. But one day, he asked his wife if she could cook something a little different. That was when she stir-fried the crabs in tomato sauce. Mr Lim thought the taste was good, except that it was a little too sweet. He suggested adding some chilli into the sauce as well. This was the beginning of a Singaporean institution. Madam Cher started making her chilli crab for friends and family, and everyone told her she should sell her chilli crab. So, in 1950, she began selling her chilli crab from a pushcart along the road.

Madam Cher's version of chilli crab is not quite the same as the one we are now familiar with. She did not put eggs or sambal in her recipe. That idea came a little later, when the owner of Dragon Phoenix Restaurant started cooking chilli crab and made some modifications to the recipe. (Incidentally, Dragon Phoenix was one of the "Four Heavenly Kings" of Cantonese cuisine at that time, along with Sin Leong, Red Star and Lai Wah Restaurant.)

By 1956, Madam Chew had progressed from a pushcart to a little shack that was lit by a hurricane lamp. Since there were coconut palms along the beach near the shack, her husband called the place "Palm Beach Seafood". By 1963, they expanded to a simple zinc-roofed building and it was around this time that chilli crab was quickly becoming a national dish.

Madam Chew's restaurant was sold off in the 1980s when her family migrated to New Zealand for 15 years before returning to Singapore. When they returned, her son Roland started working at Palm Beach Restaurant before joining his godfather at Sin Leong Restaurant. When his godfather decided to call it a day, he handed the restaurant over to Roland, who with the blessing of his godfather, subsequently renamed the place **Roland Restaurant**. This is the restaurant that sells Madam Chew's original recipe chilli crab till today. It is sweeter than the version we all know and not as rich,

because no egg is added to the sauce. With this lighter sauce, you can actually appreciate the sweetness of the crab better.

Roland Restaurant also serves up the modern version of chilli crab, which is actually pretty good as well. It is not overly spicy or sweet and the sauce is chock full of crab roe, which makes for a deadly combination with the eggs.

• • • • •

Of course, the other crab dish that must be talked about in a chapter about crabs is black pepper crab. The creation of this dish is widely attributed to the famous Long Beach Seafood Restaurant, but if you want to find the best black pepper crab around, a lot of people will tell you about this particular place where you have to ring up early in the day to book your crabs before coming down at around 5pm to start queuing for a table.

The notoriety of **Eng Seng Restaurant** is legendary. The queue is so bad that it had me intimidated for the longest time. There was also a rumour that an Empress Dowager-like figure commanded the restaurant and another Food Nazi figure would chase people away when the restaurant ran out of crabs! To make matters worse, they are usually sold out by 8pm. How to eat like that? But then again, like that, how not to eat?

When I finally got to try the black pepper crab, I found it to be strangely addictive. These black pepper crabs are not like the ones served elsewhere. The sauce is slightly sweet and not overly spicy. As Goldilocks would say, "It is just right!" It was so shiok that I ate more crabs at that one sitting, than I ever had for a long while! The lady manning the register told me that there was some secret ingredient in the black sauce, but she did not tell me what it was.

• • • • •

LESLIE'S TOP PICKS FOR CRABS

Sin Huat Seafood Restaurant
4.6/5 for crab bee hoon

The best crab bee hoon I have ever tasted! The bee hoon is not too dry nor too wet and has wonderfully soaked in the flavours of the crab, ginger and that mysterious stock.

659/661 Geylang Road (junction of Geylang Lorong 35) S389589, 6pm to midnight

Chin Huat Live Seafood Restaurant
4.5/5 for golden sauce crab and salted egg crab

My personal favourites here are the golden sauce Sri Lankan crabs, Alaskan King crabs steamed in egg white and Snow crab beehoon in superior broth.

105 Clementi Street 12 (Sunset Way) #01-30 S120105, 11.30am to 2.30pm and 5.30pm to 11pm, open everyday

Roland Restaurant
4.5/5 for chilli crab

They serve up the modern version of chilli crab, which is actually pretty good. It is not overly spicy or sweet and the sauce is chock full of crab roe.

89 Marine Parade Central #06-750 S440089, 11.30am to 2.30pm and 6pm to 10.30pm, open everyday

Eng Seng Restaurant
4.5/5 for black pepper crab

The black pepper crab here is strangely addictive. The sauce is slightly sweet and not overly spicy. As Goldilocks would say, "It is just right!"

247 Joo Chiat Road (junction of Joo Chiat Place and Still Road) S427502, 4.30pm to 8pm, open everyday

CURRY
PUFF

The modern day curry puff is a Chinese version of the Malay version of the Indian version of an English snack!

There are basically two types of curry puffs in Singapore – the Malay version, called epok epok, has a thin, crispy crust and a filling largely made of buttery curried potatoes and freshly boiled eggs. The Chinese version's crust is thicker, more buttery and more oily. The filling usually contains chicken meat as well as potatoes and eggs.

It is interesting to note that both versions are based on the Indian interpretation of an English snack. The Indian curry puff is a triangular pastry, which the Indians made for their colonial masters back in the days of the British Empire. Then, they brought it over to Singapore and the Malays took on the idea of a pastry filled with curry, but they changed the shape of the curry puff to resemble a crescent moon, the religious symbol of Islam. Then of course, the Chinese wanted to get in on the action and created a Chinese version of the Malay curry puff, with a pastry that is more buttery. So, the modern day Chinese curry puff is a Chinese version of the Malay version of the Indian version of an English snack!

Oddly, most curry puffs in Singapore are not made of puff pastry, but of shortcrust pastry. The typical Chinese version, for example Old Chang

Kee's curry puffs, are a bit too oily for me, giving me a jerlak feeling quickly. I prefer epok epok, which is much lighter, while not compromising in taste.

· · · · ·

I'm sure you've seen multi-layered curry puffs sold by 1A Curry Puff stalls all over the island, right? But did you know there are really two 1A curry puffs in Singapore – one that operates the franchise and the other that is still operated by a feisty old grandma in Henderson? This Henderson stall, called **Soon Soon Huat 1A Crispy Curry Puff**, was the originator of this particular type of curry puff. It was invented around 17 years ago by a Teochew Ah Mah, who was at that time making fried popiah and soon kueh. One day she decided to combine the two recipes, and came up with the multi-layered crispy curry puff that we are now so familiar with. The curry puff later became known as 1A Curry Puff as their stall was then at Block 1A Eunos Crescent.

The curry puffs at Soon Soon Huat are really good. The skin is crispy and thin, more like a Malay epok epok than a Chinese style curry puff. The filling is quite moist, almost as if there is a bit of gravy in it. And, I actually quite liked the sardine puff which really reminded me of the Malay version, except that you get the multi-layered crispy skin.

· · · · ·

A few people have told me that there is a shop at Sunshine Plaza that sells some of the best chicken pies and curry puffs in Singapore. Ironically, the shop's name is **Delicious Muffins**! Turns out the owner was a chef at Hilton Hotel before he started his own business. That explains why the chicken pies remind me of the ones you usually find in hotel cafes.

It is hard to find a curry puff made from puff pastry that is not overly oily. I usually avoid eating them because the combination of oil and spices gives me a bad case of indigestion. However, the curry puffs at this

Sunshine Plaza stall were great. The puff pastry was thin, but resilient, and the curry puff was chock full of buttery potatoes and chicken pieces in fragrant curry spices. Definitely one of the best puff pastry curry puffs I have come across.

. . . . .

Epok epok tastes best when eaten fresh out of the fryer. That means that you either need to get to the stall early in the morning or find a stall that has a high turnover of epok epok throughout the day, and **Killiney Curry Puff** is one stall that has just that. The filling is made with local Holland potatoes which are ideal to be fried with rempah (mixed spice paste) to produce a creamy and spicy sweet filling that goes so well with the thin and crispy crust. The final icing on the cake is a sweet and fragrant sambal. Just add a hot cup of teh tarik – simply shiok!

. . . . .

If it is Malay epok epok that you want, head on down to **Epok Epok Central** at Eunos. Do you remember the scene from the movie *Ratatouille*, when the food critic Anton was transported back to his childhood with one taste of the dish Ratatouille? Well, the epok epok here sort of did the same thing for makankaki Mr YaKwang. So, after taking the first few pictures, I gingerly held the epok epok in my hand and prepared myself to be transported into a surrealistic dream sequence as I bit into it. But I felt nothing. It could be because the curry puffs I ate growing up were from my school tuckshop, and they were a little different. That's not to say the epok epok here was not good. It was excellent. The crust was thin and crispy, and combined well with the freshly boiled egg and buttery curried potatoes. I downed about five of them before I knew it! By the way, this stall also sells very decent nasi lemak *(see chapter on nasi lemak).*

· · · · ·

Another very impressive epok epok is found at **Merpati Putih**. The family who makes these curry puffs used to have a stall at the Geylang Serai Temporary Market, where they had a picture of Minister of Environment Yaacob Ibrahim on it, but now they operate from home. They make the most impressive epok epok I have ever eaten, in that the filling is very generous. The sardine puffs have more sardines than onions. Then, there is their special order item – their heart-shaped curry puffs. Each of these huge curry puffs contains pieces of yummy chicken meat, potatoes and eggs inside.

I managed to convince Madam Junaida of Merpati Putih to make minced beef epok epok for me. After experimenting with several shapes, she finally settled on the simple "Macdonald's apple pie" shape for her beef epok epok. She seasoned the minced beef like a keema (traditional Indian meat dish), fried it till it was fragrant, and then added some potatoes. After trying it, I don't think I could eat an ordinary potato epok epok again – very shiok!

· · · · ·

It is good to know that some things never change. The **Katong Chicken Curry Puff** stall, and its offshoot, the Lagoon Chicken Curry Puff at East Coast Lagoon Food Village, have been around for 30 years. Both still use an old glass bottle as a rolling pin! The fillings of the puffs in both shops are nice and moist, not overly spicy, with a crust that is crispy, but not too buttery. Of course, finding the bits of chicken meat is like looking for Easter eggs. You know they're there, but when you find it, you still get excited. It is good to know that this good old curry puff has not changed in all these years. Great as an afternoon snack!

· · · · ·

LESLIE'S TOP PICKS FOR CURRY PUFFS

Soon Soon Huat 1A Crispy Curry Puff
4.25/5

The curry puffs here are really good – the skin is crispy and thin, more like a Malay epok epok rather than a Chinese style curry puff.

94 Henderson Road #01-276 S150094,
8am till sold out, closed on Mondays

Delicious Muffins
4.25/5

The curry puffs here are not overly oily. Definitely one of the best puff pastry curry puffs I have come across.

Sunshine Plaza, 91 Bencoolen Street
#01-51 S189652, 11.30am to 8pm,
closed on 8th, 18th and 28th of every month

Killiney Curry Puff
4.25/5

The filling is made with local Holland potatoes which are ideal to be fried with rempah (mixed spice paste) to produce a creamy and spicy sweet filling that goes so well with the thin and crispy crust.

93 Killiney Road S239536,
7am to 7.30pm

Epok Epok Central
4.25/5

The curry puffs here are excellent – the crust is thin and crispy, and combined well with the freshly boiled egg and buttery curried potatoes.

Eunos Crescent Market and Food Centre,
4A Eunos Crescent #01-09 S402004,
7am to 7pm, closed on Mondays

Merpati Putih
4.5/5 for minced beef epok epok
4.25/5 for epok epok

Try their special order item – heart-shaped curry puffs. Each of these huge curry puffs contains pieces of yummy chicken meat, potatoes and eggs inside.

Operates from home
To order, call 91653577

Katong Chicken Curry Puff
4/5

This stall has been around for 30 years and they still use an old glass bottle as a rolling pin!

Marine Parade Central Market and Food Centre,
84 Marine Parade Central #01-132 S440084,
8am to 6pm, closed on Mondays

FISH
SOUP

The End of Char Kway Teow

Healthy stuff can't be all that tasty, right? Wrong!

Every time I order fish head bee hoon soup, I will wonder, "How come the soup is white?" Someone told me that milk was added to the fish soup to make it white, and I had always imagined that this was so. So imagine my surprise when a hawker explained to me that there was no milk in fish soup!

The first step in making Cantonese style "milky" fish soup is to deep-fry the fish slices. Once fried and the oil has absorbed the fishy flavour, most of the oil is decanted, leaving just enough to mix with the soup stock. I thought the stock would be some really thick fish stock, so I was very surprised to find out that it was just a simple ginger stock! Next, the lid is put on the wok and high heat is applied until white smoke starts streaming from the edges. The ginger stock is then poured over the lid slowly. The combination of high heat, stock and oil enables the oil and water to combine together to form a milky emulsion! It takes almost five to 10 minutes to make one bowl of fish soup! And because every bowl is made individually, you can't really ask for more soup without having to wait. After the soup has turned a milky white colour, some condiments are added. The last step is the addition of Chinese rice wine just before serving. Some stalls even substitute rice wine with XO brandy.

· · · · ·

The man who explained this amazing process to me was none other than the son of the lady who originally ran a stall at Hong Kong Street. As you know, the name Hong Kong Street is pretty much synonymous with milky fish soup, in the same way that the name Jalan Kayu is synonymous with small, crispy, round prata. The man, who currently runs the **Hong Kong Street Chun Kee** at Bukit Merah, explained that his mother's stall moved to Commonwealth Avenue, and in 1997, following a newspaper article on their fish soup, business started to boom, giving rise to many of his chefs leaving to spawn their own Hong Kong Street restaurants. So that explains why there are so many restaurants named Hong Kong Street around, but the one at Bukit Merah is the original. The soup here was good, and certainly better than the fish soups you get at normal hawker centres, but I remember it being more shiok in the past.

Even though I have always called myself a Teochew Ah Hia, I think I prefer the Cantonese style "milky" fish soup to the Teochew version of fish soup, which comprises a very clear chngee (fresh) soup made from boiling fish bones, and sometimes, chicken and pork bones. (I think I can hear my ancestors all turning in their graves.) For the Teochew style fish soup, I love it when the hawker gives you generous amounts of fresh, tender fish slices, that have no fishy odour. The soup is healthy and sweeter than the milky version. I must state that I do prefer my soups with a bit of oomph, not necessarily very clean and bland. Healthy stuff can't be all that tasty right? Wrong!

· · · · ·

My first taste of the Cantonese style fish soup at **Jing Hua Sliced Fish Bee Hoon** stall was quite a "Holy Grail" experience. Forget all the hype about XO fish soup. If you've got a tasty fish soup, as in this case, you do not need to hide it behind the veil of XO brandy. This fish soup is really shiok and the best thing is that it is very affordable because it comes in individual servings. The only problem is the long queue even during off-peak periods. But take it from me, the queue is worth it.

· · · · ·

One of the best stalls for fish soup in the Central Business District is **Han Kee Fish Porridge**, which is one of the icons of Amoy Street Food Centre. This stall serves up a very tasty bowl of Teochew style fish soup that is as healthy as it is tasty! Uncle tells me that he uses only good quality Knife Brand vegetable oil, and no pork lard. He starts boiling the soup at 5am and it is only ready at 10am. For the more adventurous, you can order other parts of the fish, like the eyes, head, stomach, roe and the male equivalent of roe (which I find very hard to put down in writing).

You have to eat the dish piping hot, as you don't want to let the fish overcook. The fish is very fresh so the meat is firm, but still delicate. Unlike most other fish soups I've tried, the fish slices here come without the skin, so you don't get the chow chor (fishy) smell. The soup is really sweet and you can taste the quality of the ingredients and the effort that goes into the preparation. Uncle is another Teochew Ah Hia adamant on using only the freshest of ingredients!

· · · · ·

Another fish soup at Amoy Street Food Centre is **Piao Ji Fish Porridge**. I queued up to 40 minutes for a bowl, but unfortunately, the soup was not quite up to the high expectations of my makankakis and myself, though the

fish was very fresh and moist. The fact that each bowl was cooked individually meant that the Uncle could make sure the fish was not overcooked and maintained its juices. Good, but not nearly as good as I expected it to be.

. . . . .

If you like a bit of oomph in a clear fish soup, then you'll like the Teochew style fish soup at **Mei Xiang Fish Soup**. The soup here is full of "bits", making it slightly cloudy, but really tasty. We ordered the "black and white" version. You get nice, thickly sliced fish and pieces of fried fish, which are quite yummy though a bit on the salty side. A shiok fish soup, but not for those who like their fish soup to be clear and clean-tasting.

By the way, I heard that the owner of this stall is a Food Nazi. He doesn't allow takeaways, so if you really want to take the fish soup home, you have to bring your own container! Also, take note of the weird opening hours: 10.12am to 3.16pm! However, when I spoke to him for a while, he did seem quite nice. Maybe he turns into a Food Nazi only when he is really busy!

. . . . .

Over at **Yong Lai Fa Ji Cooked Food**, the Teochew style fish head soup is excellent. The fish is fresh and they are generous with the amount of fish they give. I especially liked the crispy tipoh (dried sole fish) which was very pang (fragrant). They make everything themselves, including the tipoh and the ikan bilis (dried anchovies) and the soup is made from boiling fish bones and chicken, for at least eight hours. They also add bittergourd to the soup, which makes it tasty and good for your cholesterol level at the same time!

This stall also serves up a mean fish head noodle soup, which is makankaki Smart's fortnightly must-eat dish. The interesting thing is that they use dried egg noodles to cook the dish. These noodles have a unique texture and taste quite savoury. They are also very generous with the chunks of batang fish head and the soup is sweeter than the normal sliced fish soup.

• • • • •

The **Hong Qin Fish and Duck Porridge** stall is widely held by some to serve up the best Teochew style fish soup in Singapore. Perhaps because it was so popular, by the time I arrived at 1pm for lunch, Uncle could only give me a few slices of fresh fish, together with slices of fried fish. The soup was very chngee (fresh), clear, light and sweet. However, the fresh fish slices were nothing to rave about. I really liked the tasty fried fish though. The seasoned batter perfectly complemented the fish meat, making it really pang (fragrant).

• • • • •

What makes **Jason's Fish Soup** special is that they serve fish skin as one of their specialties. This specialty of theirs makes me cringe, as I was brought up thinking that the skin of the fish is the part that makes it chor (gives it the fishy odour). Truth be known, the fish skin at Jason's actually tastes alright. It did not have that fishy odour that I was worried about. The texture was like soft pasta and it was a bit slimy on the inside. The soup was good and Jason spikes his soup with a generous dash of hua diao jiu (Chinese rice wine) which gave it quite a kick. Overall, the soup and the fried fish was pretty good and at $3 a bowl, I'd say it is quite good value too.

• • • • •

When you look at the mound of freshly sliced fish at **Ng Soon Kee Fish and Duck Porridge**, you immediately know that the owner is a man who cares about fresh ingredients.

THE ORIGINS OF DRUNKEN XO FISH SOUP

Who in the world would think of putting XO into fish soup? A guy who loves XO, that's who. Ricky, an XO brandy salesman, loved his drink so much that he added it to fish soup 14 years ago, and as it turned out, it worked! (Come to think of it, there is no reason why it wouldn't work. If you think of the (ang moh) creamy fish soup, which uses a European cream-based sauce, adding a dash of brandy actually does make sense.)

Ricky's version of XO fish soup which is served at **Holland Village XO Fish Head Bee Hoon** has sprouted a lot of copycats. He says you cannot simply add any XO into the soup at the end. Firstly, it has to be the best grade XO. Then, it has to be added into the soup while it is boiling and allowed to cook for a little while (the timing is a trade secret). The dash of XO just prior to serving is but the garnishing at the end of the cooking process. Ricky believes in using only the best and freshest of ingredients – he brags about how he sources his snakeheads (loi he) from Malaysia and how he only uses top grade MSG that does not give a bad aftertaste. The result is a tasty fish soup with that extra XO kick!

Ricky himself admits that he knows nuts about cooking, but somehow the addition of XO into fish soup became an instant success story. Really goes to show that success in life has to do with chance and opportunity! Ricky's stall built its reputation in a coffeeshop in Holland Drive before moving to its present location in Dover.

This is one of the few hawker stalls around which sells sliced pomfret fish soup with Szechuan vegetables. Here, you can get a nice bowl of sliced pomfret soup from $5. The fish was super fresh but you will need to request a bit more Szechuan vegetables to give the soup more kick!

The batang sliced fish soup here was also really tasty. Compared to the pomfret, the batang soup was more potent and definitely one of the tastiest fish soups I have tasted. Pity you can't get the delicate flesh of the pomfret and the potent batang soup in the same bowl! The stall owner emphasised that the soup stock is prepared from fish bones and old mother hen and they don't use any pork bones.

If you like fish soup and you have not tried this one, then you really need to add it to your list.

· · · · ·

LESLIE'S TOP PICKS FOR FISH SOUP

Hong Kong Street Chun Kee
4/5

This is the original Hong Kong Street fish soup.

125 Bukit Merah Lane 1 #01-190 S150125, 11am to 2.30pm, and 5pm to 11.30pm

Jing Hua Sliced Fish Bee Hoon
4.75/5

This fish soup is really shiok and the best thing is that you don't have to pay a bomb for it because it comes in individual servings.

Maxwell Road Food Centre, 1 Kadayanallur Street #01-77 S069184, 11am to 8.30pm, closed on Thursdays

Han Kee Fish Porridge
4.5/5

This stall serves up a very tasty bowl of Teochew style fish soup that is as healthy as it is tasty! For the more adventurous, you can order other parts of the fish, like the eyes, head, stomach, roe and the male equivalent of roe.

Amoy Street Food Centre, 7 Maxwell Road #02-129 S069111, 10am to 3pm, closed on Sundays

Piao Ji Fish Porridge
4.25/5

The fact that each bowl is cooked individually means that Uncle can make sure the fish is not overcooked and maintains its juices.

Amoy Street Food Centre, 7 Maxwell Road #02-100/103 S069111, 10.30am to 3pm, closed on Thursdays

Mei Xiang Fish Soup
4.5/5

The soup here is full of "bits", making it slightly cloudy, but really tasty.

Berseh Food Centre, 166 Jalan Besar #02-44 S208877, 10.12am to 3.16pm, closed on Saturdays, Sundays and public holidays

Yong Lai Fa Ji Cooked Food
4.5/5 for fish head noodle soup
4.25/5 for fish soup

They make everything themselves here, and the soup is made from boiling fish bones and chicken, for at least eight hours.

Circuit Road Food Centre, 79A Circuit Road #01-648 S370079, 5am to 9pm, closed on Sundays and public holidays

Hong Qin Fish and Duck Porridge
4/5

I really like the tasty fried fish – the seasoned batter perfectly complements the fish meat, making it is really pang (fragrant).

Yue Yuan Coffee Shop, 302 Sims Avenue S387516, 8am to around 2pm, closed on 1st and 15th of the month

Jason's Fish Soup
4/5

They serve fish skin as one of their specialties and it does not have that fishy odour that I'm worried about.

Market Street Food Centre, 50 Market Street #03-25 S048940, 10am to 3pm

Ng Soon Kee Fish and Duck Porridge
4.5/5 for batang soup
4/5 for pomfret soup

The soup stock is prepared from fish bones and old mother hen and they don't use any pork bones.

Aljunied Market and Food Centre, 117 Aljunied Avenue 2 #01-11 S380117, 12pm to 9pm, closed on Sundays

Holland Village XO Fish Head Bee Hoon
4.25/5

This is the stall which first started putting XO in their fish soup!

Jumbo Coffee Hub, 19A Dover Crescent S131019, 11.30am to 2pm and 5pm to 11pm, open everyday

HAINANESE CURRY RICE

NO NAME HAINANESE CURRY RICE

If you have never eaten this before, you are probably wondering how something that looks like swill could even taste good. But this stuff will definitely hit the G-spot, as in, the Gastronomic Spot.

I f you bring a foreigner to eat this dish, he might think you are pulling a fast one on him. I mean, curry gravy mixed with lor (braising sauce), then mixed with gooey stewed cabbage does not sound particularly appetising, does it? It's no wonder that Hainanese curry rice has never made it to the must-try list of "things to eat in Singapore". It just requires too much effort to convince tourists that this is a serious dish.

You will not be able to find Hainanese curry rice on Hainan Island because this is a style of cooking that is only found in Singapore. The

Hainanese were excellent cooks and were often employed by the British as well as wealthy Peranakans as chefs in their homes. They got the pork chop idea from the British and the rest from the Peranakans. Curry chicken, babi pongteh (braised pork in salted bean paste) and chap chye (stewed cabbage) are some of the Nonya dishes which have been adapted for Hainanese curry rice. Sure, other economic rice stalls might sell curry, kong bak (pork belly) and chap chye, but they always have a slew of other dishes. At a Hainanese curry rice stall, these few dishes are the main attraction and you really don't need anything else.

If you have never eaten Hainanese curry rice, you are probably wondering how something that looks like swill could even taste good. But trust me, this stuff will definitely hit the G-spot, as in, the Gastronomic Spot. Although the mixing of three gravies may sound like it will cause a collision of flavours, they go very well together! And that's not all. The texture of the gravy is gooey and thick, like tau suan (split green bean soup). It's full of cornstarch, so it's a bit like eating glue. But when you are famished, that bolus of rice and gravy slides down the oesophagus like engine oil on pistons. It's the quick and tasty way to satisfy your hunger pangs. As weird as it sounds, the deluge of three gravies flooding the rice is a heavenly combination. It works, and it works at a level that really produces an umami bomb. I feel it everytime I eat Hainanese curry rice. I really love it. I think it is one of the tastiest things on earth.

With Hainanese curry rice, you really only need three dishes – a good chicken curry, lor bak (braised pork belly) and chap chye (stewed cabbage). The rest can be side dishes which don't require a lot of skill, like fried luncheon meat and eggs. Of course, having crispy fried pork is a bonus, but the trinity of Hainanese curry rice dishes must be there.

• • • • •

There is only one word that will adequately describe the food at **No Name Hainanese Curry Rice** at Beo Crescent: Shiok! It just rolls off your tongue and I think it must also cause a release of endorphins when you say it. It is almost like uttering a vulgar expletive because it does give release to your pent up emotions when you taste something that hits the spot. The crispy pork here is like keropok (prawn crackers) – really shiok! It is crispy right through and when you add it to the plate doused in the heavenly three gravies, it is unbelievable! While the star of the show is the crispy pork, the rest of the dishes are all very good, but not outstanding. The curry chicken was very good, as was the braised pork and the stewed cabbage with "lion heads" (pork balls). As a whole, the food here makes for a very satisfying meal.

· · · · ·

I am so enamoured by the **Redhill Curry Rice** stall because its selection of dishes is a little different from other stalls, and every dish here is really shiok! If you arrange just a bit of each dish on a single plate, and decorate it nicely, you could have a 10-course degustation menu!

The first thing that got my eyes wide open was the sambal. One taste of it and it got me thinking, "What the heck did they put in this?" The sambal was sweet and savoury, not spicy. I could have eaten it simply with rice. Then there was the crispy pork that was like eating chewy keropok (prawn crackers). The contrast between the crispy pork and the soft rice drenched in savoury curry was amazing. I also tried their homemade fish paste in tau kee (dried bean sheets) braised in a soya-based sauce. I just loved the way the deep-fried tau kee soaked up the gravy! The fish rolls were also homemade – the fish paste was made from batang fish, which had a different taste from many places that use yellowtail. The texture of the fish roll was soft but bouncy. They also added a bit of minced meat into

The End of Char Kway Teow

the paste – very, very good. Finally, the braised pork was one of the best I have ever tasted. The texture was melt-in-your-mouth perfect and the kiam pang (salty and savoury) flavour of the pork really lingered at the back of my tongue even after I swallowed the tasty morsel.

Everything was good, I kid you not, and I'll be back again and again and again!

· · · · ·

At **Tian Tian Hainanese Curry Rice**, the star is undoubtedly the pork chop. Although the pork chops are not freshly fried, they are still light and crispy when you bite into them. When eaten together with the sauce, the flavours from the batter are released at the centre of your tongue and the fragrance of the marinade only hits the top of the palate after you bite into it. Pork chops like these are meant to be slowly savoured with your eyes closed. The pork chops are served together with a pea and onion gravy, which I am told, is the traditional gravy that was used before the tomato version became more commonly used. The "lion heads" (pork balls) are simmered in the same gravy used for the pork chops. They are very good, but I had a hard time trying to figure out what goes into the gravy. The lor bak (braised pork belly) is very good, but when compared to the pork chops, they are not outstanding. They are very tender, but there are better ones around. The chap chye (stewed cabbage) here is stewed till very soft and the flavour of the dried shrimp is evident. At Tian Tian, they don't have just three, but six different gravies for you to choose from – chicken curry, seafood curry, special curry, char siew sauce, pork chop gravy and lor (braising sauce). Fantastic! And you can tweak the proportions to suit your liking!

· · · · ·

Beach Road Scissor Cut Curry Rice stall is very well known among taxi drivers. It lies on a busy crossroad junction in a less savoury part of town, and it is the kind of place that makes Hainanese curry rice what it is. Dingy and dirty, the place is not pretty but the food is downright delicious. Eating here will take you back to when you were a baby. And I don't mean nostalgia. I really mean when you were a baby. They use a pair of scissors to cut up all the stuff for you and pile it all on top of the rice. The meat is in little pieces, the rice is smoldered with lots of gravy, and everything is mushy and mixed together. Yes, this is as close as you can get to eating like a baby again. Just use your spoon, scoop everything up and put it in your mouth. Minimal mastication is required. This is one of the most effortlessly tasty but superbly shiok dishes you can find.

· · · · ·

Over at Tiong Bahru, you can find a stall called **Loo's Hainanese Curry Rice** which dates back to 1946. Just because it has a history of 64 years doesn't necessarily mean it is good, but the fact that it has been around for so long should mean something. They are good because Uncle insists on doing things the traditional way. The pork chops here are coated with cream crackers instead of bread crumbs before frying. This is how my Hainanese mother-in-law does it, and if you can find a stall that still does it this way as well, then you know you have stumbled upon a Hainanese hawker who is serious about his food.

· · · · ·

No Name Hainanese Curry Rice

4.75/5 for crispy pork
4.25/5 for braised pork and
stewed cabbage with "lion heads" (pork balls)
4/5 for curry chicken

The crispy pork here is really shiok! So crispy, it is like eating keropok (prawn crackers).

40 Beo Crescent S160040,
6.30am to 3pm, closed on Wednesdays

Redhill Curry Rice

4.75/5 for sambal
4.5/5 for tau kee (dried bean sheets), fish rolls and braised pork
4.25/5 for crispy pork

It is a "Holy Grail" experience. The sambal is sweet and savoury, not spicy.

Redhill Food Centre, 85 Redhill Lane #01-95
(facing main road) S150085,
10.30am to 9.30pm, closed on Sundays

Tian Tian Hainanese Curry Rice

4.75/5 for pork chops
4.5/5 for "lion heads" (pork balls)
4.25/5 for lor bak (braised pork belly)

They don't have just three, but six different gravies – chicken curry, seafood curry, special curry, char siew sauce, pork chop gravy and lor (braising sauce).

116 Bukit Merah View #01-253 S151116,
9am to 9pm, closed on alternate Tuesdays

Beach Road Scissor Cut Curry Rice

4.5/5

They use a pair of scissors to cut up all the stuff for you and pile it all on top. This is one of the most effortlessly tasty but superbly shiok dishes you can find.

Lao Di Fang Restaurant, 229 Jalan Besar
S208905, 11am to 3.30am, open everyday

Loo's Hainanese Curry Rice

4/5 for kong bak (pork belly), chap chye (stewed cabbage) and pork chop

The pork chops here are coated with cream crackers before frying. This is how my Hainanese mother-in-law does it.

57 Eng Hoon Street #01-88 S160057,
7.45am to 2.30pm, closed on alternate Tuesdays

HAWKER
WESTERN
FOOD

The End of Char Kway Teow

Although there are many western food stalls around, only a few stand out as serving up quality stuff.

Hawker western food is a unique genre of western food. The hawkers usually have Hainanese roots, as many Hainanese men used to work on ang moh ships where they learnt how to cook western dishes. Many of the cooks in British colonial households were also Hainanese. As a result, much of the western food cooked by Hainanese hawkers is a blend of western style cooking and local cooking. If you think that fusion cuisine is a modern phenomenon, you should really consider Hainanese style food, and think again. Don't you think that Hainanese pork chop is a fusion dish? Essentially, it is pork schnitzel seasoned to suit local tastes and served with potatoes and peas. Other hawker western food dishes are typically served with baked beans and chips. In addition, the meats are marinated with a mixture of local sauces, such as, maggi seasoning, soya sauce, MSG, as well as western sauces.

Having said that, there are a growing number of western food hawkers who are using more western ingredients, like basil and tarragon, in their dishes. I guess that this is an inevitable development but this makes hawker western food lose its unique identity. Although there are many western food stalls around in our hawker centres, only a few stand out as serving up quality stuff that is affordable and delicious.

· · · · ·

The **Happy Chef Western Food** stall is famous because its owners returned from Sydney after a 15-year stay, and their restaurant was voted as one of Sydney's top 10 restaurants by the *Sydney Morning Herald*. They were in Sydney for their children's education, but now that the kids have graduated, the owners decided to move back to Singapore. They started this western food stall serving interesting items like chicken kiev and pork cordon bleu, which are to Sydneysiders what Hokkien mee is to Singaporeans.

The BBQ pork ribs are a real gem and are great value for money. You get a meaty portion of pork ribs swimming in a lovely tangy BBQ sauce, and the meat is cooked till it can be sucked off the bone. Save your calories for this one! The ribs are cut in such a way that most of the meat has been taken off the bone. The taste is close to Tony Roma's though it lacks the chargrilled flavour. Shiokadoo!

Their chicken kiev has been tweaked to cater to local tastes, as well as to make it more affordable. It was good, but could have been better if mozzarella had been used instead of cheddar. The sauce was really nice and tasted quite ang moh.

· · · · ·

If you are eating at Old Airport Road Food Centre, the **Western Barbeque** stall is definitely worth checking out. My makankakis and I tried the pork

ASTONS'
"*ieat* SUPER BURGER"

Move over, Uberburger, Singapore's got the Astons' SuperShiok Burger!

This special order burger used to be available at **Astons Specialties** only on off-peak periods, but due to popular demand, Astons has decided to stock all the ingredients to make this most magnificent of burgers. So, this marvellicious burger is now available anytime you step into Astons.

Aston decided to rename this burger in honour of the psychologically challenged blogger, yours truly, who first instigated him to create this over-the-top burger. So when you go to the restaurant, ask for the "*ieat* Super Burger". And by the way, if you have any crazy idea, do make it known to Aston through his blog, *astonsspecialties.blogspot.com* and if enough people want it, he'll name the creation after you too!

Here are 10 essential ingredients that make the SuperShiok Burger (from bottom up): (1) XL soft sesame seed bun; (2) freshly chopped sirloin steak patty 200gm, medium done; (3) Astons' homemade smoked hickory BBQ sauce (fantastic smoky, tangy flavour); (4) 2 slices of cheese; (5) 2 rashers of streaky bacon – grilled to crispy; (6) 1 fried egg; (7) lightly battered, crispy fried onion rings; (8) lettuce; (9) tomatoes; (10) mayonnaise.

Tastewise, this patty is hard to beat. Juicy and beefy, one bite and I feel like a cowboy. Yeeehah! Combined with the crispy onion frost, BBQ sauce, Astons' secret special sauce, crunchy lettuce, tomatoes, bacon and cheese this is easily the best tasting, value for money burger in town. One piece of advice, ask for extra BBQ sauce if you still feel something is missing.

chops and the chicken chops. The chicken chop is without a doubt, the star of the show. The other star was the red coloured garlic sauce that they served. It's a little sweet and tasted like the sauce from the baked beans, but mixed with fried garlic. It went well with the chicken thigh fillet which was nicely seasoned and very tender.

· · · · ·

Finally, if there were a place where hawker western food is really value for money and at the same time the best place outside of a buffet where you are guaranteed to eat till you are full, **Wow Wow West** at ABC Brickworks would be the place. The serving of fish and chips was huge. The fish was the size of a ping pong bat, and thick too! The breadcrumb crust was also well executed, such that it was crisp but not oily. The only problem is that they use cream dory, which can sometimes taste a bit muddy. I was impressed with the homemade coleslaw here, which was cold, crispy and easily better than KFC's. The tartare sauce could be a little more tangy. The other best-selling items here are the chicken chop and pork chop. Both are seasoned with western herbs, which was fine with me, though sometimes, I still prefer the more traditional marinade that has MSG. The pork loins were big – the size of a female hand – and I liked the way the meat was pan-fried till there was a nice crust on the outside.

· · · · ·

LESLIE'S TOP PICKS FOR HAWKER WESTERN FOOD

Happy Chef Western Food
4.25/5 for barbecued pork ribs
3.75/5 for chicken kiev

Returning from Sydney after a 15-year stay, the owners started this western food stall serving interesting items like chicken kiev and pork cordon bleu, which are to Sydneysiders what Hokkien mee is to Singaporeans.

Tai Hwa Eating House, 466 Crawford Lane
#01-12 S190466,
11am to 10pm, open everyday

Western Barbeque
4/5

The chicken chop is without a doubt, the star of the show.

Old Airport Road Food Centre,
51 Old Airport Road #01-53 S390051,
11am to 8pm, open everyday

Wow Wow West
4/5

The serving of fish and chips is huge – the fish is the size of a ping pong bat and thick too!

ABC Brickworks Food Centre,
6 Jalan Bukit Merah #01-133 S150006,
10.30am to 9pm, closed on Sundays

Astons Specialties
4.75/5 for *"ieat* Super Burger"

This special order burger used to be available only on off peak periods, but due to popular demand, Astons has decided put this on the menu permanently.

119/121 East Coast Road S428806,
11.30am to 10pm from Sunday to Thursday,
11.30am to 11pm on Fridays, Saturdays and
public holidays

HOKKIEN MEE

Everything gets really messy as the noodles are flagrantly swirled around the wok, with rogue bits escaping off the rim. The expectation builds as the stock gets added and the wok is covered. When the lid is lifted, you are greeted by a blossoming fragrance as the noodles and stock merge to become a familiar yellow-brown gooey mass. Absolute magic!

Hokkien mee has become, in most places, more like pasta than a true fried noodle dish. That's because in a lot of places, the noodles are not really fried, but simply cooked in the wok and then the gravy is poured over it and allowed to thicken. Just like pasta. But if you are craving a truly delicious Hokkien mee, the noodles need to be fried till slightly charred and ready to absorb all the stock that is added. Observe how long the hawker spends frying the noodles before adding the gravy. Everything gets really messy as the noodles are flagrantly swirled around the wok, with rogue bits escaping off the rim. The expectation builds as the stock gets added and the wok is covered. When the lid is lifted, you are greeted by a blossoming fragrance as the noodles and stock merge to become a familiar yellow-brown gooey mass. If the hawker gets the timing right, the result is absolute magic.

There are so many elements that work together to make a shiokadelicious Hokkien mee – crispy, fragrant pork lard bits, melt-in-your-mouth pork belly slices and a very hot wok with an expert hawker who times his frying so well that he is able to get rid of the kee (lye water) smell of the noodles, while keeping them al dente. Let's not forget the importance of a rich prawn-based stock. Some hawkers will proudly boast that they use only sua lor (sea prawns), which are sweeter and bigger than farmed prawns. (Yes, the taste of farmed prawns still fails to match how God originally created prawns to taste like. When you bite into a sua lor, you can immediately distinguish that extra sweetness in its flesh which you do not get with farmed tiger prawns.)

Some foodies will insist that Hokkien mee cooked with a charcoal fire tastes better, or that using a traditional opeh leaf to serve the noodles adds to the flavour. The humble opeh leaf comes from the inner sheath of the bark of the betel nut tree and was used extensively during the post-war years to wrap foods like Hokkien mee and chee cheong fun. We now have to import these leaves from Malaysia and they are not cheap, costing about 30 cents per sheet, which is why hawkers only give you a small piece on a plate in most places.

Then there are arguments over which type of Hokkien mee is the best. The original version was more dry and was fried with thin bee hoon. It was also eaten with sliced chillies. It was the Nonyas who came along and began cooking the noodles with more gravy and used sambal to spice up the dish. Hence, today's modern version of Hokkien mee is wet and more gooey, sometimes using thick laksa bee hoon instead of thin bee hoon. I like both versions depending on the stall I am eating at. The beauty of the thin bee hoon version is that they add the bee hoon while it is still dehydrated, so the noodles soak up all the prawn stock and are especially tasty if fried well. Perhaps this type of Hokkien mee should be called Hokkien bee hoon, since there is more bee hoon than mee! Whatever the case is, I always look out for noodles that are long, and with sufficient gravy covering each strand of noodle that has been expertly fried and sealed, for good, slurpy perfection.

Let me share with you a little tip I picked up from the hawkers: Hokkien mee is one dish that really tastes better when it is brought home because the noodles have enough time to absorb all that wonderful stock.

In 2007, I conducted an online poll on my blog and Hokkien mee came out as Singaporeans' favourite hawker dish, followed by chicken rice and bak chor mee. In order to find out which are the best of the best Hokkien mee stalls in Singapore, I ran another poll this year, where almost 1,000 readers voted. The final results showed that Nam Sing at Old Airport Road was the favourite, nudging Geylang Lorong 29 into second spot by just 28 votes. I present to you the top Hokkien mee stalls in Singapore as voted by our readers and my own take on these stalls:

(1)   Nam Sing Hokkien Fried Mee

(2)   Geylang Lorong 29 Fried Hokkien Mee

(3)   Tian Tian Lai (Come Daily) Fried Hokkien Prawn Mee

(4)   Ah Hock Fried Hokkien Noodles

(5)   Che Jian Fried Hokkien Mee

(6)   Singapore Fried Hokkien Mee

(7)   Hainan Fried Hokkien Prawn Mee

· · · · ·

The legendary status of **Nam Sing** was re-established when readers of my blog voted it the best Hokkien mee in Singapore. The Nam Sing style of Hokkien mee is the dry type, with much of the gravy being absorbed by the mee and the thin bee hoon. When I tried the Hokkien mee at this stall, I found that the mee and bee hoon were QQ (al dente) and had a very

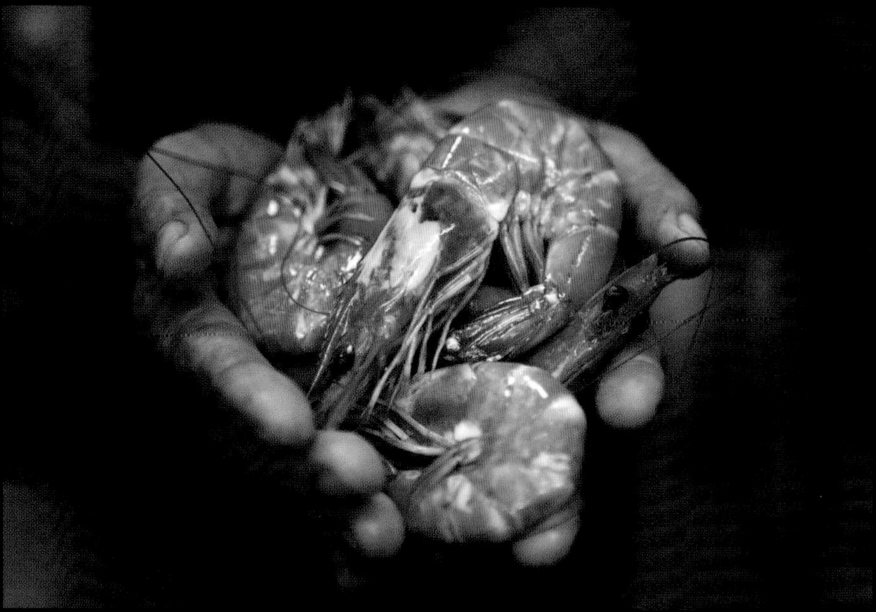

pang (fragrant) taste with each bite. I asked Uncle if the secret of his Hokkien mee was the use of special prawns, and he told me that he just uses good prawns and ikan bilis (dried anchovies) in the stock. He also told me that good control of the wok fire is crucial. The trick is to quickly seal the noodles, or else there will be a bad kee (lye water) smell!

· · · · ·

Geylang Lorong 29 Fried Hokkien Mee is not in Geylang but at East Coast Road. Alex See has been frying Hokkien mee for over 40 years and boasts that his Hokkien mee has been fried in the same style since the 1950s. The emphasis is on having a charcoal fire that heats up a special wok that is half the thickness of normal woks. That way, he can really swirl the noodles around to make sure that every strand gets equal exposure to the heat. His Hokkien mee is really fried, not just stewed. I have been patronising the stall since Mr See opened seven years ago, and this has always been one of my top Hokkien mee spots. The noodles are really shiok, but a little oily. I usually have to control myself so that I do not overeat and end up feeling really full for the rest of the day.

· · · · ·

For a Hokkien mee that is fried in the same style as Nam Sing, check out **Hainan Fried Hokkien Prawn Mee** at Golden Mile Food Centre. The noodles were fried until all the wonderful stock had been completely absorbed into the noodles and bee hoon, and sealed. Every mouthful was such a delight, and needs to be slowly savoured. This really stands out as one of the best plates of Hokkien mee I have tasted. The only letdown was the chilli, which was not quite fragrant enough and another problem is that you get a really small portion for $3.

· · · · ·

For those who prefer Hokkien mee slightly more wet, try **Tian Tian Lai (Come Daily) Fried Hokkien Prawn Mee** in Toa Payoh. The main characteristic of this Hokkien mee is its gooeyness which intensifies the crustacean taste of the stock. The noodles were well fried and the chef is no friend of pigs, so you get your lard and pork belly strips here. The prawns and sotong (squid) are tiny and only serve as garnishing. What you are going for is just a satisfying, fried noodle dish. Simple, no frills, gooey and tasty Hokkien mee.

· · · · ·

If you are looking for a truly traditional Hokkien mee, **Che Jian Fried Hokkien Mee** is the place to get it. It's got it all. The opeh leaf, the crunchy pork lard, the boiled melt-in-your-mouth pork belly, the cut chilli, and most importantly, a stock made from sua lor (sea prawns), that gives it extra sweetness. Chomp Chomp is a Hokkien mee lover's paradise, as apart from this stall, there is also Ah Hock Fried Hokkien Noodles, which also has many fans. I ate both in one sitting and to me, Che Jian edges out Ah Hock in terms of the taste of the noodles, the sea prawns, the pork belly and also the fact that they provide crispy pork lard when you request it.

· · · · ·

My first spoonful of the Hokkien mee at **Singapore Fried Hokkien Mee** was, to be completely honest, pretty unmemorable. But, that was before I added the sambal chilli and a piece of the crispy pork lard. Boom! Phwaa sayah! Shiok lah! Coming from a guy who does not usually take chilli, that is a big compliment. The sambal here was very tasty and not overly spicy. And the pork lard is one of the best I have ever tasted. Light, crispy and pang (fragrant). Why, oh why, do you have to tempt me so! The combination of the noodles, chilli and pork lard really made my day.

THE FAMOUS
HOKKIEN MEE HAWKER
WITH THE ROLEX

Who hasn't heard of the eccentric Mr Tan Kue Kim who wears a gold Rolex and long-sleeved shirt while frying Hokkien mee? He was most famous back in the 1980s when he was dishing out $15 bowls of claypot Hokkien mee and people were lapping it up without complaining. Then something happened and Kim disappeared from the scene, only to reappear in many different places, much to the confusion of Singaporeans.

What happened to Kim? Some say he had a few wives to look after and they sapped up all his money. Others say he gambled his fortune away on horses. Then there is the question of the different stalls that have sprouted up across the island with the same brand name. Are they genuine? As luck would have it, I spied a man frying Hokkien mee wearing a long-sleeved shirt at **Kim's Hokkien Mee** one day! So, I got my golden chance to clear up all this mystery. Turns out that Mr Tan is quite a personable man who is not camera shy. Yes, he was still wearing his gold Rolex too. So I asked him the $69,000 question – what happened to him? What brought down the Kim Empire? Was it the gambling or the bickering wives? (Yes, I actually asked him that.) The actual reason he told me turned out to be relatively mundane. At the peak of Kim's popularity, he bought a building in Geylang, which made him lose a lot of money because one of the ground floor tenants was supposed to move out, but did not. As a result of the financial disaster, he decided to retire for a while. Kim now operates a number of stalls across the island. His sons are in charge of the stalls, but they are all under the Kim umbrella. No family feud, no juicy gossip, just a simple family business.

Oh and he also categorically stated that he has only one wife.

Kim's Hokkien mee is pre-fried, left to rest and then re-fried when you order your plate. According to Mr Tan, this is done as the noodles taste better this way, not to save time. He uses only sua lor (sea prawns) and the best sotong (squids), which he proudly showed me. The noodles are QQ (al dente) firm and the tasty stock beautifully coats each strand. Also, crispy pork lard is liberally sprinkled on top of the dish! Although the Hokkien mee was good, I felt it has lost a bit of the magic it had when it was at its prime. However, kudos must go to Mr Tan who quite readily agreed to cook up a special version of Hokkien mee for me – sio bak (roasted pork) claypot Hokkien mee! They also sell a claypot abalone version of Hokkien mee and an XO Hokkien mee (XO here stands for extra oysters) at the 37 Joo Chiat Place stall.

. . . . .

Ah Hock Fried Hokkien Noodles is perhaps more popular than Che Jian at Chomp Chomp Food Centre. The Uncle frying the noodles has been doing it for 30 years, and yes, there is that element of authenticity in his Hokkien mee. Perhaps it had something to do with his white hair, which was flying in the wind like a modern-day Beethoven conducting a symphony while he cooked, or the queue of people waiting in line. Somehow, all these visual cues added to the whole Hokkien mee experience. Tastewise, the noodles were very good – Ah Hock uses thin bee hoon and the noodles were well fried. I was a little disappointed that there was no pork lard or pieces of pork belly, which would have added that extra oomph.

. . . . .

Finally, if you are at East Coast Park enjoying the sea breeze and feel a craving for Hokkien mee, head on down to **Sheng Hokkien Mee**. Uncle Loh has been frying Hokkien mee since 1958, when he was just 15 years old and was working as an apprentice for a Hokkien mee seller. After five years, he struck out on his own, with a pushcart along Tanjong Rhu. His style is the thin bee hoon kind of Hokkien mee. Although I have eaten at his stall several times, I never really found it outstanding until this one particular night when the noodles were exceptionally tasty and well fried. The portion was excellent and came with nice, juicy medium-sized prawns. Overall, a great place to get a plate of old school Hokkien mee.

. . . . .

LESLIE'S TOP PICKS FOR HOKKIEN MEE

Nam Sing Hokkien Fried Mee
4.6/5

ieat readers vote this to be the best Hokkien mee in Singapore.

Old Airport Road Food Centre,
51 Old Airport Road #01-32 S390051,
11am to about 8pm when everything is sold out,
closed as and when Uncle feels tired

Geylang Lorong 29 Fried Hokkien Mee
4.6/5

Alex See has been frying Hokkien mee for over 40 years and boasts that his Hokkien mee is fried in the same style as that of the 1950s.

396 East Coast Road S428994,
11.30am to 9.30pm, closed on Mondays

Hainan Fried Hokkien Prawn Mee
4.6/5

The noodles are fried until all the wonderful stock has been completely absorbed into the noodles and bee hoon, and sealed.

Golden Mile Food Centre, 505 Beach Road
#B1-34 S199583, 11am to 2pm, 3pm to 9pm,
closed on Wednesdays

Tian Tian Lai (Come Daily) Fried Hokkien Prawn Mee
4.5/5

The main characteristic of this Hokkien mee is its gooeyness, which intensifies the crustacean taste of the stock.

Toa Payoh West Market and Food Court,
127 Toa Payoh Lorong 1 #02-27 S310127,
9.30am to 9pm, closed on Mondays

Che Jian Fried Hokkien Mee
4.5/5

The Hokkien mee here has got it all. The opeh leaf, the crunchy pork lard, the boiled melt-in-your-mouth pork belly, the cut chilli, and most importantly, a stock made from sua lor (sea prawns), giving it extra sweetness.

Chomp Chomp Food Centre, 20 Kensington Park
Road Stall 11 S557269 (left hand side towards the
back), 5.30pm to 1am, open everyday

Singapore Fried Hokkien Mee
4.5/5

The pork lard, oh the pork lard, is one of the best I have ever tasted. Light and crispy and pang (fragrant).

Whampoa Drive Makan Place (Whampoa Food
Centre), 90 Whampoa Drive #01-32 S320090,
4pm to 1.30am, open everyday

Ah Hock Fried Hokkien Noodles
4.25/5

A little disappointing because their Hokkien mee has no pork lard or pieces of pork belly, which would have added that extra oomph.

Chomp Chomp Food Centre, 20 Kensington Park
Road, Stall 27 S557269, 5.30pm to midnight,
closed once a fortnight

Sheng Hokkien Mee
4.25/5

A great place to get a plate of old school Hokkien mee.

East Coast Lagoon Food Village,
1220 East Coast Parkway Stall 12 S468960,
12pm to midnight, open everyday

Kim's Hokkien Mee
4.25/5

Who hasn't heard of the eccentric Mr Tan Kue Kim who wears a gold Rolex and long-sleeved shirt while frying Hokkien mee?

62B Jalan Eunos S419510,
11am to 1am, open everyday

HOR
FUN

Searing hor fun properly, to get it just burnt, but still soft and slippery, is a skill that differentiates the experts from the wok wannabes.

The state of fried hor fun in Singapore is pretty lacklustre. It is one of those uncelebrated staples that never makes it onto the recommended list of any cze cha menu. Hor fun is always on the "in case you don't want to spend more than $3 for your meal" list. As a result, there really aren't that many "star" hor fun out there.

In the past, hor fun used to be cooked using a charcoal fire. But these days, gas stoves are used instead because of safety reasons. However, hor fun cooked using a charcoal fire tastes different from one that is cooked using a gas stove. With a charcoal fire, the whole wok gets really hot, whereas with a gas-fired wok, only the bottom of the wok gets heated. It makes a big difference when you are trying to sear the kway teow. Searing hor fun properly, to get it just burnt, but still soft and slippery, is a skill that differentiates the experts from the wok wannabes. It does not even require pork lard. Simply a hot wok, oil, kway teow and skill. Indeed, gone are the days of Fei Lao (Old Fatty), who was famous for his charcoal-fired wok and incredible seafood hor fun wrapped in opeh leaf, which was the best hor fun in the Eastern part of Singapore.

My quest for the ultimate hor fun has two criteria: first, the noodles must be slightly charred and so tasty it can be eaten on its own. (Finding good wok hei flavour is very hard these days because some Singaporeans prefer not to have their noodles charred due to health reasons.) The noodles cannot be a matted mass, but must be soft, lively, smooth and flavoured with wok hei. Second, the gravy cannot be ordinary – it must have the flavour that makes you think, "What the heck did they put in this?"

· · · · ·

The legendary hor fun hawker, Fei Lao (Old Fatty), may have passed on, but his legacy lives on with his nephew helming the wok at **Changi Lorong 108 Fei Lao Seafood**. While the nephew tries to emulate everything his famous uncle used to do, he is limited by the lack of a charcoal-fired wok, 40 years of wok skill and the trend of modern Singaporeans trying to cut down on their cholesterol. Still, the wok hei flavour of the hor fun was good and the sauce tasty. Overall, one of the more memorable hor fun around, though not as legendary as the original Fei Lao's.

· · · · ·

For beef hor fun, I always look forward to juicy tender pieces of beef that are not overly marinated, such that they taste like fish cake, or worse, like sponge. I still like some bite in my beef, but it should be tender and not require a mastication marathon. The gravy for beef hor fun should have oomph – lots of black beans, chilli and pepper. Shiok!

The beef hor fun at **Lorong 9 Beef Kway Teow** in Geylang has a special place in my heart since I first laid tongue (and eyes) on it over 10 years ago, when I was still a Medical Officer working in the General Surgery unit at Changi General Hospital. Ten years on, it is still my favourite beef kway teow, despite much criticism that Auntie no longer puts in effort because she is so famous and popular. While it is probably true that standards have dropped, this stall in my opinion still dishes out one shiok plate of beef hor fun – the sauce is irresistibly tasty, and the beef super tender.

· · · · ·

It is unusual that one of the best wok hei flavoured hor fun is not found at a hawker stall, but in a good old Hainanese coffee house! **Prince Coffee House** at Coronation Plaza, to be exact. The beef was very nicely flavoured and wonderfully tender without being too spongy. The most impressive plate of beef hor fun I have had in ages and the whole experience is definitely not to be missed!

· · · · ·

Teck Hin Fried Hor Fun is another good hor fun stall I can recommend. When you order the hor fun, Uncle will fry it fresh over a super-heated wok so as to infuse the hor fun with wok hei flavour, before frying the ingredients. The sauce is not prepared when you order. Instead, it is prepared beforehand and simply spooned over the freshly fried hor fun. I loved the hor fun and the sauce but found the ingredients over-tenderised and lacking flavour. It would have been perfect if the beef had a bit more bite and the prawns were not so springy. Otherwise, I really enjoyed the hor fun.

· · · · ·

While Madam Leong of **Nam Seng Wanton Mee** is a hawker legend more famous for her wanton mee *(see chapter on wanton mee)*, her venison

hor fun is also excellent and pretty well-known. The sauce is really good – it is addictive and very satisfying. However, I was less enthusiastic about the hor fun, which lacked wok hei flavour. When I highlighted this to Madam Leong, she said that it was because her landlords do not allow her to use a gas stove on the premises, so they have to cook the hor fun on an electric hotplate! Still, it is one of the tastiest hor fun around.

· · · · ·

The other way of preparing hor fun is to blend it and serve it with a sauce and a variety of toppings. In Singapore, we call this "Ipoh hor fun", a dish which I am told, does not exist in Ipoh. The beauty of a good Ipoh hor fun is the wonderfully slippery hor fun that leaps into your mouth and slides down your throat with minimal friction and maximum satisfaction.

For an Ipoh hor fun that will make you return again and again, try the chicken cutlet hor fun at **Wing Kee Ipoh Hor Fun** in Changi Village. This is a seriously enjoyable, tongue-tingling, lip-smacking experience that is worth the trip to the end of Singapore! The hor fun was really smooth, while the chicken cutlet was crispy on the outside and oh-so-juicy and savoury on the inside. Combined with that sauce, ooooh that sauce… Simply shioka-delicious! I found out later that Wing Kee's hor fun is served with a sauce that is made from boiling old mother hen for many hours. This is the real star of Changi Village Food Centre and I have been fantasising about going back again!

· · · · ·

Mention Mei Ling Food Centre and one stall comes to mind – **Shi Hui Yuan Hor Fun Specialty**. This is makankaki Liverpool's favourite hor fun stall. The kway teow was excellent and you can tell from the taste of the gravy that it is still made with much passion. I suspect that they never make a batch of sauce from scratch. There will always be some left over every day, to which they will add new ingredients, to make gravy for the next day. That means that theoretically, there might be molecules of stuff in there from 1969 when they first started!

Although the lady boss suffered a stroke and is now unable to cook, she is still at the stall supporting her husband and daughter, the latter of which has returned from Hong Kong to take over the stall. That means we get to enjoy her dish for at least another generation. If you are a fan of hor fun, this is one place you must make a point to visit. I highly recommend the pork ribs, mushroom and chicken feet hor fun.

· · · · ·

Lee Tong Kee Ipoh Sar Hor Fun is probably one of the most well-established Ipoh hor fun stalls in Singapore. Lee Tong Kee started selling hor fun in 1948 in Kuala Lumpur, and then opened a branch in Tanjong Pagar in 1969. The hor fun here is really smooth and slippery, just like Ipoh hor fun should be. The sauce is a closely guarded secret made by Mr Lee's daughter everyday. While it was tasty and complemented the hor fun well, I thought it lacked oomph. However, I was really bowled over by the ngau lam (stewed beef brisket) hor fun, which was one of the best versions of this dish I had come across. The gravy was a classic ngau lam, spiked with a good dose of Chinese five-spice powder. The only complaint was that I did not get some melt-in-your-mouth tendons that day.

Here is a little tip shared by makankaki Tiantianchi, one of the most knowledgeable foodies I know. Drizzle some of the prawn oil that is provided at Lee Tong Kee over your hor fun and it will bring the dish to the next level!

· · · · ·

Finally, I was suitably impressed by the Ipoh hor fun at **Funan Weng Ipoh Hor Fun**, not just because of the hor fun, but also because of the story

behind the stall. This humble stall started out as a wanton mee stall at the legendary hawker street, Hock Lam Street. Hock Lam Street used to be where Funan Digitalife Mall currently stands, and together with some of the original stalls, Funan Weng relocated back to the Funan food court, which occupied the whole of the top level of Funan Digitalife Mall, when the shopping mall opened. (That food court has since closed down.) Upon relocation, Mr Ho Weng changed his father's wanton mee stall into an Ipoh hor fun stall and his creation was so popular, he was even featured on television for it. In 1993, when Funan underwent major renovation, Mr Ho relocated to Ghim Moh and his son, Mr Ho Kuen Loon, began learning how to make his father's secret sauce for Ipoh hor fun. But that's not all – as an enterprising new generation hawker, the young Mr Ho, who was a Harvard graduate and previously a Chief Financial Officer (CFO), decided to take his father's stall to a whole new level. He opened a modern eatery so that his father's Ipoh hor fun could be introduced to a new generation of Singaporeans.

Funan Weng Ipoh Hor Fun at Maxwell Road was thus born. In air-conditioned comfort, you can get to try this unique Ipoh hor fun recipe. What makes this hor fun stand out is a dollop of specially brewed herbal dark soya sauce, which is added before the hor fun is bathed in the conventional light hor fun gravy. The dark soya sauce gives the hor fun a kick that you do not get elsewhere. However, if you are not big on anything herbal, you might find the taste a little overpowering.

By the way, this eatery also serves gourmet sui gao (prawn dumplings) containing no MSG. They taste pretty good!

• • • • •

LESLIE'S TOP PICKS FOR HOR FUN

FRIED HOR FUN

Changi Lorong 108 Fei Lao Seafood
4.25/5

The legendary hor fun hawker, Fei Lao (Old Fatty), may have passed on, but his legacy lives on with his nephew helming the wok.

86 Bedok North Street 4 #01-165 S460086, 11am to 2pm and 5pm to 10pm, closed on alternate Tuesdays

Lorong 9 Beef Kway Teow
4.5/5

This stall in my opinion dishes out one shiok plate of beef hor fun – the sauce is irresistibly tasty and the beef is super tender.

237 Geylang Lorong 9 S388756, 4.30pm to 2.30am, open everyday

Prince Coffee House
4.5/5

It is unusual that one of the best wok hei-flavoured hor fun is not found in a hawker stall, but in a good old Hainanese coffee house!

Coronation Shopping Plaza, 587 Bukit Timah Road #02-15 S269707, 11am to 9pm, open everyday

Teck Hin Fried Hor Fun
4.25/5

I love the hor fun and the sauce but found the ingredients over-tenderised and lacking flavour.

Ghim Moh Market and Food Centre, 20 Ghim Moh Road #01-44 S270020, 10am to 3pm, closed on Mondays

Nam Seng Wanton Mee
4.5/5

The venison hor fun here is excellent, but lacks wok hei flavour.

Far East Square, 25 China Street #01-01 S049567, 8am to 8pm, closed on Sundays

IPOH HOR FUN

Wing Kee Ipoh Hor Fun
4.6/5

This is a seriously enjoyable, tongue-tingling, lip-smacking experience that is worth the trip to the end of Singapore!

Changi Village Market and Food Centre, 2 Changi Village Road #01-04 S500002, 10.30am to 11pm from Mondays to Fridays, 8am to midnight on Saturdays and Sundays

Shi Hui Yuan Hor Fun Specialty
4.5/5

I suspect that they never make a batch of sauce from scratch – there will be some leftover every day, to which they will add new ingredients, and make gravy for the next day. That means there might be molecules of stuff in there from 1969!

Mei Chin Road Market, 159 Mei Chin Road #02-33 S140519, 7.30am to 2pm, closed on Mondays and Tuesdays

Lee Tong Kee Ipoh Sar Hor Fun
4.5/5 for ngau lam hor fun
4/5 for Ipoh hor fun

I am really bowled over by the ngau lam hor fun, which was one of the best versions of this dish I have come across.

2/8 South Bridge Road S058827, 10am to 9pm, open everyday

Funan Weng Ipoh Hor Fun
4.5/5 for sui gao
4/5 for hor fun

What makes this hor fun stand out is a dollop of specially brewed herbal dark soya sauce, which is added before the hor fun is bathed in the more conventional light hor fun gravy.

32 Maxwell Road #01-07 S069115, 11am to 9pm, closed on Sundays

KOPI
AND
TOAST

The End of Char Kway Teow

There is something very Singaporean, even very patriotic about ordering a cup of kopi C siew dai and drinking it with kaya toast.

I never really got used to lattes and cappuccinos, even though I spent seven years in Australia. We had one of those espresso machines at home and for a while we went crazy over frothing milk. But at the end of the day, when the dust settles, we will still go back to using the trusty old coffee-stained coffee sock. Call me Ah Beng, call me Ah Peh, call me an anti-barista coffee ignoramus, I don't care. Nothing beats a cup of kopi C (coffee with evaporated milk) brewed in a sock! Smooth, sweet, syrupy and brimming with pang-ness (fragrance). When you pay $5 for a cup of cappuccino, you are actually paying $4 to sit in a nice cafe environment, 50 cents to satisfy your caffeine craving and 50 cents to arouse your sense of smell and taste. In Australia, you can get a good cappuccino for as little as $2, so I often wonder why it is so much more expensive in Singapore.

In polls conducted on my blog, 46.7 per cent said they preferred kopi, while 32.5 per cent liked western style coffee. Indeed, there is something very Singaporean, even very patriotic about ordering a cup of kopi C siew dai (coffee with evaporated milk and less sugar) and drinking it with kaya toast. It just makes you feel very local. How many of us take pride in bringing our foreign guests for a cup of kopi and teaching them how to order it properly? I find it most interesting to try to explain the meaning of kopi O tid loh (extra strong black coffee with sugar). Honestly, a hot cup of kopi C with kaya toast is the best $2 you can ever spend on afternoon tea.

But even though I would choose a good old-fashioned cup of kopi over cafe latte any day, the only problem is that on so many occasions, the places that sell cheesecakes and croissants do not sell kopi, and likewise, the coffeeshops that sell kopi would definitely not sell cheesecakes and croissants!

· · · · ·

According to the Singapore Book of Records, the original **Killiney Kopitiam** shop at 67 Killiney Road is Singapore's oldest existing Hainanese coffeeshop, having been around since 1919. The shop used to be called Qiong Xin He and was a typical Hainanese joint that served really good kopi and kaya toast. In 1993, it was bought over by Mr Woon who changed the name to Killiney Kopitiam and started expanding operations. Fortunately, Mr Woon managed to persuade Ah Gong and two other Hainanese men, who were all working at the coffeeshop at that time, to continue serving the kopi and kaya toast at the Killiney Road premises.

Apparently, Ah Gong brewed the best kopi at Killiney Kopitiam and had been making kopi there for the longest time. Unfortunately, Ah Gong retired in 2004 and went back to Hainan Island before passing on at the age of 86 in 2007, after having served close to a million cups of kopi (assuming

GOOD MORNING NANYANG CAFÉ

he made 500 cups a day for 54 years with two weeks' break each year.) You don't get people like Ah Gong anymore, so I thought I should mention him, as a little tribute to his contribution to our Singapore food heritage.

I used to think that franchising and expansion were bad for preserving Singapore food heritage. There are some franchises out there which I feel have deviated too far from the original. However, with Killiney, somehow they have managed to preserve a part of our heritage that would otherwise have been lost back in 1993. Now at least, I can still get a good cup of kopi accompanied by kaya toast that is up to standard at several locations around Singapore.

Not sure whether it was just the placebo effect, but my wife and I felt that the kopi C (coffee with evaporated milk) we had at the Killiney Kopitiam at Killiney Road was the best cup of Hainanese style kopi we have ever had, compared to the other Killiney shops that we frequent. It was smooth, aromatic and very fragrant, with only a slight tinge of bitterness and acidity.

Here's a little tip from the regular customers of Killiney Kopitiam – rather than ordering the usual kaya toast, get there first thing in the morning and try their fresh bread with butter and kaya. Incidentally, their fragrant kaya is homemade with freshly squeezed coconut milk. The freshly sliced bread is super soft and you can really savour the taste of the butter and kaya, while nibbling on the soft texture of the bread.

· · · · ·

If you like kopi, you have to try the one at **Good Morning Nanyang Café**. After going around tasting the various famous kopi places, I have to say that the kopi here ranks as one of the best. It is smooth, creamy and fragrant, with very little bitterness or acidity. It is just the way I like it. Don't just take my word for it, ask any of the Uncles sitting around who come three times a day to get their kopi fix!

This place is also unique because it is the only place I know of in Singapore where you can get freshly baked scones with kopi and teh C (tea with evaporated milk). The scones here are light and fluffy but the problem is, they don't serve clotted cream! On the plus side, you can choose to have your scones with kaya if you want. In addition, this stall sells kaya toast made with ciabatta! The bread is really light and fluffy on the inside, but crispy on the outside. I was amazed how well it went with butter and homemade kaya. And if you are trying to limit your cholesterol intake, you can choose to have your toasted ciabatta with a whole range of wonderful preserves, including orange marmalade with cognac, and four fruits marmalade with strawberry and champagne. You can also choose from different types of ciabatta – the orange ciabatta stood out for me (it's got caramelised orange peel in it!), as did the pumpkin seed ciabatta. Eating kaya with pumpkin seed ciabatta was like eating bread with kway chee (dried pumpkin seeds) but without having to peel the kway chee yourself.

· · · · ·

For a real blast from the past, try a cup of kopi at **Chin Mee Chin**. When you step into Chin Mee Chin, you will feel like you are stepping back to a time when life was simpler, and the Indonesians were still happily giving us sand to push the beachfront further away. I just love such old and quaint makan institutions. Everything about this place is just so original, from the fact that they still heat their coffee over a charcoal fire, to the fact that they still bake their own buns and scones at the back of the shop. The tiles on the walls remind me of my childhood days of living in a 3-room HDB flat in Toa Payoh. The only thing that was missing from the whole scene was the old Hainanese man in his pajama pants making coffee. Instead, coffee was made by a lady who looked as if she should be working at a fashion consultancy!

The kopi here is excellent, full-bodied, robust with little acidity, and though I stopped drinking coffee because of my reflux problem, this is one kopi I make an exception for. They make only a few types of bread and pastries in the bakery and all of them are very old school. In the morning, the favourites here are the custard puffs and luncheon meat buns. The buns may not look as nice as the ones in the fancy new bakeries, but they sure taste good. The raisin buns with thick slices of butter had that quality that gets me enticed just by looking at them.

. . . . .

One sip of the kopi at **Coffee Hut** and makankaki SCS Butter was hooked. He said it was the best kopi he had tasted around the area. There was that spiciness when the coffee first hit the palate, followed by the full-bodied taste of the evaporated milk and coffee, finishing off with a lingering aroma at the back of the throat after swallowing.

The kaya toast was delightfully light, crispy and crumbly on the outside but soft on the inside. The butter was the right consistency and not overly thick, while the kaya was fragrant but not sickly sweet. Stall owner Roland revealed to us the fine art of toasting bread. He said he only uses fresh bread rather than day-old or two-day-old bread, which is easier to handle because it is stiffer. The extra effort results in better tasting bread, which is fluffy on the inside and crumbly on the outside. The kaya toast is definitely worth coming here for.

. . . . .

When makankaki Damien mentioned to me that **Seng Hong Coffeeshop** at Lengkok Bahru still steams its lohti (traditional bread), I got really excited! And it gets better. Not only were they steaming their lohti, they were still

The End of Char Kway Teow

boiling water from an ancient pot which, I am told, is at least 70 years old! Rest assured, they clean the pot and decant the water at the end of the day, so it is not like one of those legendary braising sauces where the pots are never washed out, and theoretically, you could be eating bits of sauce from great grandpa's days.

The steamed bread was very shiok! And with the peanut butter, it was one of the best things I had ever eaten. Warm and super soft, it was so good, I had to order a second serving even though I just had lunch! The kopi here was thick, full-bodied, creamy and fragrant. The shop traces its origins back to Tong Ya at Keong Saik Road. 40 years ago, the third son of the owner of Tong Ya left to open his coffeeshop here. Like Tong Ya, the coffee can be a bit on the bitter side, but this can be fixed easily with the addition of evaporated milk.

· · · · ·

Tong Ya Coffeeshop at Keong Saik Road is an iconic place to have a cup of kopi. It is one of the few coffeeshops that is recognised by the building that houses it. Tong Ya has a long history and used to roast their own beans. Though they no longer do this, they still retain their secret blend of coffee beans, which are sourced from different suppliers to protect the secret. The kopi is fragrant with little acidity but with a good bitter taste to it. The crispy kaya toast here is one of the best around, but you have to know what to order. If you simply order kaya toast, you will get the thick sliced toast. They have several grades of kaya toast here, so make sure you order the grade A kaya toast. This is the one that has been toasted and re-toasted several times to achieve super crispy and brittle bread. It is excellent with cold butter and homemade kaya, which has a nice pandan fragrance and is the pale green lumpy type. I prefer this version to the smooth, brown version.

The stall owner at **Yue Yuan Coffeeshop** said they were originally from the Singapore Airlines Cargo House Canteen, where they have been brewing kopi for over 20 years. They were very famous for their kopi and ice kachang (ice and beans). Although they don't roast their own coffee beans, they have a secret blend of coffee powder that comes from various sources. The final result is a full-bodied coffee, aromatic, mellow and creamy, with little acidity.

I had to try the ice kachang (ice and beans) after the stall owner boasted its fame. They ran out of peanuts, so the ice kachang was topped with strawberry puree instead. The ice and syrup tasted normal, but buried under the avalanche of shaved ice lay stuff that made this dessert really special: mushy, homemade red beans. The beans were perfectly done, just the way I liked them. The skin of the beans was soft and there was a good proportion of beans and paste. I also ordered the hong dou ping (red bean ice), which is just ice and kachang (beans) drizzled with a generous amount of Carnation milk. Simple but really yummy.

· · · · ·

LESLIE'S TOP PICKS FOR KOPI AND TOAST

Killiney Kopitiam
4.75/5 for kopi
4.25/5 for bread

Besides serving smooth, aromatic and very fragrant kopi, their fresh bread with butter and kaya is really good too.

67 Killiney Road S239525,
6am to 11pm on Mondays and Wednesdays to Saturdays, 6am to 6pm on Tuesdays, Sundays and public holidays

Good Morning Nanyang Café
4.5/5 for kopi
4/5 for scones with kaya and ciabatta with kaya
4.25/5 for orange ciabatta and pumpkin seed ciabatta

This place is unique because it is the only place I know of in Singapore where you can get freshly baked scones with kopi and teh C (tea with evaporated milk).

Chinatown Point, 133 New Bridge Road #03-01 S059413, 8am to 8.30pm from Mondays to Fridays, 10.30am to 8.30pm on Saturdays, Sundays and public holidays

Chin Mee Chin Coffee Shop
4.75/5 for kopi
4.25/5 for raisin buns

Everything about this place is just so original – from the fact that they still heat their coffee over a charcoal fire, to the fact that they still bake their own buns and scones.

204 East Coast Road S428903,
8.30am to 4pm, closed on Mondays

Coffee Hut
4.5/5 for kaya toast
4.25/5 for kopi

The kaya toast is delightfully crispy and crumbly on the outside but soft on the inside. The butter is the right consistency while the kaya is fragrant but not sickly sweet.

Berseh Food Centre, 166 Jalan Besar #02-43 S208877, 7am to 4pm, closed on alternate Saturdays or Sundays

Seng Hong Coffeeshop
4.5/5 for steamed bread
4.25/5 for kopi

The steamed bread is warm, soft and very shiok! And with the peanut butter that is spread on it, it is one of the best things I have ever eaten.

58 Lengkok Bahru S150058,
6am to 6pm, closed on alternate Sundays

Tong Ya Coffeeshop
4.5/5 for kopi
4.5/5 for kaya toast

Make sure you order the grade A kaya toast, which has been toasted and re-toasted several times to achieve super crispy and brittle bread.

36 Keong Saik Road S089143,
11am to 2.30pm and 5.30pm to 10.30pm from Mondays to Fridays, 11am to 2.30pm and 5.30pm to 11pm on Saturdays and Sundays, closed on alternate Wednesdays

Yue Yuan Coffeeshop
4.5/5 for ice kachang (ice and beans)
4.5/5 for hong dou ping (red bean ice)
4.25/5 for kopi

They don't roast their own coffee beans, but they have a secret blend of coffee powder. The final result is a full-bodied coffee, aromatic, mellow and creamy, with little acidity.

302 Sims Avenue Lorong 27 S387516,
8am to 10pm, open everyday

KWAY
CHAP

The End of Char Kway Teow

Most of the colorectal surgeons I know crave for kway chap after a long day in surgery!

If you're the sort that does not like to waste food, then you would be very happy with kway chap. Every part of the pig is eaten in this dish, including the rectum, fallopian tubes, small and large intestines as well as the skin and the meat. Nothing is wasted. Incidentally, a big plate of kway chap can also serve as a practical lesson for first-year medical students who can try to identify the different parts of a pig's anatomy, which is very close to the human anatomy. The pig's anatomy is so close to human's that pig valves are used in valve replacement surgery for humans!

When eating kway chap, I look out for good lor (braising sauce) – it must be pang (fragrant). The kway (flat noodles) must be smooth, and my favourite bits are the skin and pork belly. I know a lot of colorectal surgeons who love kway chap and they often go for the small and large intestines. When we study western medicine, the rectum is always regarded as the end

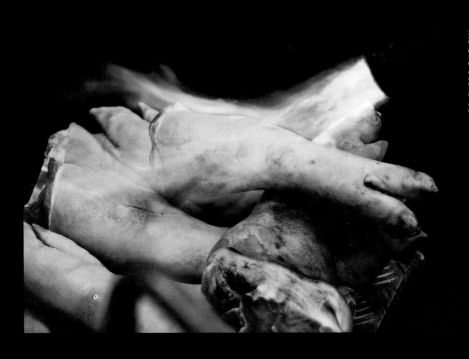

of the alimentary system, which starts from the mouth. The Chinese on the other hand call the rectum "da chang tou" which means the "head" of the large intestines. See where the priorities of the two cultures lie?

· · · · ·

There is a little stall in Haig Road Food Centre that does not have any newspaper clippings or awards of any sort, but they have been cleaning out pig innards for more than 30 years. The pig's da chang (large intestines) at **Yong Li Cooked Food** stall are so clean that they do not have any foul smelling taste at all. I immediately spotted the secret, thanks to my years of studying histology and anatomy in medical school. (Ya, right!) The secret is, the old lady laboriously turns the large intestine inside out and painstakingly strips off the mucosal layer, which is the part that comes in contact with fecal matter. This extra step results in a clean-tasting da chang that everyone can appreciate.

· · · · ·

The kway chap at **To-Ricos Guo Shi** is one of the most famous in Singapore as evidenced by the perpetual queue outside the shop. The flavour of the braising sauce was very pang (fragrant). Uncle told me that he torches the pig's trotters and leaves them overnight. Then, he comes in the morning and braises the trotters for only an hour and a half. I would have thought it took longer! Overall, this is a yummy kway chap not to be missed, if you are hungry for some spare parts.

· · · · ·

Over at Serangoon Gardens, **Garden Street Kway Chap** is one of those heritage hawker stalls with a sterling reputation. So naturally my expectations were very high. For me, this was a good kway chap but not exceptional.

Their hordes of regular customers would surely beg to differ. The braising sauce was good, the kway (flat noodles) was smooth, but no one item stood out. Having said that, everything was definitely above average. I also found out that there would be good kway chap for us to enjoy for at least one more generation, because the son has taken over the stall from his father.

. . . . .

Tong Lok Kway Chap at Pasir Panjang serves excellent pig innards. Uncle takes a lot of pain to wash the intestines so you get no off-putting flavour. The braising sauce is good and all the intestines have been braised till absolutely velvety. But the real killer for me was the ter kah (pig's trotters). Unlike other hawkers, Uncle chops up the trotters first before braising them in a special thick caramel-like spiced gravy till the collagen from the trotters is turned into that sticky slimy goodness that we all love. Aiyoh, only one word can adequately describe it. SHIOK!

. . . . .

Finally, check out **Chuan Lai Guo Zhi Wang**. When I went, there were lots of people eating there, even though it was after lunch hour, and the stall had all kinds of newspaper write-ups and reviews pasted on its window. Unfortunately, the food was not quite to my liking. The lor (braising sauce) was thick and gooey, with a strong herbal taste. The duck was tender and was one of the better ones I have tasted, but the pork belly had a smelly pork taste that I could not stand. Do check it out yourself to see if you agree with me!

. . . . .

LESLIE'S TOP PICKS FOR KWAY CHAP

Yong Li Cooked Food
4.75/5

The pig's da chang (large intestines) at this stall are so clean that they do not have any foul smelling taste at all.

Haig Road Food Centre,
14 Haig Road #01-33 S430014,
7am to 2pm, open everyday

To-Ricos Guo Shi
4.25/5

The kway chap here is one of the most famous in Singapore as evidenced by the perpetual queue outside the shop.

Old Airport Road Food Centre,
51 Old Airport Road #01-135/36 S390051,
11.30am to 4.30pm, closed on Mondays

Garden Street Kway Chap
4/5

This is one of those heritage hawker stalls with a sterling reputation. The braising sauce is good and the kway smooth.

Serangoon Gardens Market and Food Centre,
49A Serangoon Garden Way, Stall 21 S555945,
8am to 3pm, closed on Mondays

Tong Lok Kway Chap
4.5/5 for braising sauce and all the intestines
4.6/5 for ter kah (pig's trotters)

The real killer for me is the ter kah (pig's trotters). Uncle chops them up before braising them in a special thick caramel-like spiced gravy till the collagen is turned into that sticky slimy goodness.

114 Pasir Panjang Road S118539,
7am to 2pm, closed on Sundays, Mondays and public holidays

Chuan Lai Guo Zhi Wang
3.75/5 for duck
3/5 for lor (braising sauce)
2/5 for pork belly

The duck is tender and is one of the better ones I have tasted, but the pork belly has a smelly pork taste that I cannot stand.

560 Macpherson Road S368233,
8am to 12.30am, open everyday

LAKSA

YOU'VE GOT A FRIEND (ODE TO LAKSA)

(Sung to the tune of "You've Got a Friend" by James Taylor and Carole King)

When you feel that something's missin',
Some imbalance deep inside,
And your tongue has got that cravin'
You just can't hide…

You're trying hard to study,
Your exams are round the bend
But you just can't satisfy
Those hunger pangs…

Chorus
You just get in the car
And no matter how near or far,
Searching for, that bowl of Laksa…

Hae Bee, Oil, Chilli and Ha'am,
Flows down your throat, it's so *pang*,
Hits you right there! Yeah yeah yeah
You've got a friend…

*To listen, log on to the blog and search for
"You've Got a Friend (Ode to Laksa)"*

Nothing quite hits the spot like a good bowl of laksa.

The very first time I ate Katong laksa, I was still in Junior College, dating my ex-girlfriend Rockett Girl (who is now my wife). It was one of those extreme epicurean epiphanic experiences (E⁴), so vivid that I can recall the taste of the hae bee (dried shrimp) sediments on the tip of my tongue today. (Or, maybe it was the combination of the wonderful laksa and the extra delectable company that made the experience unforgettable?)

At that time, there weren't as many Katong laksa stalls as today. In fact, only one stall can officially claim the name of "Katong laksa". The story goes like this: the real granddaddy of Katong laksa was a legend of extraordinary proportions (in laksa lore anyway), a man named Janggut who used to peddle his laksa at Marine Parade jetty in the 1950s. When he neared retirement, his son opened a stall at 49 East Coast Road and called it Marine Parade Laksa. Janggut sold laksa there only on weekends. It was around that time that George's father (George being the current owner of Katong Laksa at 1 Telok Kurau Road) learnt the recipe from Janggut and started peddling his laksa along the streets. Eventually, he settled in Chai Chee and registered his stall as "Katong Laksa" in 1982 – and he has the business certificate of registration to prove it!

While it used to be that Katong laksa referred to a specific shop in Katong serving special Nonya style laksa that you ate with a spoon (the laksa bee hoon is cut up so that you can scoop it up with a spoon), nowadays, "Katong laksa" has become like a brand name – it refers to a certain style of Nonya laksa which is meant to be eaten with just a spoon. There are so many Katong laksa stalls around. At the height of the Katong laksa craze, there must have been about four or five stalls all competing for the Katong laksa crown. When I first ate there 20 years ago, it was just a stall in an old coffeeshop. Then, the stall moved across the road, then another stall came and occupied the old stall, then another one opened next door and so on, until there were about four or five stalls all in the same junction. These days, there are three stalls vying for customers at that junction, and lots more Katong laksa stalls have been set up throughout the island.

Nothing quite hits the spot like a good bowl of laksa. If there was an umami scale, laksa would be rated nine out of ten, while hospital porridge specially ordered for a hypertensive, diabetic, heart bypass patient would be one out of ten. One thing I always find lacking in my bowl of laksa is chicken

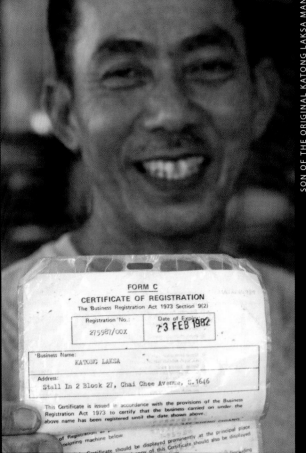

SON OF THE ORIGINAL KATONG LAKSA MAN

meat, so it always helps to order a plate of chicken meat from a nearby chicken rice stall to add to laksa. I love my laksa gravy with a lot of hae bee (dried shrimp) sediments. The gravy can range the whole spectrum – from watery ones to thick and gritty ones. I love them all, but whatever it is, the gravy must have oomph. Unfortunately, laksa is not the healthiest of dishes, and the no-holds-barred, gimme-your-best-shot versions are usually not something I would recommend for those who have problems with indigestion or cholesterol. That is why I do appreciate the more soupy laksa gravies, which allow me to finish a whole bowl without feeling too jerlak or unhealthy!

· · · · ·

Of the three stalls competing in Katong for the "Katong laksa" crown, my favourite is **328 Katong Laksa**. The laksa gravy is still one of the best around, although I must admit that it used to be even better in the days when Lao Ban Niang was cooking it only for her one stall. The best part back then was finding the minced up hae bee (dried shrimp) at the bottom of the bowl of soup. Nowadays, it is minced too fine, such that you can't really enjoy the grainy bits in your mouth. Nevertheless, this is still one satisfying bowl of laksa.

· · · · ·

The **Katong Laksa** stall at Telok Kurau is the only stall that can officially claim to have first registered under the name "Katong Laksa". The laksa here is very popular with the locals though not as well known as the stalls at Ceylon Road. The gravy is nice and savoury, and as good (or some say better) than the other more famous stalls. I thought it could do with a lot more hae bee (dried shrimp) in the gravy.

· · · · ·

If you still want to eat laksa that is cooked the traditional way atop a charcoal fire, you better hurry down to **Sungei Road Laksa** before it goes the way of the dodo! The owners here are very generous with the amount of haam (cockles), so lovers of this mollusk will be very happy. The distinct characteristic of this laksa is that the gravy is much lighter than what I am used to. It has flavour without being too jerlak. Personally, I feel that the laksa I had that day did not meet up to expectations befitting its legendary status. But that's me against the 10 or 20 customers who had turned up to eat laksa at 3pm that afternoon!

· · · · ·

Finally, I would heartily recommend the laksa at **Famous Sungei Road Trishaw Laksa**. This laksa comes with a very light gravy that is more soupy than thick. You can drink a lot of it without feeling jerlak. However, that does not mean that the flavour was compromised. The soup was still quite fragrant and had the savoury sweetness of the hae bee (dried shrimp), which I enjoyed. As Hong Lim Food Centre is under renovation, Uncle and Auntie will be taking a rest until early 2011.

· · · · ·

LESLIE'S TOP PICKS FOR LAKSA

328 Katong Laksa
4.5/5

The laksa gravy is still one of the best around, although it seemed even better in the days when Lao Ban Niang was cooking it only for one stall.

216 East Coast Road S428914,
8am to 10pm, open everyday

Katong Laksa
4.25/5

This stall at Telok Kurau is the stall that can officially claim to have first registered under the name "Katong laksa".

1 Telok Kurau Road
(opposite SPC Petrol Stration) S423756,
8am to 3.30pm, open everyday

Sungei Road Laksa
4.25/5

The owners here are very generous with the amount of haam (cockles), so lovers of this mollusk will be very happy.

Jalan Shui Kopitiam, 27 Jalan Berseh #01-100
S200027, 9am to 6pm, closed on first
Wednesdays of every month

Famous Sungei Road Trishaw Laksa
(Closed till Q1 2011)
4.25/5

This laksa comes with a very light gravy that is more soupy than thick. You can drink a lot of it without feeling jerlak.

Hong Lim Food Centre,
531A Upper Cross Street #02-67 S510531,
10.30am to 6.30pm, closed on Sundays

LOR
MEE

For me, the shiokness of lor mee comes from nibbling on the crunchy, salty, and savoury fried nuggets of flavoured batter coated in the slimy, sweet, garlicky, and sourish sauce. It is not easy to get so many textures and tastes in perfect balance. But when it happens, you have a bowl of gooey goodness to behold.

You could categorise hawker food in several ways. One could be called the "Superstars of Hawker Cuisine", which would consist of dishes like chicken rice, Hokkien mee, laksa and satay, which are must-eats for tourists who come to Singapore. The next category would be the "Unsung Heroes of Hawker Cuisine", which are the dishes that most Singaporeans love, but are lesser known to non-locals. These would be dishes like bak chor mee, wanton mee and fish soup. Then, there would be the category called "Sinful Hawker Food", in which char kway teow or oyster omelette would feature as prime culprits.

Now which category would lor mee be placed under? I guess it could go under "Less Popular Hawker Dishes with Long Queues". Under this category, I would also put satay bee hoon. These are dishes where there are a few popular stalls that command super long queues, but few hawkers seem interested to steal a piece of the pie.

Lor mee is a Hokkien dish that originated from Xiamen in Fujian province. However, like many of our hawker dishes, even though lor mee has its origins in China, it has since evolved into something unique to Singapore, such that it is nothing like the version you get in Xiamen today.

The beauty of lor mee lies in the contrast of textures. The most prominent is the contrast between the sticky, gooey, slimy sauce and the crunchy, fried bits. For me, the shiokness of lor mee comes from nibbling on the crunchy, salty, and savoury fried nuggets of flavoured batter coated in the slimy, sweet, garlicky, and sourish sauce. It is not easy to get so many textures and tastes in perfect balance. But when it happens, you have a bowl of gooey goodness to behold.

· · · · ·

The owner of **Bukit Purmei Lor Mee**, Mr Teo, has been selling lor mee since the 1970s. He gets the balance of tastes and textures just right and produces mighty tasty bowls of lor mee. Mr Teo told me that his lor (braising sauce) is made from pork bones, spices and egg whites. It is made fresh every morning when he gets to the stall at 5am. By 7.30am, it is ready to be served. Aside from the lor, the other two ingredients, which act as supporting actors, are the chopped garlic and black vinegar. The vinegar is also specially flavoured with a secret blend of spices and this very important condiment gives the lor a well-balanced and rounded taste which coats the whole palate.

Here is a little tip for those who are visiting the stall for the first time. The standard bowl of lor mee comes with sliced lean lor bak (braised pork belly), crunchy bits, ngoh hiang (fried pork rolls), pork chops and char siew (barbecued meat). If you want an extra special lor mee, ask Mr Teo for his special stash of braised pork belly which he prepares for his regulars. He told me that people nowadays try to avoid fatty meat, which is why he serves lean braised meat. But for the ultimate bowl of lor mee, his regulars know that the secret is in the braised pork belly!

· · · · ·

There are few lor mee stalls that have as long a legacy as **Yuan Chun Famous Lor Mee**. While I was queuing up for my bowl of lor mee, I met a man who told me he had been eating lor mee at this stall for over 40 years! He was only a little boy when he first started, and till today this is the only lor mee stall he ever eats at. He has been eating here since the stall was still along Boon Tat Street, before it moved to its present location at Amoy Street in 1984. He remembered that as a student, he used to be able to buy lor mee for 20 cents – those were the days when you could buy just noodles bathed in lor (braising sauce), without any other ingredients.

The lor mee here is quite unique. Unlike a lot of places where the lor (braising sauce) is sort of transparent and gluey, the lor here is thick, but not as sticky. I think they use something other than tapioca flour to thicken the lor. However, it is still very heavy, and people with weak chopstick skills might struggle a little to pull the thick and flat noodles up to mix with the sauce. The sauce itself is very flavourful and the combination of the sauce with the pork belly and fried prawn cakes is excellent. However, I found the kee (lye water) smell of the noodles a little overpowering, and would have liked more sauce to go with the noodles.

· · · · ·

For the stall **Lor Mee 178** at Tiong Bahru Market, the special draw is the famous shark meat fritters which are added to the lor mee. I don't think shark meat is that unique in taste. It tastes like any other white fish to me! But the lor (braising sauce) is very tasty and the stall gives lots of crispy crunchy stuff that is awesome with the lor. I also really like their crispy meat fritters – very pang (fragrant). There are some things I miss though, like braised pork, ngoh hiang (fried pork rolls) and braised egg.

· · · · ·

If you are hungry and yearning for an affordable meal that can fill you up, head down to **Wei Nan Wang Hock Kian Lor Mee** at Market Street, and you can have a nice big tasty bowl of lor mee with lots of ingredients. The sauce is not overly thick and has got a sourish tang to it. The crispy fried stuff soaked in the lor (braising sauce) was quite shiok.

The couple who sells the lor mee here have a romantic story to tell. They started selling lor mee at Bugis Street 40 years ago and are still manning the stall together after all these years. They are happily married and are selling their dish at almost the same price as years ago!

· · · · ·

Finally, I also checked out **Xin Mei Xiang** because many told me that this place was fantastic and the last time I dropped by, the lor mee was sold out. My level of expectation was very high, and indeed, the gravy was good, but it was definitely not the kind of "Holy Grail" experience that I was led to believe it would be. The ingredients were also good, but not tongue tingling. The fried snapper they added on top was generous, but tasted a bit fishy. One good thing, though, was the black vinegar which was really smooth and piquant. Overall, sadly, I have to say that this stall is a bit over-rated. But then again, taste is subjective, so do check it out for yourself!

· · · · ·

LESLIE'S TOP PICKS FOR LOR MEE

Bukit Purmei Lor Mee
4.5/5

The vinegar here is specially flavoured with a secret blend of spices and this very important condiment gives the lor (braising sauce) a well-balanced and rounded taste which coats the whole palate.

109 Bukit Purmei Avenue #01-157 S090109, 7.30am to 3.30pm, closed on Mondays

Yuan Chun Famous Lor Mee
4.25/5

The lor (braising sauce) here is quite unique – thick, but not as sticky. So people with weak chopstick skills might struggle a little to pull the thick and flat noodles up to mix with the sauce.

Amoy Street Food Centre, 7 Maxwell Road #02-79/80 S069111, 8.30am till around 4pm when sold out, closed on Mondays and Tuesdays

Lor Mee 178
4.25/5

The special draw at this stall is the famous shark meat fritters which are added to the lor mee.

Tiong Bahru Market and Food Centre, 30 Seng Poh Road #02-58 S168898, 6am to 9.30pm, closed on Wednesdays

Wei Nan Wang Hock Kian Lor Mee
4/5

The crispy fried stuff soaked in the lor (braising sauce) is quite shiok!

Market Street Food Centre (also known as Golden Shoe Food Centre), 50 Market Street #03-03 S048940, 9.30am to 3.30pm

Xin Mei Xiang
3.75/5

Sadly, this stall is a bit over-rated. The ingredients are good, but not tongue tingling, and the fried snapper they add on top is generous, but tastes a bit fishy.

Old Airport Road Food Centre, 51 Old Airport Road #01-116 S390051, 7am to 2.30pm, closed on Thursdays

NASI
LEMAK

The End of Char Kway Teow

Personally, my idea of the perfect breakfast is a cup of teh tarik, a plate of epok epok, and nasi lemak. That is what I miss most when I am overseas.

Nasi lemak is one of those simple but shiok dishes that satisfies you when you are craving for something seriously lemak (rich and savoury) after being on a salad and fruit diet all day. Good nasi lemak needs to be made with a good grade of rice – the sort with bite. You should be able to taste and smell the coconut and pandan leaves emanating from the rice, and the sambal tumis (stir-fried sambal) should be on the sweet side, yet have a wonderful savoury taste that hits the umami spot. The key to a great nasi lemak is freshness. The best nasi lemak stalls usually have long queues and as a result, the rice and chicken wings are often served fresh and piping hot. When the rice is hot, the fragrance of the coconut cream wafts through the air and the combination of the warm coconut-flavoured rice and the sambal tumis is so shiok! One trick is to always choose a nasi lemak stall that has a high turnover of customers, to ensure that the food will be hot and the chicken wings crisp.

· · · · ·

When I first tasted the nasi lemak at **Selera Rasa Nasi Lemak**, I thought to myself, "At last! A nasi lemak that is really shiok!" This nasi lemak is so shiok that I was told the Sultan of Brunei will tar pau (takeaway) it back to the embassy when he comes to Singapore! Check out the rice here. This is the first time I have tried nasi lemak made with basmati rice! The basmati rice gives it a lighter texture, better flavour and the grains are beautifully separated. It is also better for diabetics since basmati rice has a lower glycaemic index, so it does not cause the sugar levels to rise as quickly as jasmine rice. The sambal is equally shiok and you should not miss the sambal cuttlefish that they offer as an optional side dish. The best nasi lemak I have tasted so far!

· · · · ·

At **Epok Epok Central** stall in Eunos, all I needed to do was to catch a whiff of the steaming rice to know that this nasi lemak was good. The sambal tumis (stir-fried sambal) was also very shiok and on the sweetish side, which should be the case for a good plate of nasi lemak. The chicken wings were well marinated with lots of tumeric and ginger, so they were very good, but I would advise you to be there around lunchtime in order to get them freshly cooked. You can also buy the pre-packed nasi lemak that comes with rice, ikan bilis (dried anchovies) and a choice of egg or ikan kuning (fried fish) for $1.20. They put in special effort to sandwich the chilli between two pieces of banana leaves for that added fragrance. Sedap lah brudder! (delicious, man!) This place also sells very good epok epok *(see chapter on curry puff)*.

THE NASI LEMAK BATTLE AT CHANGI VILLAGE

Those who have been to Changi Village for a meal may have noticed three nasi lemak stalls there – **International Nasi Lemak** is the one with the longest queue. Then, there is **Mizzy's Corner** and **Sri Sujana**, which are right next to each other. So, which is the best? Honestly, my opinion is that the standard of nasi lemak at International is about the same as the other two, so the real question to ask is, "Which one should I go for if I can't be bothered to queue up for International Nasi Lemak?"

I first tried Mizzy's. I felt the rice here was nice but like most of the stalls here, they did not use jasmine rice, so the rice came out all broken, light and dry. I liked the sambal, which was sweet and very savoury. The chicken wings were yummy and well marinated, but they were fried half an hour ago, and thus were not so crispy.

As for Sri Sujana's nasi lemak, as far as I could see, the only difference was that Mizzy's used a deeper plate. The rice at Sri Sujana had a stronger pandan flavour which I enjoyed, but once again, the rice could have been better if they had used a better grade of rice. The chicken wings were fresh out of the wok and tasted great! But the chilli was a letdown. It was sort of homogenous, without that nice layer of chilli oil on top, and had a burnt taste.

The conclusion? There is no perfect nasi lemak at Changi Village! The best strategy is to go for the one with the highest turnover, especially when it comes to the chicken wings, which are all great when served fresh!

. . . . .

If you live in the West and are looking for a good plate of nasi lemak late at night, then you would probably head to **Boon Lay Power Nasi Lemak**. That would explain why there seems to be a perpetual queue of 20 people lining up for this stall's nasi lemak. We were there from 10pm to midnight and the queue never seemed to wane! One thing to note is that this is not traditional nasi lemak. The traditional version uses broken local rice which is dry and very light, with little bite. This nasi lemak uses jasmine rice, which retains moisture much better. The chicken wings here are fresh, but not particularly spectacular. This is one very satisfying plate of nasi lemak. However, there is no compelling reason to make the journey all the way to the West for this stall, unless you happen to be in the region.

. . . . .

Bali Nasi Lemak in Geylang is a good place to satisfy your nasi lemak craving and they serve really excellent curry. Aside from the very good curry chicken, the brinjal and sayur lodeh (coconut vegetable stew) were excellent. The rice was fragrant, though not the best I have tasted, and the sambal was the sweeter version, which I prefer. This place is also famous for its black chicken wings – chicken wings coated in a sweet and savoury kecap manis (Indonesian soya sauce) based sauce. The sauce is very shiok but I found the chicken wings a bit overcooked and dry that night. Some have raved about the petai (bitter beans), but I find it too bitter for my palate.

. . . . .

LESLIE'S TOP PICKS FOR NASI LEMAK

Selera Rasa Nasi Lemak
4.5/5

This nasi lemak is so shiok that I was told the Sultan of Brunei tar pau (takeaway) it back to the embassy when he comes to Singapore!

Adam Road Food Centre, 2 Adam Road #01-02 S289876, 7am to 10pm, open everyday

Epok Epok Central
4.25/5

This stall puts in special effort to sandwich the chilli between two pieces of banana leaves for that added fragrance.

Eunos Crescent Market and Food Centre, 4A Eunos Crescent #01-09 S402004, 7am to 7pm, closed on Mondays

Boon Lay Power Nasi Lemak
4.25/5

This stall does not sell your traditional nasi lemak. They use jasmine rice, which retains moisture much better.

Boon Lay Place Market and Food Centre, 221 Boon Lay Place #01-06 S641221, 5pm to 2am, open everyday

Bali Nasi Lemak
4/5

This place is famous for its black chicken wings – chicken wings coated in a sweet and savoury kecap manis-based sauce (Indonesian soya sauce).

2 Geylang Lorong 15 (Geylang side) S388596, 6pm to 4am, open everyday

International Nasi Lemak
3.5/5

The nasi lemak stall with the longest queue at Changi Village.

Changi Village Market and Food Centre, 2 Changi Village Road #01-57 S500002, 9.30am to 3.30pm, 6pm to midnight from Mondays to Fridays, 9.30am to 7.30pm on Saturdays and 9.30am to midnight on Sundays

Mizzy's Corner
3.5/5

The chicken wings are yummy and well marinated, but they are fried beforehand, they are not so crispy.

Changi Village Market and Food Centre, 2 Changi Village Road #01-55 S500002, 7am to 4pm, open everyday

Sri Sujana
3.5/5

The chicken wings were fresh out of the wok and tasted great! But the chilli was a letdown.

Changi Village Market and Food Centre, 2 Changi Village Road #01-54 S500002, 7am to midnight, closed on Mondays and Tuesdays

NASI
PADANG

RUBIAH MUSLIM FOOD NASI MELAYU

The End of Char Kway Teow

There is nothing quite like a good plate of rice drenched in a coconut-laden gravy. And it doesn't get better than nasi padang.

The first word that comes to mind when I think of nasi padang is "Rendezvous". The next image that forms in my mind is the really shiok yellow-green chicken korma (Indonesian chicken curry) that the original Rendezvous Restaurant used to dish out. Nasi padang might mean many things to different people, but for me, it is all about the chicken korma, which is sometimes known as gulai ayam, ayam korma or ayam opor. This was the dish my parents used to order for me because as a kid, I would not eat stuff that was too spicy. The first taste of it changed my life forever. I still remember it today and use it as a yardstick to gauge all other nasi padang. The creamy, citrus-coconuty flavour of that non-spicy curry was incredible, but unfortunately, it is not so easy to come by nowadays.

My other favourite nasi padang dish is bergedil (fried mashed potato fritters). I can down half a dozen of these fried mashed potato fritters at one go, especially when I have chicken korma (Indonesian chicken curry) gravy to drown them in. Simple dish it may be, but it delivers maximum satisfaction especially when served freshly fried. A good bergedil is made from local potatoes which tend to be buttery and slightly sweet. The potatoes should be roughly pounded so that they are still a little chunky and should be moist and savoury on the inside. There is nothing quite like a good plate of rice drenched in a coconut-laden gravy. And it doesn't get better than nasi padang. A plate of rice, half a dozen bergedil and a big plate of chicken korma equals maximum oomph for me!

· · · · ·

My makankakis and I were sitting at the Geylang Serai Market and Food Centre, and during the entire hour we were there, we noticed a perpetual queue outside the **Hajjah Mona Nasi Padang** stall. Out of curiosity, I ordered a few dishes. Then I understood why people were queuing. The first mouthful of the chicken korma (Indonesian chicken curry, called ayam opor at this stall) was like a "Holy Grail" moment. The gravy was so full of lemon grass that the fragrance wafted out of your nostrils like the flames of a fire-breathing dragon. Seriously, from the ayam opor to the beef rendang to the sayur lodeh (coconut vegetable stew), you could taste the passion and quality of the dishes in each mouthful.

· · · · ·

The other nasi padang stall at Geylang Serai Market and Food Centre with a long queue is **Sinar Pagi Nasi Padang**. You can easily spot it by the numerous awards pasted on the front of the stall. True enough, the food was delicious – I liked the chicken bumbu, which is fried chicken covered in grated coconut, also known as kerisik. Another dish I would order again is the chicken rendang – the gravy had a special oomph and it went very well with the rice. The bergedil (fried mashed potato fritters) was also a little chunky, moist and savoury on the inside, just the way I like it.

· · · · ·

Of course, when you talk about nasi padang, the famous eatery **Nasi Padang Sabar Menanti II** immediately pops to mind. Even though this stall is called Sabar Menanti II, it is quite different from the original Sabar Menanti just across the road at Kandahar Street. Having tasted the food from both stalls, I would say that this is one restaurant where the offshoot is better than the original.

The chicken korma (Indonesian chicken curry, called opor ayam at this stall) was shiok! The gravy was almost like the one at the original Rendez-vous Restaurant. Spoon the gravy over the bergedil (fried mashed potato fritters) and I would gladly trade my ribeye steak with you (New Zealand ribeye, but not wagyu, ok?) The creamy, green chilli and tumeric scented gravy is definitely one of the top 10 yummiest dishes in my book! The beef rendang here is the dry type with chunks of tender beef coated with a fragrant spicy paste that contains kaffir lime and tumeric leaves to give it a nice spicy citrus flavour. Mak Cik uses yellow Holland potatoes to make the bergedil, so it is real sweet and creamy.

· · · · ·

Warong Nasi Pariaman is another very famous nasi padang eatery. Located at North Bridge Road since 1948, the current stallholder is the third-generation, but Mr Jumrin insists that the stall's traditional recipes continue unadulterated and they remain faithful to the original Padang recipes. The yellow-green curry chicken is known as ayam pangang here, though it has

AN EXCELLENT INDONESIAN NASI PADANG RESTAURANT

When I visited Bali in 2009, the food did not leave much of an impression on me. Even the world famous Ibu Oka in Ubud failed to live up to my expectations. But a visit to **Cumi Bali Indonesian Restaurant** along Tanjong Pagar Road reignited my interest in Indonesian cuisine! Cumi Bali has been around for 21 years. It was previously at Duxton Road and its chef-cum-owner Fiona, is a passionate person who cooks for the love of food.

Let me cut the long story short and tell you that the sate ayam madura (chicken satay) here is one of the best things I have tasted. Maybe it is because I am partial to the sweet, savoury flavour of kecap manis (Indonesian soya sauce) marinade, but the tender, sweet and smoky pieces of chicken really hit the spot! As for the beef rendang, while not your classic fiery red and spicy version, it was still very good. The tender beef was stewed in a gravy that had a wonderful combination of spices which you probably need both hands and toes to count. The ikan bakar (chargrilled fish) looked very promising but it was the one dish I felt could have been much better. This dish was basically a whole fish barbecued in an otah paste. The paste was too raw and grassy-tasting for me, but the fish was very nice and had a smooth texture. Finally, the sup buntut (oxtail soup) had a nice flavour although the oxtail could have been cooked a bit longer so that the meat would come off the bone more easily.

Cumi Bali is definitely worth visiting if you are looking for a curry meal!

the taste and appearance of chicken korma (Indonesian chicken curry) – the chicken is first cooked in the gravy, then grilled and left to dry. The gravy is poured over the chicken just before serving. I found the caramelised, char-grilled flavour of the spices on the chicken skin really shiok, but the gravy was too light. The beef rendang is another signature dish of the stall. I was told that this style of beef rendang is served in Padang, Indonesia. The meat is cooked till it is almost dry and easy to shred. It is quite fiery and should appeal to those who like more heat in their food.

· · · · ·

The **Rubiah Muslim Food Nasi Melayu** stall is frequented by makankaki Cactuskit and has a perpetual queue from the time it opens. If you like sotong (squid) with roe, you will definitely want to make a beeline for this stall. I found it amazing that the three or four servings that we ordered were full of roe, much to the delight of my makankakis. Plus, what I really did enjoy was the peanuts with ikan bilis (dried anchovies) which were excellent, as was the bergedil (fried mashed potato fritters). The sayur lodeh (coconut vegetable stew) was quite average, but Cactuskit raved about the assam fish (fish in tamarind juice) here.

· · · · ·

LESLIE'S TOP PICKS FOR NASI PADANG

Hajjah Mona Nasi Padang
4.5/5

The gravy of the chicken korma (Indonesian chicken curry) is so full of lemon grass that the fragrance wafts out of your nostrils like the flames of a fire-breathing dragon.

Geylang Serai Market and Food Centre,
1 Geylang Serai #02-166 S402001,
8am to 7pm, closed on Wednesdays

Sinar Pagi Nasi Padang
4.5/5 for chicken rendang
4/5 for bergedil (fried mashed potato fritters)
3.5/5 for chicken bumbu (fried chicken in grated coconut)

You can easily spot this stall by its numerous awards pasted on the front of the stall.

Geylang Serai Market and Food Centre,
1 Geylang Serai #02-137 S402001,
9am to 10.30pm, closed every fortnight on
Mondays and Thursdays

Nasi Padang Sabar Menanti II
4.5/5 for chicken korma (Indonesian chicken curry) and bergedil (fried mashed potato fritters)
4.25/5 for beef rendang

Having tasted the food from both stalls, I would say that this is one restaurant where the offshoot is better than the original (Sabar Menanti).

747 North Bridge Road (at the junction of
Jalan Kledek) S198715, 6am to 5pm,
closed on Sundays and public holidays

Warong Nasi Pariaman
4/5 for beef rendang
4.25/5 for chicken korma (Indonesian chicken curry)

The beef rendang is another signature dish of the stall. I was told that this style of beef rendang is served in Padang, Indonesia.

738 North Bridge Road S198706,
7.30am to 3pm, closed on Sundays and
public holidays

Rubiah Muslim Food Nasi Melayu
4.25/5
(Makankaki Sumosumo gave 4.5/5 and makankaki Smart gave 4.75/5)

If you like sotong (squid) with roe, you will definitely want to make a beeline for this stall.

Whampoa Drive Makan Place (Whampoa Food
Centre), 90 Whampoa Drive #01-34 S320090,
10am to 6pm, closed on Sundays

Cumi Bali Indonesian Restaurant
4.75/5 for beef rendang and
sate ayam madura (chicken satay)
3.75/5 for ikan bakar (chargrilled fish)

The sate ayam madura (chicken satay) here is one of the best things I have tasted. Cumi Bali is definitely a place worth visiting.

66 Tanjong Pagar Road S088487,
11am to 2.30pm and 6 to 9.30pm,
closed on Sundays

NGOH
HIANG

Ngoh hiang is not exactly the most friendly food for your arteries. So, if you are going to clog your arteries anyway, you don't want to clog them with lousy ngoh hiang, right?

Have you ever wondered why ngoh hiang is called ngoh hiang? Meaning "five flavours" in Hokkien, ngoh hiang was brought to Singapore by our Hokkien forefathers from the Fujian province in China. The original ngoh hiang comprised five different types of fritters – prawn, pork rolls, pork liver rolls, egg rolls and pork sausage. Hence, the name "five flavours".

As time went by, other stuff that could be deep-fried was added and served with the same dipping sauce, for instance, tofu, fishballs, sotong balls and rolls of many different flavours. Hey, I am not complaining, except that it is increasingly hard to find hawkers who make their own ngoh hiang these days. With the advent of commercially available ngoh hiang, most stall owners have opted to be ngoh hiang traders, instead of ngoh hiang chefs. So, when I find passionate hawkers who still endeavour to make their own ngoh hiang, I like to support them and write about their efforts. Of course, their ngoh hiang has to be nice as well!

If it is hard to find handmade ngoh hiang, it is even harder to find handmade Teochew ngoh hiang. Most ngoh hiang stalls sell commercially made Hokkien style ngoh hiang. Teochew ngoh hiang uses a lot of water chestnuts – there are liberal quantities of water chestnuts in the prawn rolls and water chestnut slices. Teochews also love yam, so they add yam into their pork rolls. There are times when being hao lian (proud) and ngerng (stubborn) can be an asset, and this is the case when it comes to making your own food. Teochews have this common personality trait when it comes to food – they just feel it is their God-given duty to produce quality food for their customers.

Having tasted handmade ngoh hiang, I am getting really spoilt and refuse to waste my precious calories on factory-made ones any more. In general, ngoh hiang is not exactly the most friendly food for your arteries. The items are made of pork fat, liver, eggs, MSG and salt – all very artery-clogging, if you ask me. So, if you are going to clog your arteries anyway, you don't want to clog them with lousy ngoh hiang, right?

· · · · ·

At **Lao Zhong Zhong Five Spice Stall**, you can find Teochew Ah Chiks and Ah Sohs busily wrapping ngoh hiang. Mr Tan, the owner, refuses to buy ngoh hiang from suppliers for two reasons. He feels that such ngoh hiang is of poor quality and secondly, most of the suppliers only provide Hokkien style ngoh hiang. Of the 10 or so items offered at this stall, only the tofu is bought from a supplier. This stall even makes its own pork sausages from pork thigh meat. The crispy prawn fritters are so light and crisp, they just melt in your mouth after the first bite! The heh chor (prawn roll) is definitely the world's second best (the world's best has not been found yet)! Full of crunchy and sweet water chestnuts, if you are feeling a little depressed, just eat two of these and you are guaranteed to feel better! The ngoh hiang has pork mixed with yam in it, which gives it a subtle sweet flavour. Phwaa say! They are also famous for their lo mei (parboiled) squid. Another item you just have to save up calories for is their water chestnut slice, which is made of egg, flour, water chestnut and pork lard. Not for those with cholesterol problems, but one bite of it and all your troubles will be gone! Must try! Finally, the chilli is not overly spicy and is made of sweet plum sauce, sesame oil, black vinegar and peanuts. I don't usually like chilli with my ngoh hiang, as I prefer the sweet sauce, but this one was really phwaa say!

Since Lao Zhong Zhong moved from Jackson Centre to its current location at Tai Thong Crescent, I feel the food is not as awesome as it used to be. Perhaps I am psychologically programmed to think that food served in an old coffeeshop tastes better than food in a clean, modern environment. Still, the ngoh hiang here remains much better than the commonly available factory-manufactured variety and is definitely worth a try.

· · · · ·

The **Hup Kee Wu Xiang Guan Chang** stall, also known as China Street Fritters, serves very unique ngoh hiang that has red colouring on the inside. Really tasty, but a tad small. The pink sausages were handmade and tasted much better than the normal factory ones. They were some of the best I have ever tasted. The soft pink stuff was really tasty and the pork was shiok. I don't usually go for liver, but the liver here was highly recommended by the *ieatishootipost* forummers. It was quite good! The liver did not have too strong a "liver-y" taste and there was koo chai (chives) in it. I also tried the egg slice which was decent but nothing to rave about.

The handmade Teochew ngoh hiang at **93 Wu Xiang Xia Bing** is not as spiced up as the usual ngoh hiang. So for me, it did not have the kick of a spicy full flavoured pork roll, but both my makankakis liked it because they liked the freshness of the taste. There were a couple of the chef's own inventions that you will not find anywhere else. One that is worth mentioning is the tofu egg fritters – it was refreshing to have ngoh hiang that was silky soft on the inside. Very novel!

· · · · ·

The **Five Spice Prawn Fritter** stall at Zion Road is another stall that stubbornly hangs on to tradition and makes all the five foundational items – prawn fritters, pork rolls, pork liver rolls, egg rolls and pork sausage – from scratch. They do, however, outsource the fishballs and tofu. I have never seen anyone else make prawn fritters on the spot, which might explain why this stall is so popular. In fact, this stall is so popular, it only opens for two hours every day, from 11am to 1pm! The items at this stall tend to be more savoury than sweet. While most ngoh hiang comes with sauce that is pinkish and sweet, the sauce served here is more like the sauce for lor mee. Apart from the prawn fritters, which I found quite special, albeit a bit oily, the rest of the items were good, but not spectacular.

· · · · ·

LESLIE'S TOP PICKS FOR NGOH HIANG

Lao Zhong Zhong Five Spice Stall
4.25/5

The heh chor (prawn roll) here is definitely the world's second best (the world's best has not been found yet)!

Lao Zhong Zhong Eating House,
29 Tai Thong Crescent (corner of Tai Thong Crescent and Siang Kiang Avenue) S347858,
11.30am to 11.30pm, closed on
alternate Mondays

Hup Kee Wu Siang Guan Chang
(also known as China Street Fritters)
4.5/5 for ngoh hiang and pink sausages
4/5 for liver
3.5/5 for egg slice

This stall serves very unique ngoh hiang – with tinges of red on the inside. Really tasty, but a tad small.

Maxwell Road Food Centre,
1 Kadayanallur Street #01-64 S069184,
12pm to 8pm, closed on Mondays

93 Wu Xiang Xia Bing
4/5 for ngoh hiang and
tofu egg fritters

There are a couple of the chef's own inventions that you will not find anywhere else. One that is worth mentioning is the tofu egg fritters.

Toa Payoh Lorong 4 Hawker Centre,
93 Toa Payoh Lorong 4 #01-33 S310093,
12pm to 9pm, closed on Thursdays

Five Spice Prawn Fritter
4/5
(Makankaki Sumosumo gave 4.5/5 and makankaki Smart gave 4.75/5)

This stall is so popular, it only opens for two hours every day!

56 Zion Road S247781,
11am to 1pm, open everyday

OYSTER
OMELETTE

What do you get when you fry the best oysters, sweet potato flour, eggs, fish sauce and homemade chilli sauce in a hot pan full of the best lard? The yummiest and most artery-clogging concoction invented by man, that's what!

Oyster omelette is a high calorie, high cholesterol dish, so when you eat it, make sure that the calories are worth it. From my point of view, the dish has such simple ingredients – it is essentially starch and eggs fried in oil – yet some hawkers can get it dreadfully wrong. In particular, the consistency of the starch can go wrong, so skills and experience are necessary to get it right.

The flavour of the dish comes simply from the eggs, oil, oysters and fish sauce. I feel that a good oyster omelette need not be bathed in chilli to taste good. The texture, on the other hand, is a bit more complex. There's got to be just the right balance of crispy-starchy, chewy-starchy, sticky-starchy and crispy brown egg bits! A good oyster omelette is crispy on the outside, yet still sticky with a good amount of fried eggs on the inside. That contrast of crispyness and sticky-starchiness, together with the contrast of fresh, juicy oysters is out of this world (when it is done right)!

When I was young, I never liked oysters or cockles, so I grew up just eating the sticky paste with the egg. That version of oyster omelette, where they add sweet potato flour, is known as orh luak or orh jian. You only realise how yummy a simple omelette is when you are out in the jungle during reservist training and someone starts frying eggs. Of course, I also enjoy orh neng (oyster egg) which contains no sticky sweet potato flour. The taste of fluffy tender eggs with oysters is fantastic. Orh neng is more wet than orh luak (oyster omelette), and the fried eggs soaked in the juice from the oysters, chilli and lard is absolutely (and literally) to die for! Of course, the high level of cholesterol and oil in this dish is the reason why one should only eat this gu gu jip pai (once in a long, long time). And if you ever order a version that is mediocre, it would be better not to eat it rather than to try and finish it just because you were taught never to waste food. In my opinion, it is sometimes better to waste food than to spend a bomb on medical costs later!

· · · · ·

The most satisfying oyster omelette I have eaten was at **Ah Chuan Oyster Omelette**. The oysters were big, juicy and fresh, and the texture of the dish was just perfect. The only thing I could think of that would make it even better was if Uncle had fried it in pork lard. Oyster omelette is one of those dishes I try to avoid eating too much of because it really isn't all that healthy. So if I were to have a craving for oyster omelette, this is the one stall I would head for to guarantee that my calories are not wasted.

• • • • •

The owner at **Ah Hock Fried Oyster Hougang** is another Teochew Ah Hia who insists on using the best oysters from South Korea, the best sweet potato flour from China, and the best eggs from Swee Choon egg farm in Choa Chu Kang. Everything must be grade A. The only thing he does not make himself is the lard, but he insists that he gets only the best ready-made lard available. The orh neng (oyster egg) here was better than the orh luak (oyster omelette), but both were definitely exceptional and worth trying.

• • • • •

You may be pleasantly surprised by the oyster omelette at **Tong Siew Fried Rice** at Pek Kio Market and Food Centre. It is a rather straightforward dish, essentially a plain omelette that is topped with oysters which has been fried in a rather nice chilli paste. Not many places actually make them this way. It is not too oily, unlike the usual orh luak, and is a nice side dish to order.

• • • • •

If, however, you are craving an oily oyster omelette that has been fried to the crisp, head down to the **Oyster Omelette stall at Nam Heng Restaurant**. The oyster omelette here is very popular and Uncle still adheres to the oyster omelette credo of "really hot pan with lots of good lard!" (In Teochew, this is jiak tia gao lar!) Uncle is very old school, and putting all warnings of cholesterol aside, he produces crisp oyster omelettes that are sinfully good.

· · · · ·

There is a perpetual queue outside the **Hup Kee (Orchard) Oyster Omelette** stall at Makansutra Gluttons Bay. Although I had heard mixed reviews about this place, I liked the fact that the eggs and starch were fried till really crispy. The oysters were also quite plump and tasted quite fresh.

· · · · ·

Finally, I am including the **No Name Stall** at Bedok in my top picks because first of all, it is a halal stall, which is quite uncommon, and secondly, because the orh luak (oyster omelette) here is not too oily. And of course, the oyster omelette here actually tastes quite good. What I like is that they manage to get the paste really nice and crispy. However, the oysters are a tad tiny, so orh luak afficionados would probably not look favourably on them.

· · · · ·

LESLIE'S TOP PICKS FOR OYSTER OMELETTE

Ah Chuan Oyster Omelette
4.75/5

Oyster omelette is one of those dishes I try to avoid eating too much of. But if I were to have a craving for it, I would head for this stall to guarantee that my calories are not wasted.

Kim Keat Palm Market and Food Centre, 22 Toa Payoh Lorong 7 #01-25 S310022, 3pm to 9pm, closed on Tuesdays

Ah Hock Fried Oyster Hougang
4.75/5 for orh neng (oyster egg)
4.5/5 for orh luak (oyster omelette)

The owner is a Teochew Ah Hia who insists on only using grade A ingredients.

Whampoa Drive Makan Place (Whampoa Food Centre), 90 Whampoa Drive #01-54 S320090, 11am to 12am, closed on Wednesdays

Tong Siew Fried Rice
4.25/5

The oyster omelette here is essentially a plain omelette topped with oysters which have been fried in a rather nice chilli paste. Not many places actually make them this way.

Pek Kio Market and Food Centre, 41A Cambridge Road #01-23 S211041, 11am to midnight, closed on Wednesdays

Oyster omelette stall at Nam Heng Restaurant
4/5

Uncle still adheres to the oyster omelette credo of "really hot pan with lots of good lard!" (In Teochew, this is jiak tia gao lar!)

Nam Heng Restaurant, 949 Upper Serangoon Road (at junction with Simon Road) S534713, evenings till 10pm, open everyday

Hup Kee (Orchard) Oyster Omelette
4/5

The eggs and starch are fried till really crispy. The oysters are also quite plump and fresh.

Esplanade Mall, Makansutra Gluttons Bay, 8 Raffles Avenue #01-15, Stall K S039802, 6pm to 3am, open everyday

No Name Stall
3.75/5

This is a halal stall and the orh luak (oyster omelette) here is really nice and crispy but not oily.

Bedok Food Centre (Bedok Corner), 1 Bedok Road S469572, open everyday

PAU

The End of Char Kway Teow

To me, a good pau must have the rustic homemade feel of thick, soft fluffy skin. The meat in the pau should be juicy and savoury. It definitely helps if the stall roasts its own meat, like char siew, giving it a nice, smoky charred flavour.

I am so relieved there has been a resurgence of handmade pau in recent years, such that we do not have to be subjected to calorie wastage at the hands of factory-made pau. Prior to this, the standard of pau in Singapore was really going downhill, and I was getting fed up of eating poorly disguised protein molasses wrapped in a synthetic skin. Even today, there is still a lot of commercially made pau sold in our coffeeshops. But there is light at the end of the tunnel – slowly but surely, more handmade pau is not only being made, but also being franchised out to coffeeshops.

I have loved pau since I was a kid. I remember one of the best da pau (big pau) I ever ate was at the corner coffeeshop along Serangoon Road just before you turn left to get onto the PIE (diagonally opposite Jackson's Food Centre). They used to mix pork and chunks of chicken with the bones still intact. If you were lucky, you might even get a chicken wing! It was one of those things that I would save my pocket money for and look forward to eating right after school. Sadly, I have no idea where this stall has disappeared to.

The household names for pau in those days were Tanglin Pau and Tiong Bahru Pau. They were very good and us boys (my two brothers and I) would often look forward to driving out to buy Teck Kee Tanglin Pau. The fat man logo at the bottom of each pau was a signal for our salivary juices to start flowing. As with most businesses, when these two established brands expanded, the quality dropped, but they still make some of the better pau around, though these days, it is the good old "mom and pop" stalls that excite me the most.

To me, a good pau must have the rustic homemade feel of thick, soft fluffy skin. The meat in the pau should be juicy and savoury. It definitely helps if the stall roasts its own meat, like char siew, giving it a nice, smoky charred flavour.

· · · · ·

There is only one pau stall in Singapore that has the audacity to call a small pau a big pau and charge you a dollar for it. **Tanjong Rhu Pau & Confectionery** is the stall I am referring to, and despite the smaller sizes of their pau, there is always a queue outside the stall, around the clock. I have looked high and low for a cheaper alternative to this pau, but none have come close. It remains in a league of its own and as long as it remains there, suckers like me will continue to keep our mouths shut and obediently fork out our dollars for these tasty morsels.

There is just something inexplicable about the taste of this da pau (big pau). The combination of the soft sweet skin and the juicy savoury meat just makes the tastebuds resonate with excitement with each bite. And since most people can finish one pau in two mouthfuls, one is never enough.

The char siew pau here is one-third the size of the da pau (big pau), while the yuan yang pau, which contains lotus paste, red bean paste and salted egg, is excellent too. Although small, both pau are still much better than the factory-made ones and so, they get high marks from me!

. . . . .

The da pau (big pau) at **Man Ji Handmade Pau** is easily the juiciest pau in Singapore – and it's chock full of crunchy turnips, which I love. There is no egg in it and the meat filling is a little on the sweet side, which some may not like. Tastewise, if it just had a bit more oomph, I would have given it the same rating as Tanjong Rhu Pau.

. . . . .

Over at ABC Brickworks Food Centre, the handmade char siew pau at **Guang Ji Bao Zai** is really shiok. The char siew filling is juicy and sweet, and you can taste its chargrilled flavour. The hands that have been making pau here have been doing so for over 30 years. It's amazing how fast you can make a pau after so much practice. Uncle originally started when he was in his teens and has not looked back since. He still roasts his own char siew in a charcoal oven, which is why his char siew filling is so good. The other reason is that he used to sell char siew and sio bak (roasted pork) before settling down to make pau. The da pau (big pau) were also commendable but I think it is the char siew pau that steals the show.

. . . . .

As mentioned earlier, I grew up eating **Tiong Bahru Pau** and even though the franchise serves up pau that are no longer as great as they used to be,

INNOVATIVE
PAU HAWKERS

Having tasted so many pau, I am glad to say that some hawkers these days are really passionate and innovative about making pau – the owners of Godzilla Handmade Tim Sum & Da Pau and D'Bun are just two bright shining examples of this.

The concept for the Godzilla da pau (big pau) was birthed in 2006 when I met Mr and Mrs Cheng and remarked how nice it would be to have those gigantic pau that you often see along the highway while driving in Malaysia. They took on the idea and it became such a success that when they moved location, they decided to rename their stall **Godzilla Handmade Tim Sum & Da Pau!**

The Godzilla da pau (big pau) is XL-sized – each pau is roughly equivalent to eight standard-sized char siew pau. I call it the "social pau" because it is so big, there is no way you can finish it on your own! It's not the most beautiful pau in the world, but it never fails to impress the first time you behold one. It will spark two extreme responses – the food lovers will hardly be able to wait to sink their teeth into one, while the more petite eaters would be appalled by the size of it.

When you break open the pau, you are immediately greeted with a savoury bouquet of juicy chunky meat, one whole salted egg, one whole egg, mushrooms and sausages. The meat tastes very fresh and the salted egg, mushroom and Chinese sausages combine very well.

Another innovative pau hawker is the owner of **D'Bun**, Mimi. Her curry pau's curry is very mild, so even kids can eat it. I love eating bread with curry, so this combination of "curry" and "pau" is actually not all that far-fetched. It is good, but could be even better if the curry had a bit more umami kick. D'Bun also makes yuan yang pau – it is not readily available these days, and is made from red bean paste, lotus paste and salted egg yolks. They use a special layered skin for this pau which I felt was just slightly too thick.

they still deserve mention, since they are better than factory-made ones. The distinctive feature of Tiong Bahru Pau is the lack of egg in the da pau (big pau). Despite this, I have always liked their meat filling. The da pau used to be my favourite, though the skin has become thicker and more dry over the years. Thankfully, the char siew pau is still very good and one of the best around – the char siew is very tasty and still retains that distinctive smoky flavour. Again, the skin could be thinner, but overall, it is still something you could showcase to overseas visitors.

Incidentally, Tiong Bahru Pau also serves up delicious siew mai (steamed meat dumplings), although I remember them tasting better in the past too.

· · · · ·

The Teochews are famous for many dishes, but pau is not one of them. Still, the pau at **Teochew Handmade Pau** in Toa Payoh is special because the Teochew Ah Hia here has taken liberties with what we know as pau, and given it his own Teochew twist. Firstly, the pau here are tiny and the skin very thin. These pau are made for enjoyment, not to fill up the tummy, it seems. The kong bak pau (braised pork pau) is the most popular pau here, and you have to call them to reserve this pau otherwise it is usually sold out by noon. I found the kong bak pau tasty, though a bit dry. They are small, so you can finish it off in two mouthfuls (or one, if there's no one around to see how big you can open your mouth.)

This stall is also famous for its char siew pau, but I didn't think too much of it as it lacked charred flavour. However, the da pau (big pau) was good – not super juicy, but it had a very different flavour from the typical ones, and is definitely worth trying if you like da pau.

· · · · ·

Makankaki Liverpool had raved about the char siew pau at **Hong Ho Phang Hong Kong Pau** so I had to check it out. Unfortunately, while the char siew filling was good, it did not live up to the description that Liverpool had given. I did however find the vegetarian pau quite good. The filling was made of turnip and hae bee (dried shrimp), and is a great alternative to meat pau whenever you need to cut down on your cholesterol. This place also has fantastic fan choy (rice steamed with char siew) and lo mai kai (steamed glutinous rice with chicken). The fan choy is really good and probably the only significant fan choy I have tasted in my life.

. . . . .

LESLIE'S TOP PICKS FOR PAU

Tanjong Rhu Pau & Confectionery
4.6/5 for da pau (big pau)
4/5 for char siew pau and yuan yang pau

The combination of the soft sweet skin and the juicy savoury meat just makes the taste-buds resonate with excitement with each bite.

7 Jalan Batu #01-113 S431007,
12.30pm to 8pm, closed on Sundays

Man Ji Handmade Pau
4.5/5

The da pau (big pau) here is easily the juiciest pau in Singapore and it's chock full of crunchy turnips.

327 Hougang Avenue 5 S530327,
6am to 1pm, open everyday

Guang Ji Bao Zai
4.5/5

The handmade char siew pau here is really shiok to eat – the char siew filling is juicy and sweet, and you can taste its chargrilled flavour.

ABC Brickworks Food Centre,
6 Jalan Bukit Merah #01-135 S150006,
10am to 10pm, closed on Thursdays

Tiong Bahru Pau
4/5 for da pau (big pau)
4.25/5 for char siew pau and siew mai (steamed meat dumpling)

The distinctive feature of Tiong Bahru Pau is the lack of egg in the da pau (big pau).

Tiong Bahru Market and Food Centre,
30 Seng Poh Road #02-18/19 S168898,
7.30am to 9pm, closed on Mondays

Teochew Handmade Pau
4/5 for da pau (big pau) and kong bak pau (braised pork pau)
3.5/5 for char siew pau

The kong bak pau (braised pork pau) is the most popular pau here, but you have to call them to reserve it, otherwise it is usually sold out by noon.

Toa Payoh West Market and Food Court,
127 Toa Payoh Lorong 1 #02-02 S310127,
open 6am to 2pm from Mondays to Saturdays,
6am to 12pm on Sundays

Hong Ho Phang Hong Kong Pau
4/5 for char siew pau and vegetarian pau
4.5/5 for fan choy
4.25/5 for lo mai kai (steamed glutinous rice with chicken)

The vegetarian pau is quite good – the filling was made of turnip and hae bee, and a great alternative to meat pau whenever you need to cut down on your cholesterol.

5 Telok Kurau Road S423758,
7.30am to around 4pm, closed on Mondays

Godzilla Handmade Tim Sum & Da Pau
(Closed temporarily and moving to a new location. Check for updates on my blog!)
4/5 for Godzilla da pau (big pau)
4.25/5 for kong bak pau (braised pork pau)

One Godzilla da pau (big pau) is roughly equivalent to eight standard-sized char siew pau!

Orient Success Coffee House,
623 Elias Road, Stall 5 S510623, 6.30am to 8pm,
open everyday, but only till 1pm on Tuesdays

D'Bun
4/5 for curry pau
3.75/5 for yuan yang pau

They sell really interesting pau like curry pau and yuan yang pau which is not readily available these days.

358 Joo Chiat Road (junction of Marshall and Joo Chiat Road) S427603,
8am to 10pm, open everyday

POPIAH

I love my popiah loaded with crunchy bits, and folded tightly, looking like it's going to burst at the seams.

Popiah is the ultimate side dish – it goes well with everything and is relatively healthy and tasty. I am always tempted to buy one or two for everyone to share, whenever I go to a hawker centre in groups. If you think about it, popiah is the Chinese version of the donar kebab or the burrito and consequently, the way I see it, it is meant to be eaten whole, rather than cut up into bite-sized pieces. The reason why I say this is because a "wrap" is designed to be eaten on the go – in the past, you should be able to grab your popiah in one hand while the other hand is holding onto the reins of your horse. However, these days, it is standard operating procedure to cut popiah into bite-sized pieces and eat them with chopsticks. This does not really make sense to me – inevitably, some filling will drop out during transit from plate to mouth. How wasteful!

For me, good popiah must have nice, soft, chewy skin that leaves a sweet carbo aftertaste. Good skin is paramount – it is what separates the wheat of fantastic popiah from the chafe of so-so popiah. I especially love it when the hawker makes his own popiah skin, though this is quite rare these days. Next, good popiah must be packed with a generous amount of ingredients – sweet and savoury turnip filling and let's not forget those unidentified heavenly crunchy bits. I love my popiah loaded with crunchy bits, and folded tightly, looking like it's going to burst at the seams. When you put all the ingredients of popiah together, you get a wonderful matrix of flavours and textures. Chewy (skin), crunchy (crispy bits), juicy (turnips), crispy (lettuce and beansprouts), sweet (sauce) and spicy (chilli), and the contrast between the warm filling and cool vegetables. This is the beauty of an expertly rolled, fully packed and turgid popiah.

· · · · ·

If you are a popiah lover, you have no excuse not to try the popiah at **Kway Guan Huat Joo Chiat Original Popiah and Kueh Pie Tie**. Not only is this eatery a part of Singapore's food heritage – it can trace its roots all the way back to 1938 when its food was sold from a push cart – the popiah here is simply shiok. The skin is nice and transluscent, yet it holds all that filling without breaking or allowing the sauce to ooze out. The texture of the skin is chewy and leaves a wonderful sweet carbo aftertaste upon chewing. The second most important ingredient, the turnip filling, is savoury sweet and has wonderful umami oomph. It's no wonder, as they actually de-shell Sri Lankan crabs and add the crabmeat into the filling. You can't see the meat, but you can definitely appreciate the crustacean sweetness. Finally, the homemade crispy bits add a sweet crunch to the popiah.

There is only one thing I am not quite happy about. The filling is microwaved just before making the popiah. I feel that traditionally, it should be scooped up while still bubbling in a pot. This would have made it even juicier.

The best thing about the popiah here is that it is fully customisable as well. They sell the standard version, but if you just want the premium stuff, just ask Zita, the Lao Ban Niang, to pack you the works. You even get to choose from not just one, but four different types of crunchy bits. Heavenly! Zita also welcomes her customers to bring their own stuff to put into the popiah, and apparently some have added seaweed before!

Finally, you can actually have a go at rolling your own popiah, if you want to. They sell popiah sets where you get the filling in a claypot and all the ingredients, so that you can roll it yourself. Ingenious. Rockett Girl and I tried making our own popiah, and when we got the Lao Ban Niang to do another one for us, boy was there a difference! Turns out there is an art to folding popiah well. It's got to do with the proportion of ingredients and also how you roll the popiah. One of the crucial things that I observed was the initial side fold. Lao Ban Niang brought both sides to meet each other in the middle before proceeding to roll the popiah. That seemed to make the popiah very full and the double layer of skin gave me more skin to chew on in every bite.

Kway Guan Huat also sells sets that you can bring home to have your own popiah party. Finally, I was told that the President's maid comes regularly to tar pau (takeaway) popiah home – so this popiah also has the seal of Presidential approval!

• • • • •

The strength of the popiah at **Qi Ji Poh Piah** lies in the skin – literally. Although it is super thin, it is amazingly resilient. Even when you tar pau (takeaway), it doesn't get soggy, but retains its chewy, slightly gummy texture. I derive a lot of pleasure from chewing on the skin, which is almost like chewing gum. The filling is marvellous too. The layer of crunchy stuff gives a good bite while the turnips are moist and sweet.

• • • • •

Although popiah originated from China, we have a version that really is unique to our little island or, at least, among the Peranakans living along the Malayan Straits. There are not many places outside of a Peranakan home where you can find this style of popiah, but thankfully **Glory Catering** at East Coast Road makes such a popiah and is about the only place in Singapore I found that still makes egg skin.

When you first eat this version of popiah, you might not really take to it because it is slightly different from the ones we are used to. For one, they don't use the fried crunchy bits and secondly, they use freshly ground chilli instead of the chilli sauce found in a typical Hokkien popiah. The skin is not your typical popiah skin but one that is much like a crepe. The texture is more tender, like the skin of kueh dah dah (Nonya dessert) and is less dry than the common popiah skin. Try it soon, because apparently, this is an old style of making popiah skin that is all but disappearing.

. . . . .

The popiah at **Old Long House Popiah** is almost legendary. The skin is homemade, so it is nice and chewy. The ingredients are fresh and the crispy bits are really crispy. A good popiah, but not quite as good as it gets.

. . . . .

Ruby Poh Piah is quite well known among my makankakis, so I gave it a try. Auntie uses two pieces of popiah skin to wrap the popiah and the skin is quite good. The ingredients are generous except for the ever-important crunchy stuff. All in all, quite a good value popiah to eat while you are at Whampoa, but not something I would drive all the way there for.

. . . . .

The popiah at **Miow Sin Popiah and Carrot Cake** at Lavender came highly recommended by *ieatishootipost* forum members, so I had to try it. I got really excited when I saw a whole bowl of crispy bits displayed at the stall. But as the lady began to make my popiah, I noticed the popiah skin had the words "Made in Kaki Bukit" printed on it! And it was the factory-made type that looked really synthetic! My heart dropped to the floor and bounced back up again. Such a popular popiah stall using machine made skin? Well, turns out the popiah was not too bad, but it was not exceptional either. Really, someone should just resurrect the whole popiah industry and bring back handmade popiah skin! The convenience of the synthetic popiah skin has lured too many hawkers over to the dark side!

· · · · ·

For those of you who have never seen how popiah skin is made, head to the second floor of Margaret Drive Food Centre and check out **Queenstown Poh Pia**. You can witness how the hawker puts his whole hand into a big vat of gooey flour mix and then just slaps it onto a hot griddle. He then deftly retracts his hand, leaving the thin popiah skin on the griddle. Repeat this a few hundred times and you would have a leaning tower of popiah skin!

This stall has been featured on *asiaone.com* as one of the four best popiah stalls in Singapore. Apart from the handmade popiah skin, the filling is the classic sweet sauce, chilli, braised turnip, beansprouts, eggs and crunchy sweet bits.

Sadly, I have yet to find the preeminent popiah in Singapore. My dream popiah would have handmade skin. It would be huge, with extra crunchy bits, crispy pork floss, black sesame seeds, nice king prawns and XO lup cheong (waxed Chinese sausages). When will my dream be fulfilled?

· · · · ·

LESLIE'S TOP PICKS FOR POPIAH

Kway Guan Huat Joo Chiat Original Popiah and Kueh Pie Tie
4.6/5

The best thing about the popiah here is that it is fully customisable. They also sell popiah sets you can bring home to have your own popiah party.

95 Joo Chiat Road S427389, 10am to 8pm, closed on Mondays (but takeaway is available on Mondays)

Qi Ji Poh Piah
4.5/5

The popiah skin here is super thin, yet amazingly resilient.

Funan DigitalLife Mall, 109 North Bridge Road #01-17 S179097, 9am to 8.30pm, open everyday

Glory Catering
4/5

They sell Nonya style popiah here, which uses egg skin unlike the Hokkien style popiahs.

139 East Coast Road S428829, 8.30am to 8.30pm, closed on every Monday except public holidays

Old Long House Popiah
4.25/5

The popiah skin is homemade, so it is nice and chewy.

Kim Keat Palm Market and Food Centre, 22 Toa Payoh Lorong 7 #01-03 S310022, closed on Mondays and Tuesdays

Ruby Poh Piah
4.5/5

Auntie uses two pieces of popiah skin to wrap the popiah and the ingredients used are really generous.

Whampoa Drive Makan Place, 90 Whampoa Drive #01-53 S320090, 12pm to 8pm, closed on Wednesdays and Thursdays

Miow Sin Popiah and Carrot Cake
4/5

The popiah was not too bad, despite the fact that the skin was the factory-made type and looked really synthetic.

Lavender Food Square, 380 Jalan Besar #01-04 S209000, open till midnight, closed on alternate Wednesdays

Queenstown Poh Pia
3.5/5

This stall has been featured on *asiaone.com* as one of the four best popiah stalls in Singapore.

Commonwealth Avenue Food Centre, 40A Commonwealth Avenue #01-484 S140040, 10am to 10pm, open everyday

PRATA

The secret to a really good prata is simply passion and technique.

Ah prata, one of my all time favourite breakfast foods. It might have something to do with how my Pa used to bring me to the coffee-shop at Toa Payoh Lorong 8 to eat prata. If I remember correctly, $1 used to buy you 10 pratas and you could bring an egg to the prata man for him to add it in for you.

Unfortunately, with the proliferation of 24-hour prata joints, the standard of prata in Singapore has been waning, and in some places, it is just plain bad. The reason is simple – it has to do with ownership and passion. In the past, men from India used to come to Singapore to etch out a living for themselves. So, they would open a prata shop and through sheer hard work, make a name for themselves. These days, the guys flapping the prata are all hired from India and Malaysia. Unless the boss correctly incen-tivises them, it is difficult to ensure quality.

Many people have told me that the dish we Singaporeans call roti prata, (also known as roti canai in Malaysia) does not exist in India. One of my patients confirmed that this is not true. Prata does exist in India, but only in a small part of Southern India, and predominantly in Chennai. Over there, this dish is simply called prata. Indian migrants brought this dish to Singapore where it became known as roti prata. The Malaysians however, named this dish roti canai which means "bread from Chennai". If you still doubt that this dish is available in India, consider this: most of the men who make prata in Singapore are foreign workers from Southern India. Do you really think that we brought them all the way here to teach them how to make prata? It's like bringing the Chinese over to teach them how to play ping pong right?

There are actually many variations of the ever popular prata in Singapore – on one end of the spectrum is the soft chewy type and on the other end, the super crispy type. Thasevi at Jalan Kayu made famous the small, round crispy type of prata, and now, the name "Jalan Kayu" has become synonymous with prata and is used to describe that style of prata. My ultimate prata has to be big, thick and crispy on the outside, but fluffy and chewy on the inside. These are my criteria for making the ultimate prata:

- The stall needs to make its own prata dough. (I always look out for a big red plastic tub with two Indian men shaping the dough in the stall. Conversely, one of the tell tale signs that a prata shop is going to deliver a pedestrian prata is when you spot a cardboard box with the dough all stacked up uniformly inside. The final product will reek of that cheap trans fat laden margarine! There is something about dough that is mixed and kneaded by hand that gives it that special taste. With so much commercialisation of prata dough these days, it is getting hard to find handmade prata, and hence, such pratas should rightly be called artisanal pratas.)
- It helps if the prata chef is skilful and obliging.
- A big enough work area is key.
- Ask for two doughs and specify that you want your prata thick and fluffy.
- Stick around when they start flipping and specify you want them to flip the prata as big as possible, and then fold into many layers.

- Make sure they allow the prata to rest for at least two minutes before frying.
- Fry the prata in ghee (QBB brand).
- Finally, eat the prata hot, or as soon as it hits your plate!

Why not try my method the next time you order prata? I usually have to describe my requests with my best Indian accent, together with head-bobbing and animated hand motions!

Although prata is a favourite breakfast dish among Singaporeans, there is a certain level of mystique about it because the process of flipping the dough seems difficult, and so, not many people would even attempt to do it at home. Why would you want to make it at home if it is so readily available outside at relatively cheap prices? I can think of three reasons:

(1)   Most of the pratas you eat at the stalls contain high levels of trans fat since they are made with cheap margarine and usually contain more oil than is necessary. When you make prata at home, you can use olive oil and limit the amount of oil used.

(2)   When you can make your own prata, you can add ingredients which you will never find outside, for example, luncheon meat. You can even organise parties and get your friends to bring toppings and design their own murtabak!

(3)   Because nobody believes you can.

I actually did my own research on how to make prata and even learnt how to flip it like a pro! Now our family enjoys hot piping prata that is made from olive oil at home. The full recipe and videos on how to make prata from scratch can be found on my blog.

· · · · ·

But back to my top picks for prata stalls. To me, the prata at **Sin Ming Roti Prata** is how prata should be. It is shatteringly crisp on the outside, but

chewy and fluffy on the inside, leaving a buttery sweet taste at the back of the palate after you work through the satisfying chew. It is as flakey as a croissant on the outside and as chewy as sourdough bread on the inside. As an added bonus, the stall also sells curry rice, so you get a selection of different curries to go with your prata.

Faizal is a young man who still hangs onto the traditional recipe where the dough is mixed and kneaded by hand, then rested for an hour before being moulded into dough balls. He is a third generation prata seller. His grandfather started selling prata when he arrived in Singapore. The recipe was passed down to his father, who moved the stall to Cluny Road, and then to Sin Ming. Faizal, under the watchful eyes of his father, has been trained to take over the stall.

· · · · ·

Mr Abdul Aziz of **Riyadh Muslim Food** takes pride in making his own dough and flipping his own prata. His father was the one who started the famous Thasevi which made Jalan Kayu prata a household name. When he parted ways with his brother, he started up this little stall in Defu Lane. That was 20 years ago and Mr Abdul is still doing much the same as his father had done.

The pratas here are hard to beat. As with the Jalan Kayu pratas, they are small, but crispy, flakey and very flavourful. Mr Abdul still hand kneads his dough, saying he has no space to put a mixer in his small shop. He still adds QBB pure ghee to his dough to give that savoury buttery taste, as well as Carnation evaporated milk. The other ingredients are Prima's Ikan Terbang brand flour, salt and sugar. The most important ingredient in making prata is the flour and almost all the good prata stalls in Singapore use Prima's Ikan Terbang flour, which is specially formulated for roti prata. So, if you manage to see a sack of Ikan Terbang hidden in the corner of the stall, you know that the owner makes his own dough at the stall. The best thing about this stall is that the owner insists on making the prata only when you order – so you are assured of fresh pratas all the time. If you love prata, this is one place you have to visit.

· · · · ·

The prata at **The Prata House** is a no-holds-barred, eat-at-your-own-risk prata which I would only recommend to younger people with no history of coronary heart disease. From the rich yellow dough, which is evidence of the amount of margarine used, to the fact that they literally deep-fry the prata in Vanaspati butter flavoured vegetable oil, you know this prata is really good for your palate but bad for your heart!

This prata is of the super crispy variety. When you bite into its crisp texture, it just dissolves in your mouth. It was heavenly together with the curry. The butter flavoured vegetable oil does make it very tasty but for the life of me, I cannot believe that an artificially flavoured palm oil product can be good for you, even if it is vegetable oil. Very tasty, but very sinful.

· · · · ·

When I first tasted the prata at **Syed Restaurant** at Simpang Bedok, I had to tell myself, "Be still my trembling taste buds! Now this is a prata worthy of praise!" Crispy on the outside, light and fluffy with micro-thin layers of dough on the inside, this is probably the best prata I have had in terms of texture. Unfortunately, tastewise, the prata faltered. Instead of a buttery, savoury flavour, the taste of cheap margarine was predominant. They also use commercial dough here, so unfortunately, I cannot give the prata top marks.

· · · · ·

Over at **The Prata Place** at Thong Soon Avenue, the prata is excellent and the stall has a wide range of curries to complement the dish. This is one

THE MIGHTY MURTABAK!

The **Singapore Zam Zam Restaurant** is probably the most well-known murtabak stall in Singapore. It is certainly one of the oldest I know that is still in the same spot since its inception, 102 years ago. When I walked in, the chef was flipping the most gigantic and awesome murtabaks I had ever seen! The way they make their murtabak is a bit different from other places. In addition to an extra layer of pre-fried prata kosong, which they put at the base of the murtabak, they also add an extra egg on top of the folded murtabak and sprinkle minced mutton before frying. The result – a massive murtabak with crispy fried mince topping!

Behold the murtabak! I really liked the crispy, savoury topping of the mutton, but felt that it was not as savoury and tasty as it could be. Texture wise, it was crispy on the outside and chewy on the inside, so no complaints in that area.

Makankaki Damien swears that the chicken murtabak is to die for and he is 100 per cent spot on. The chicken murtabak was so yummy, because a lot of that tasty gravy had already been infused into the dough by the time they served it. Only one word to describe it – shiokadelicious!

of the most comfortable places to get a nice prata with a cup of teh tarik because it is air-conditioned. Although they brand themselves as a crispy prata place, the crispyness is no way like The Prata House. Instead, it is crispy on the outside and fluffy on the inside, just the way I like it.

· · · · ·

Casuarina Curry Restaurant at Upper Thomson is a famous prata stall that has revamped, transforming from a little coffeeshop to an air-conditioned restaurant that has taken over the space of two shops. I always get a bit apprehensive when facilities are upgraded because sometimes, it means that the food gets altered as well, and usually for the worse.

Still, we were suitably impressed when the prata was served because it really did look light and flakey on the outside, which is what Casuarina is famous for. The texture was good, but the prata was severely lacking in taste. My makankakis and I thought it was pretty bland, lacking the nice buttery taste I remembered from past visits. Overall, it was still better than most pratas out there, but not as good as it was before.

· · · · ·

Finally, my list of top picks is rounded off by my review of **Thasevi Famous Jalan Kayu Prata Restaurant**. Everyone wants to call themselves Jalan Kayu prata, when in fact this restaurant does not have any branches! Thasevi made this style of prata famous – the small, round, and crispy type. The prata here is good – crispy on the outside, flakey on the inside, and surprisingly, not too oily! My only complaint is that it is too small, such that you really need to eat at least four to satisfy a prata craving. The curry was very tasty too, and complemented the prata well.

· · · · ·

LESLIE'S TOP PICKS FOR PRATA

Sin Ming Roti Prata
4.75/5

It is shatteringly crisp on the outside, but chewy and fluffy on the inside, leaving a buttery sweet taste at the back of the palate after you work through the satisfying chew.

24 Sin Ming Road #01-51 S570024,
6am to 7pm, open everyday

Riyadh Muslim Food
4.6/5

The best thing is that the owner insists on making the prata only when you order – so you are assured of fresh pratas all the time.

Soon Soon Lai Eating House, 32 Defu Lane 10, Stall 12 S539213, 6.30am to 7pm, closed on every last Wednesdays of the month

The Prata House
4.5/5

This prata is of the super crispy variety – when you bite into its crisp texture, it just dissolves in your mouth.

246 Upper Thomson Road S574370,
open 24 hours everyday

Syed Restaurant
4.25/5

Crispy on the outside, light and fluffy with micro-thin layers of dough on the inside, this is probably the best prata I have had in terms of texture.

326 Bedok Road (Simpang Bedok) S469496,
open 24 hours everyday

The Prata Place
4.25/5

The prata is crispy on the outside and fluffy on the inside, just the way I like it.

1 Thong Soon Avenue (Springleaf Estate) S787431, 7.30am to midnight, open everyday

Casuarina Curry Restaurant
4/5

The texture was good, but the prata was severely lacking in taste, as it was pretty bland and lacked a nice buttery taste.

126 Casuarina Road (off Upper Thomson) S579514, 7am to 11.30pm on weekdays, 7am to midnight on weekends and eve of public holidays

Thasevi Famous Jalan Kayu Prata Restaurant
4/5

The prata is crispy on the outside, flakey on the inside, and surprisingly, not too oily.

237/239 Jalan Kayu S799461,
open 24 hours everyday

Singapore Zam Zam Restaurant
4.5/5 for chicken murtabak
4/5 for mutton murtabak

The chicken murtabak was so yummy. Only one word to describe it – shiokadelicious!

697 North Bridge Road S198675,
8am to 11pm, open everyday

PRAWN
MEE

The End of Char Kway Teow

When you feel you need to eat something really hot, soupy, savoury and yummy, a nice bowl of prawn mee will satisfy that craving like nothing else can!

Afull-bodied robust soup with a powerful prawn flavour. That's what I look for when it comes to prawn mee. The soup should be savoury and have oomph, without being overly salty. The stock should be made from prawns, though nowadays some places add "secret" ingredients such as dried scallops, crabs and other goodies. It really does make a difference to add sua lor, which is wild prawns that are harvested from the sea. Unlike farmed tiger prawns, wild sea prawns have a special sweetness and texture that is hard to beat.

. . . . .

The success of prawn mee rises and falls with the quality of the soup. And sometimes, the standard of the soup varies throughout the day. If you get your soup just before the hawker refills it with fresh stock, you are bound to be in for that wonderful umami rush, because the soup has been enriched by the previous blanches of prawns. Other than the prawn or seafood stock itself, you also need good fried shallots and freshly fried pork lard.

But there are other elements, like tender pork ribs and freshly procured noodles that are not pasty, but still have some bite. The chilli powder used for the dry version of prawn mee is also important. I know of at least one stall, The **Old Stall Hokkien Street Famous Hokkien Mee** at Hong Lim Complex that specially prepares its chilli powder by frying it with dried prawns. The taste is very distinctive. It is so good that the hawker even sells the chilli powder. When you feel you need to eat something really hot, soupy, savoury and yummy, a nice bowl of prawn mee will satisfy that craving like nothing else can!

· · · · ·

While the other prawn mees I have tried tend to have soups that are really salty and tastes like lots of MSG was added, the prawn mee at **Wah Kee Prawn Noodles** is different. This is one of the best prawn mee stalls I have found in Singapore. Their noodles had a unique taste that I could not identify initially. I just knew that it was a spectacularly pleasing taste and it wasn't predominantly MSG. It was only after finishing a bowl of soup that I realised what it was – the unique taste you get in lobster bisque.

The owner was tight-lipped about what goes into the soup. But after much pestering, he did reveal that it contained six seafood ingredients, and no pork bones. I also found out that he fries the prawn heads and shells, and squeezes out all the yummy stuff. Uncle has one big advantage – his son-in-law sells seafood at Tekka Market so he always gets the first pick of the best prawns. Indeed, the prawns here are some of the biggest prawns I have ever seen – so sweet and juicy. The noodles were also excellent. I had the dry mee pok, and the texture and taste of the noodles were equally spectacular.

Take the freshest prawns and mix them with a lot of passion and pride, and you get one very special and potent prawn broth. You must try this prawn mee – pamper yourself and order the $10 or $15 version of this dish to get the supreme soup and the full works!

· · · · ·

The first thing that strikes me when I order from **Noo Cheng Adam Road Prawn Noodle** stall is the quality and size of the prawns. These are not the common bred tiger prawns that you get at most stalls. They are sua lor (sea prawns), with flesh that is tender and really sweet! We tried both the dry and soup versions. While the soup version lacked oomph, the dry version was super shiok! The chilli was more savoury than spicy, and it had that X-factor that kept me thinking about it even after I left. The owner said that besides using good belachan (shrimp paste), the other secret ingredient was good quality Indian spring onions. And here's another tip: for those who have a bit of extra cash to spend, you can try their special giant prawn noodles, where you get foot long Goliath prawns at $25 a bowl!

· · · · ·

Incidentally, there is also a **Noo Cheng Adam Road Prawn Mee** branch at Zion Riverside Food Centre. At this branch, the soup version definitely beats the one over at Adam Road! Those looking for an umami rush will be very pleased.

· · · · ·

River South (Hoe Nam) Prawn Noodles Eating House has been in business for a long time. There is a good reason why their prawn mee is very, very tasty – they don't have any gimmicks. You won't find giant king prawns here. You just get your traditional prawn mee with options for pork ribs,

RIVER SOUTH (HOE NAM) PRAWN NOODLES

pig's tail and abalone. And best of all, the prices are not exorbitant. Why is the soup so good? The owner says it is because they sell many bowls of noodles a day, so they have to boil more prawns in the stock. More prawns, more taste. It's that simple. Apart from prawns, the other main ingredient in the soup is pork bones. The soup is simmered for over 24 hours to extract all the flavour from the prawns and pork bones. Other ingredients? A bit of soya sauce and a secret spice mix.

· · · · ·

The soup at **Joo Chiat Prawn Noodle** stall at Crane Road is simply marvellous, though to be fair to the other stalls, I had it just before closing time and by that time, the soup seemed more concentrated, having had a whole morning's worth of prawns enjoying their spa in the soup. The other really shiok thing was the pork ribs. They were just tender enough to bite without being too soft, such that the meat falls off the bone. Plus, the meat was really pang (fragrant). My only complaint was that they didn't serve nice long prime ribs, so there were more bones than meat, and the prawns were fresh but they only offered medium-sized prawns here.

By the way, this Joo Chiat stall is part of the Prawn Mee Trinity in Singapore, comprising the Beach Road Prawn Mee at East Coast Road, the Jalan Sultan Prawn Mee near Kallang MRT station and itself. All three stalls are spinoffs of the famous Beach Road Prawn Mee, which was started by this stall owner's father over 50 years ago when he migrated from Xiamen to Singapore. (I review all three stalls in the Prawn Mee Trinity in this chapter). The East Coast stall is owned by the Joo Chiat stall owner's eldest brother's son and the one at Kallang is owned by her older sister's son! For all three stalls in the trinity, their soup versions are better than their dry versions.

· · · · ·

Part of the Prawn Mee Trinity in Singapore, the **Jalan Sultan Prawn Mee** stall serves up a great prawn mee. Like the other stalls in the Prawn Mee Trinity, the soup version here is better than the dry version, having a wonderful oomph when you drink it. Unlike the stall at Joo Chiat, this stall gives you the option of ordering jumbo king prawns to satisfy your prawn craving. The pork ribs here are big, tender and very shiok.

· · · · ·

Finally, my review of prawn mee would not be complete without including the famous **Beach Road Prawn Noodle House**, which is part of the Prawn Mee Trinity in Singapore. Beach Road Prawn Mee was the best prawn mee I knew of before I started my blogging adventure. But as I began to taste other famous prawn mees, Beach Road Prawn Mee kept being pushed down lower and lower on my top 10 list of prawn mees. It is, no doubt, the most famous prawn mee among the general public. But ask any of our makankakis and most will be able to tell you more than a handful of places where you can get a better bowl of prawn noodles.

My last few visits to Beach Road have left me a bit disappointed. I found that the soup had lost its complexity and tasted like it lacked a few ingredients. Visually, it was still very impressive, with huge jumbo prawns adorning the bowl, but this is more style than substance.

On one occasion, I was showing Penang blogger C K Lam around and we were along East Coast Road eating Geylang Lorong 29 Hokkien Mee, which I was confident was something that Singapore had that Penang could not beat. With C K, it is always a competition to see which country's food reigns supreme. Since we were in the area, I decided to tell her about Singapore's most famous prawn mee, with the caveat that there were still better ones around. As you would expect, her first reaction to the jumbo prawn noodles was an expression of smugness to tell me that once again,

Penang had won. I had to admit defeat because the soup tasted more like the dishwater the hawkers in Penang used to wash their bowls. (When you have tasted prawn mee in Penang, you will understand what I mean. In comparison, the soup is full-bodied and tastes like the concentrated liquid version of prawn crackers.) Ours is like American coffee compared to their espresso.

But then, salvation appeared when the owner came and introduced himself to us. When he found out we were having a Singapore-Penang food competition, he immediately went back to the stall and came out with a bowl of specially prepared wild tiger prawn soup. When C K tasted it, she immediately said this was what prawn mee should taste like. The soup was very much more concentrated and had that wonderful umami kick that one would crave for in a good prawn noodle broth. The owner went on to tell us that we should order our prawn mee without beansprouts the next time, because they dilute the taste of the soup.

I think Beach Road Prawn Mee is still good, but you can taste it at its best only if the person you order from can convey your special order to the people cooking your food. When the boss is there, the taste can be quite phenomenal. That goes to show that nothing beats knowing that the hawker you are ordering from is still personally cooking your bowl of noodles.

· · · · ·

LESLIE'S TOP PICKS FOR PRAWN MEE

Old Stall Hokkien Street Famous Hokkien Mee
4.25/5

The owner specially prepares the chilli powder by frying it with dried prawns. It tastes so good that they even sell the chilli powder.

Hong Lim Complex Temporary Market and Food Centre, 10 Upper Pickering Street #01-11 S058285, 9am to 7pm, closed on Thursdays

Wah Kee Prawn Noodles
4.8/5

The prawns here are some of the biggest prawns I have ever seen – so sweet and juicy.

Pek Kio Market and Food Centre, 41A Cambridge Road #01-15 S211041, 7.30am to 2pm, closed on Mondays

Noo Cheng Adam Road Prawn Noodle
4.6/5

The chilli is more savoury than spicy and it has got that X-factor that kept me thinking about it that night.

Adam Road Food Centre, 2 Adam Road #01-27 S289876, 9.15am to 4pm and 6.30pm to 2am, open everyday

Noo Cheng Adam Road Prawn Mee
4.5/5

At this branch, the soup version definitely beats the one over at Adam Road!

Zion Riverside Food Centre, 70 Zion Road Stall 4 S247792, 11am to 11pm, open everyday

River South (Hoe Nam) Prawn Noodles Eating House
4.5/5

Why is the soup so good? The owner says it is because they sell many bowls of noodles a day, so they have to boil more prawns in the stock. More prawns, more taste.

31 Tai Thong Crescent (facing Jackson Centre) S347859, 6.30am to 4.30pm, closed once a month on Mondays

Joo Chiat Prawn Noodle
4.6/5

The other really shiok thing here is the pork ribs – they are just tender enough to bite without being too soft that the meat falls off the bone.

Xin Hua Ji Food House, 15 Crane Road S429812, 7am to 3pm, closed on Tuesdays

Jalan Sultan Prawn Mee
4.5/5

This stall gives you the option of ordering jumbo king prawns in order to satisfy your prawn craving.

2 Jalan Ayer (off Geylang Lorong 1, opposite Kallang MRT station) S347859, 8am to 3.30pm, closed on Tuesdays

Beach Road Prawn Noodle House
4.5/5 for tiger prawn special
3.5/5 for original bowl

The owner tells us that we should order our prawn mee without beansprouts, because they dilute the taste of the soup.

370 East Coast Road S428981, 8am to 4pm, closed on Tuesdays

ROASTED MEATS

CHAR SIEW, SIO BAK AND ROAST DUCK

There is nothing more sinful and shiok than burnt fat with caramelised sugar!

I t is hard to find an exceptional roast duck or sio bak (roasted pork) in Singapore, but great char siew (barbecued meat) is easier. My idea of what shiokadelicious char siew should be thickly cut, tender, marbled and juicy, with nicely charred and caramelised bits of fat on the outside and have a melt-in-your-mouth texture when you bite into it. With each bite, you should be able to appreciate the smell of smoky charcoal.

It is mind-boggling how many different versions of excellent char siew I have come across. Conventional wisdom dictates that char siew is made by marinating pork with the simple combination of fish sauce, sugar, white pepper and red colouring. But on-the-ground experience has shown that char siew need not be red; some versions are dark brown or even black. And the ingredients used to make a good char siew varies. One Teochew hawker revealed to me that he uses tau cheo (salted bean paste) and malt to make his delicious char siew, while Fatty Cheong uses oyster sauce and caramelised sugar. I even found a third version that adds yao chai (Chinese herbs) in the marinade!

Despite the different versions, there is general consensus that to yield the best char siew, the hawker must use specific cuts of pork, typically the pork shoulder (the part just behind the neck) which is commonly known in Singapore as wu hua rou, meaning "five flower pattern pork". I think it is called so not because there are five layers of meat and fat, but because when you look at the cross section of the meat, the white coloured fat vaguely resembles the ancient Chinese character 5. But, according to Fatty Cheong, the most prized cut of pork to make char siew is the pig's armpit, which is also known as bu jian tian, meaning "never see the sky". Technically, this is the part between the shoulder and belly, so the meat and fat are nicely layered like belly meat, tender and springy at the same time, and full of flavour.

· · · · ·

The char siew at **Fatty Cheong** is easily one of the best versions of char siew in Singapore, and very reasonably priced. Fatty Cheong uses only pork from Brazil (Malaysian pork is still banned in Singapore), and offers a choice of both lean and marbled versions of char siew. His char siew is dipped intermittently during the roasting process in a marinade of soya sauce, sugar, oyster sauce and tau cheo (salted bean paste) to ensure that a thick, transluscent and caramelised layer coats the char siew. His charcoal oven ensures the pork gets that characteristic smoky flavour. Fatty Cheong's char siew is always tender and juicy. The sio bak and roast duck here are both very good, but it is his char siew that has that extra oomph to keep you salivating when you think of it.

Why is the shop called Fatty Cheong? Well, it turns out that it may be a case of self-fulfilling prophecy. When Mr Cheong started his shop 14 years ago, he was a slim young man. I think he must have chosen the name Fatty because he used to be an apprentice at Fatty Ox, a famous roast duck stall that has closed down. Since then, he has tweaked his char siew recipe to suit local tastes.

· · · · ·

The char siew at **Lee Kheong Roasted Delicacy** in Chinatown was so good that I had to close my eyes to fully concentrate on the sweet savoury aroma of the pork. I have only come across one other char siew that is even more tok kong (superlative) but that was Ming Kee, in Kuala Lumpur! Finally, another char siew that might just rival Fatty Cheong's!

The sio bak at Lee Kheong was also very good, but not what I was expecting, based on makankaki Liverpool's glowing review. However, to be fair, I had gone on a day when the sio bak had just about run out, so I did not get the best piece.

· · · · ·

At **Kay Lee Roast Meat Joint**, the Lao Ban Niang marinates her char siew with yao chai (Chinese herbs)! Eleven herbs and spices to be exact, just like Colonel Sanders! The Lao Ban Niang is a colourful character and is fiercely passionate about the Zhu Jiang heritage of her char siew and roast duck. (The only thing I love more than people with passion is expressive people with passion!) She does not use any MSG in the marinade, and insists that her sauce is the only one of its kind in Singapore, and of course, the best! "When you taste it, it leaves a karm karm (astringently sweet) taste in your mouth and you won't get thirsty from it," she lectures. Even her method of chopping the duck is special. She chops it diagonally, insisting that it makes a difference to the texture of the meat.

FATTY CHEONG

The char siew here is very shiok and most importantly, they use armpit meat which is beautifully marbled. It is wonderfully tender and chewy at the same time. As for the duck, I thought it was one of the best ducks I have tasted in Singapore, though my makankaki SCS Butter begged to differ. I agreed with him that it did lack that extra oomph, but the special thing about it was that the skin was crispy, and that sets it apart from a lot of other roast ducks in Singapore. The sio bak was also very good. The skin was crispy and the meat had enough spice and salt. Unfortunately, we had it in the afternoon, so it was not fresh out of the oven, or it would have been even better! One down side of Kay Lee's roasted meats is that they tend to be on the pricey side, which is why I have not crowned it the king of roasted meats.

· · · · ·

When you see a stall with a long queue in Singapore, it is usually because of two reasons. The first one is of course the food is very good. But the second reason is because the food is not only good, but also cheap. Singaporeans do have a nose for a good deal, and some stalls generate a queue because of competitive prices. (Of course, the food has to be of an acceptable quality as well!) I think the **New Rong Ge Liang Hong Kong Roast** stall falls into the latter category. Both the char siew and the sio bak here are very good, but not good enough to generate a long queue. The queue here is therefore due to their reasonable pricing. The roast duck is very good and certainly one of the best I have tasted. The meat is fragrant, not gamey, and very tender. At $15 for half a duck, the price is reasonable and certainly offers a compelling reason to join the queue! Guess everyone knows a good deal when they see one!

· · · · ·

Toh Kee stall in Chinatown serves up another of Singapore's zhao pai (famous) roast ducks and the name is almost synonymous with People's Park Centre. The first thing that strikes me is how much darker its roast duck is – yes, it is the Dark Lord of roast ducks, almost half black rather than the usual burnt sienna colour. Underneath that crispy dark skin is very tender and highly agreeable duck meat. Definitely one of the better roast ducks around. I especially liked the braised soya beans that accompanied the platter. Not many places provide them nowadays. The next best thing was the sio bak, which had very crispy skin with tender and fragrant flesh. We were not overwhelmed, or even "whelmed" by the char siew though. It was tasty, but a little dry.

· · · · ·

If you ask any foodie where the best char siew in Singapore is, quite a few will mention **Alex Eating House**. Unfortunately, as with a lot of other eateries in Singapore, the owner has now trained a whole troupe of foreign workers to tend the shop while he takes time to smell the roses, so I was unable to get any background stories from them. (I don't know about you, but when I see a stall being operated by foreigners, my expectations always drop a notch.) In any case, Alex Eating House has always been well known for its char siew and it is indeed quite good, although when I tried it at around 2pm, the meat was a little dry. Still, the sauce was very good and definitely one of the better ones around. The sio bak was okay, but the skin was not as crispy, though the meat was flavourful. I am sure there are many fans of this restaurant that come here often, but for me, the char siew is not compelling enough for me to make the trip back, since there are other stalls that are more accessible.

· · · · ·

The **Jiu Jiang Shao La** stall at Ghim Moh had many fans recommending it, so I had very high expectations. However, my first plate of roast duck, sio bak and char siew was anything but stellar. The marinade was very good but the meat a tad dry. Thankfully, when I decided to order another portion, I got some bu jian tian pork (pig's armpit), and that really saved the day – the fatter cut of char siew was juicy and I rather enjoyed the bits of caramelised charred fats.

· · · · ·

Some people like Bill Gates want to rule the world. Others, like Phua Chu Kang want to rule Singapore, JB (Johor Bahru) and Batam. But for Johnny Teo of **Fong Kee Roast Duck**, all he wants is to rule Toa Payoh. With two roast meat stalls strategically placed in Toa Payoh, residents need not worry about where to get their char siew and roast duck fix. And Johnny said he has no intention of moving out of the boundaries of the Big Swamp (Toa Payoh means "big swamp" in the Minnan dialect).

The roast duck at Fong Kee is set apart from the rest by its sauce, which is quite shiok, and the sesame seeds add more savoury goodness to the flavour. The char siew was just above average the first time I tasted it, but improved to be juicy, tender and well caramelised the second time I had it. However, the sio bak lacked juiciness and umami kick both times I had it. Despite having a crispy skin, the flesh was dry.

· · · · ·

LESLIE'S TOP PICKS FOR ROASTED MEATS

Fatty Cheong
4.75/5

The char siew here is easily one of the best in Singapore, and very reasonably priced.

ABC Brickworks Food Centre,
6 Jalan Bukit Merah #01-120 S150006,
11am to 8.30pm, closed on Thursdays

Lee Kheong Roasted Delicacy
4.75/5 for char siew
4.25/5 for sio bak

We have only come across one other char siew that is even more tok kong (superlative) than the one served here, but that is Ming Kee, in Kuala Lumpur!

People's Park Cooked Food Centre,
32 New Market Road #01-1040 S050032,
10am to 4pm, closed on Tuesdays

Kay Lee Roast Meat Joint
4.5/5 for char siew and roast duck
4.25/5 for sio bak

Lao Ban Niang says that her sauce is one of its kind in Singapore, and she marinates her char siew with 11 kinds of yao chai (Chinese herbs).

125 Upper Paya Lebar Road S534838,
10am to 7pm, closed on Tuesdays

New Rong Ge Liang Hong Kong Roast
4.5/5 for roast duck
4/5 for char siew and sio bak

The roast meats here are cheap and tasty. The roast duck is exceptionally good – the meat fragrant, not gamey, and very tender.

269B Queen Street #01-235 S182269,
9am to 8pm, closed on 1st Wednesdays of
every month

Toh Kee
4.5/5 for roast duck
4/5 for sio bak
3.5/5 for char siew

The first thing that strikes me is how much darker the roast duck is – yes, it is the Dark Lord of roast ducks, almost half black rather than the usual burnt sienna colour.

People's Park Cooked Food Centre,
32 New Market Road #01-1014 S050032,
10.30am to 7pm, closed on Mondays

Alex Eating House
4.25/5 for char siew
4/5 for sio bak

The char siew sauce was very good and definitely one of the better ones around.

Chye Sing Building, 87 Beach Road #01-01
S189695, 9am to 6pm, open everyday

Jiu Jiang Shao La
4/5 for sio bak and roast duck
4.25/5 for char siew

The pig's armpit cut of char siew was really good. Instead of being too dry, the fatter cut of char siew was still juicy and I rather enjoyed the bits of caramelised charred fats.

Ghim Moh Market and Food Centre,
20 Ghim Moh Road #01-45 S270020,
10.30am to 2pm, closed on Wednesdays

Fong Kee Roast Duck
4.25/5 for char siew and roast duck
3.75/5 for sio bak

The roast duck at Fong Kee is set apart from the rest by its sauce, which is quite shiok, and the sesame seeds add more savoury goodness to the flavour.

SATAY

I love satay that is juicy after grilling, and made from chunky whole pieces of thigh meat. I prefer the meat to be on the sweet side, with the fragrance of the marinade, made from a combination of spices including lemon grass, generously assaulting my olfactory nerves as I survey my meal.

Satay is one of the must-try dishes in the minds of many tourists that visit Singapore. Yet, I find that satay in Singapore caters to the mass market. Go to Lau Pa Sat or East Coast Lagoon Food Village, and you will be spoilt for choice by the large number of satay stalls. Unfortunately, the choice is between the bad and the so-so. I can't even name one great satay stall at these two so-called Satay Clubs. Gone indeed are the days when the word Esplanade used to conjure up thoughts of piping hot satay by the sea, rather than two big inedible durians. People fondly remember from those days the good old Satay Club where names like Fatman Satay reigned supreme. Since then, our present day Satay Clubs are all but a shadow of what the original one was like.

Perhaps the problem with these Satay Clubs is that business is good and the stalls do well enough by enticing customers with a perfunctory, "Satay, sir?" In other words, they don't see the need to put in effort to improve their satay. It is the problem of complacency mixed with contentment – a lethal concoction for blah food. Then, there is another problem – most Singaporeans do not want chicken skin in their satay. I am not saying that eating chicken skin is good for you; you should not eat too much of it, especially if you have high cholesterol levels or are overweight. What I am saying is that the same people who frown upon eating chicken skin in satay also happily munch on BBQ chicken wings, chicken rice and Wagyu beef. It's a form of gastronomic hypocrisy. As a result, you don't see any chicken skin in satay in Singapore, whereas such satay is still widely available in Malaysia. And then we complain that the satay is better across the Causeway!

I love satay that is juicy after grilling, and made from chunky whole pieces of thigh meat. I prefer the meat to be on the sweet side, with the fragrance of the marinade, made from a combination of spices including lemon grass, generously assaulting my olfactory nerves as I survey my meal. To create a great peanut sauce is also quite an art. I love my sauce thick, chunky, with a generous amount of coarsely ground peanuts. Of course, satay and sauce made at the stall is usually better than those bought from suppliers!

One thing to bear in mind is that there really are two types of satay in Singapore. One made by the Chinese and the other by the Malays. The Chinese style satay features a zebra crossing pattern of lean meat followed by fat. The marinade for Chinese style satay, or more accurately, Hainanese style, usually has some saffron and Chinese "five spice" in it. These spices make it distinct from the Malay style. You can also find pineapple puree in the dipping sauce.

For the best Hainanese style satay, head down to **Chuan Kee Satay** at Old Airport Road. This is traditional Hainanese style satay, which is pork satay served with peanut gravy that comes with pineapple slush. The flowery bouquet from the freshly grilled skewers was too much of an unbearable tease and the first bite was like getting infatuated all over again. The meat was really tender and coated with spicy golden syrup that hinted strongly of lemon grass and coriander. Fantastic.

The elderly couple manning this stall told me that they have been dishing out satay for almost 50 years. Uncle started out by helping his father sell satay along the streets of Geylang, when he was just five years old. These days, the waiting time for this stall's satay on weekends is around 45 minutes!

· · · · ·

Even though they are a satay supplier, **Kwong Satay** is not to be missed. One of the secrets is that Kwong insists on using saffron ($6,000 per kg) in the marinade, which makes it very aromatic. The peanut sauce comes with crushed pineapple which would please most foodies. However, I felt the sauce could have been more "peanuty" to make it even more shiok. The ketupat (compressed Malay rice cakes) was very nice as they used pandan leaves instead of coconut. Have a sniff before you pop it into your mouth!

When Kwong Satay agreed to my idea of doing a Kushiyaki style pork belly satay, I was ecstatic! At the taste-test of this "*ieat* creation", the majority gave this new type of satay extremely high marks, including myself. The satay was almost 2½ times the size of normal satay. Furthermore, it is made from pork belly meat, which is more expensive than pork loin.

· · · · ·

THE EAST COAST SATAY CHALLENGE

One of the things that really frustrates me every time I visit East Coast Lagoon Food Village is that I never really know which of the 10 Malay style satay stalls is really the best. I always end up ordering randomly from whoever does the best touting that night. So, being a Scienty-Fienty (the nemesis of the Arty-Farty) type of guy, there was only one solution to the problem – do an experiment! A randomised, double-blinded, controlled trial to find out which satay is indeed the best! Well, sort of.

What I did was to mobilise a dozen test subjects, order satays from every stall there and taste-test each one to find out whether there was a clear favourite. Our unwitting but intrepid test subjects were all experts in their own right – each with at least 20 years of experience in eating. (Of course, that's just counting biological age. The true "eating" age of some of them far exceeds their biological age, as evidenced from the subcutaneous storage of unused calories!)

We decided to taste-test only chicken satay since that was the most popular choice. Each judge graded both the satay and the quality of the peanut sauce. You would think that with seven satay stalls (three of the 10 stalls were closed that night) all competing for the same customers, competition would be stiff. The unfortunate truth was that a lot of them tasted quite similar and most of them were quite lacklustre. Our judges were penning down more phrases like "terrible", "no taste at all" and "not marinated enough", rather than adoring accolades. There was, however, a real difference in the quality and style of the peanut sauces that were provided. These ranged from "watery, burnt nutty taste" to "consistent" and "can taste peanut".

Three of the seven stalls sampled procured their satay from suppliers, but some made it a point to make their own peanut sauce. It seemed to me that the sellers were trying to differentiate their products with their sauces, rather than with the satay itself.

The good news is that there was a clear winner that night – our judges rated the satay from **Musa Ikan Bakar BBQ** stall as the best, with comments like "tender and plump", "tastes good" and "can taste the chicken". The accompanying peanut sauce was thick and chunky, with generous amounts of coarsely ground peanuts.

I was pleasantly surprised and delighted to find **Rosraihanna Soto and Satay**, a little stall run by a very pleasant Mak Cik at Golden Mile. She serves one of the best satays I have eaten in a long time. I think some may find it a little on the sweet side, but I enjoyed the fresh fragrant aroma of the lemon grass, and the tender, juicy pieces of chicken thigh meat that had been marinated just right, such that they were full of flavour, but still tender and juicy.

When you plunge the satay into the sauce, you will know that you are eating something made with passion. The evidence is undeniable – the pieces of uneven peanuts in the gravy show that the lady bothered to roast her peanuts before pounding them by hand, rather than buying them ready-ground or even grinding them in a food processor. One of the best sauces around!

· · · · ·

Warong Sudi Mampir is one of those satay stalls that does not need to open at night and in fact, it closes two days a week. I think that says it all. At 3pm in the afternoon, almost every table in front of the stall has a plate of satay and the hawkers are grilling satay to fulfill take-home orders of hundreds of sticks or more!

Pak Cik recommended I try the beef tripe satay. What I liked most was the marinade and the good thing about tripe is that it absorbs the marinade very well, so that you can taste the zesty lemon grass and other spices in the meat. What I didn't like was that they used chicken breast meat for the chicken satay. I also found the mutton a little on the tough side, but it was still very yummy. The satay sauce was very commendable – lots of chunky peanuts and very sedap!

· · · · ·

LESLIE'S TOP PICKS FOR SATAY

Chuan Kee Satay
4.75/5

The satay meat is really tender and coated with spicy golden syrup that hints strongly of lemon grass and coriander. Fantastic.

Old Airport Road Food Centre,
51 Old Airport Road #01-85 S390051,
6pm till sold out, open at 1pm on Sundays,
closed on Mondays and Thursdays

Kwong Satay (original stall)
4.75/5 for kushiyaki style
pork belly satay
4.5/5 for pork satay

One of the secrets of Kwong Satay is that the hawker insists on using saffron in the marinade. They also serve an *'ieat creation'*, the Kushiyaki style pork belly satay!

Sing Lian Eating House,
549 Geylang Lorong 29 S389504,
5pm to 11pm, closed on alternate Wednesdays

Rosraihanna Soto and Satay
4.5/5

One of the best satay sauces around!

Golden Mile Food Centre,
505 Beach Road #B1-19 S199583,
12pm to 10pm, closed on Sundays

Warong Sudi Mampir
4.5/5 for beef tripe satay
4/5 for mutton satay
3.5/5 for chicken satay

The satay sauce was very commendable – lots of chunky peanuts and very sedap!

Haig Road Cooked Food Centre,
14 Haig Road #01-19 S430014,
10.30am to 7pm on weekdays,
10.30am to 5pm on weekends,
closed on Wednesdays and Thursdays

Musa Ikan Bakar BBQ
4/5

The best satay stall out of the seven stalls we tried at East Coast Lagoon Food Village.

East Coast Lagoon Food Village,
1220 East Coast Parkway, Stall 51 S468960,
4pm to past midnight, closed on Mondays

TEH TARIK

The End of Char Kway Teow

Take a sip and let the sweet aroma of comfort flow down your throat. Gulp, smack, ahhh! Ain't nothing like a good teh tarik.

There is nothing quite like a cup of hot teh halia (ginger tea) to wash down all that oil after eating stuff like nasi lemak and biryani. The tannin in the tea acts as an astringent to wash down the flavours, the fat in the milk binds with capsaicin (the substance in chilli that causes a burning sensation) which eases the heat, the sugar triggers the release of substances from the tongue that also eases the burning sensation and the ginger helps to relieve bloatedness and aid digestion. Wow! Which brilliant fellow came up with this wonderful after-your-spicy-dinner drink?

We don't know who, but we certainly can say that teh halia ultimately has its origins in China. This is because tea is originally from China, while ginger is native to both China and India. It was the British traders who smuggled tea out of China to India, to start their own tea plantations. Their attempt to ease the trade deficit caused by too many Britons liking tea, and too little Chinese liking anything English is the reason that tea became a popular drink in India.

I love the smooth taste of teh tarik and the strong ginger punch of teh halia. Take a sip and let the sweet aroma of comfort flow down your throat. Gulp, smack, ahhh! Ain't nothing like a good teh tarik. While you can try to make this drink yourself at home, it's not going to be the same. Let me explain why. First, you have to boil water the traditional way – in a big aluminium pot. Next, you have to put a piece of muslin cloth (make sure it's been used at least a few hundred times) over a smaller aluminium pot and pour a mound of fragrant strong tea dust from a big plastic sack (probably from India, Indonesia or Malaysia, but definitely not Lipton) into the pot. Next, add water till all the tea dust floats up and almost overflows. Strain the tea into a big stainless steel cup, add evaporated and condensed milk, and get ready to tarik (pull the tea)! Pulling the tea adds bubbles into the tea and cools it down. (Oh, it also helps if you are Indian. Adds authenticity, if you know what I mean!) Trust me, I have tried doing this at home, with the same ingredients, but it is just not the same. Best way to get your teh tarik fix is to leave it to the experts.

· · · · ·

Want to drink Presidential teh tarik? Come to **Hilmi Sarabat Stall** at Marine Parade and you too can feel like the President, at least for 10 minutes. Although this stall is open throughout the day, the Presidential teh tarik is only available till 12.30pm because it has to be made by a particular man, who is code-named Michael Bolton to protect his real identity, and he only works till then.

The first time I went there, I had teh halia made by Michael Bolton's partner, who was on the afternoon shift, and it was very, very good! There was enough punch from the ginger, the tea was strong, and it was creamy and smooth. Sip, gulp… Aaah! The second time I went there, the Presidential teh tarik man was on duty – maybe it was just psychological, but the brew was indeed befitting of royalty. Full-bodied and fragrant, with an

THE ULTIMATE TEH TARIK EXPERIMENT: DOES TARIKING THE TEH MAKE A DIFFERENCE?

I have always wondered whether tariking the teh (pulling the tea) actually makes a difference to the taste itself. Apart from cooling it down, and making the foam on top, does the extra air in the tea actually make it taste better? Well, I decided to put the question to the test. So, in true scientific fashion, I did a totally unrigorous, randomised, uncontrolled trial – the type that could never be published in any respectable journal. This experiment was done at the **No Name Sarabat Stall**.

The hypothesis:

Tariking the teh does affect its taste, making it more delectable to the palate.

The design:

Two cups of tea were prepared using a common container so that the amount of condensed milk, tea and water were the same. One cup was then decanted into a mug without tariking. The other underwent three tariks at a distance of a man's arm. It was then decanted into another absolutely identical mug. Unsuspecting subjects were first asked to taste both teas with their eyes opened, then with their eyes closed. They were then asked if they perceived a difference in taste. A bottle of mineral water was provided to cleanse the palate in between tastings.

The results:

- Makankaki Tag was given two sips of the non-tariked tea. He claimed that the first one tasted better than the second.
- Our second judge was given the tariked one first, then the non-tariked one. She claimed the first was the non-tariked one and the second one the tariked one.
- Makankaki Camemberu was similarly given the tariked one first and the non-tariked one next. She got it right the first time, but could not repeat her feat the second time.
- Makankaki Liverpool was given two sips of the non-tariked tea. He said the first was tariked and the second was non-tariked.
- I was honest enough to just say I could not tell the difference.

The conclusion:

There is no doubt that we have proven the hypothesis to be false.

However, in an interesting turn of events, one of my blog readers later wrote in to explain that tariking the tea does actually make it taste different because the protein degradation of the milk changes through the pulling process. Simply adding hot milk to hot tea, or cold milk to hot tea, will not make the milk change in the same way. The reader ended off with an emphatic, "Trust me, I'm a scientist."

So, it appears there is some scientific basis for teh tarik tasting different from normal teh. But still, the difference was perhaps not great enough for my makankakis and myself to pick up on consistently!

excellent post-gustatory ginger punch. It really put the tiger in the tank. So good, I had to order a second cup.

. . . . .

Over at Far East Square, the teh tarik at **Mr Teh Tarik Cartel** certainly fulfilled my criteria for a good teh tarik. It was smooth and creamy, the taste of the tea was strong enough and it flowed down the throat so smoothly. It's no wonder that there is a perpetual queue outside the stall.

. . . . .

There aren't many places in Singapore where people still boil their water in an aluminium pot over a gas fire. So if you want to drink teh tarik that is both robust and rustic, **Sri Vijaya Restaurant** is one of the places to find it. This place gives you a sense of what teh tarik must have tasted like when your grandfather still had a head of black hair. It really is one of the best around.

. . . . .

Rafee's Corner at Amoy Street is a very popular stall for teh tarik – they are popular for their teh halia, but on the day we tried it, it did not really hit the mark for me. However, the teh tarik was very good. The tea was smooth and creamy, and the tea flavour was robust without being too "waxy".

. . . . .

Finally, the continuous queue outside the **Taj Mahal** stall certainly caught my attention. The teh halia was surprisingly refreshing. Unlike others I have tasted before, this one was not overly milky and had a good balance of ginger and tea flavours. Perfect for washing down all that oil and spices!

. . . . .

LESLIE'S TOP PICKS FOR TEH TARIK

Hilmi Sarabat Stall
4.6/5 for teh made by "Michael Bolton"
4.5/5 for teh made by
"Michael Bolton"'s partner
The Presidential teh tarik was full-bodied and fragrant, with an excellent post-gustatory ginger punch.

Marine Parade Central Market and Food Centre,
84 Marine Parade Central #01-146 S440084,
5.30am to 11pm (Presidential teh tarik is
available only till 12.30pm)

Mr Teh Tarik Cartel
4.5/5

It was smooth and creamy, the taste of the tea was strong enough and ooh, it flowed down the throat so smoothly.

Far East Square, 135 Amoy Street #01-01
S049964, 7am to 9.30pm, open everyday

Sri Vijaya Restaurant
4.5/5

If you want to drink a teh tarik that is both robust and rustic, this is one of the places to find it.

229 Selegie Road S188344,
6am to 10pm, open everyday

Rafee's Corner
4.25/5

The tea was smooth and creamy, and the tea flavour was robust without being too "waxy".

Amoy Street Food Centre,
7 Maxwell Road #02-85 S069111,
6.30am to 6pm on Mondays to Fridays,
6.30am to 2pm on Saturdays and Sundays

Taj Mahal
4.25/5

The teh halia here is perfect for washing down all that oil and spices after a meal!

Adam Road Food Centre,
2 Adam Road #01-15 S289876,
open 24 hours everyday

No Name Sarabat Stall
4/5

The ambience of this unassumingly quaint little shop, manned by two elderly men with distinguished beards really adds to the whole teh tarik experience.

21 Baghdad Street S199660, 6.30am to midnight,
open everyday

TEOCHEW PORRIDGE

TEOCHEW MUAY

The End of Char Kway Teow

Nothing satisfies like a nice bowl of hot porridge on a cold rainy day. There is no doubt about it — Teochew porridge is comfort food!

The wonderful thing about Teochew porridge is the fact that it is just plain, hot and watery. I think the reason Teochews like their porridge watery might be because they were poor in the past, so all they could do was to add more water to their rice if they wanted to have more porridge.

The enjoyment of Teochew porridge, also known as Teochew muay, comes from gulping down the hot porridge after you have taken a mouthful of the often salty accompanying dishes, like fermented beancurd or chye poh (preserved radish) omelette. One or two mouthfuls of porridge are good enough to cleanse the palate of that small amount of kiam (saltiness). And the experience of the warmth of the porridge sliding down your gullet – nothing satisfies like a nice bowl of hot porridge on a cold rainy day. There is no doubt about it – Teochew porridge is comfort food!

A good bowl of Teochew porridge has got to have the right proportion of water and rice. A Teochew porridge connoisseur can tell immediately if a particular Teochew muay stall is worth eating at by just eyeing the bowl of porridge. Firstly, what we want to see is the "swa ga hai" (mountain and sea), which basically means that the porridge is watery, but not overly watered down. Secondly, the rice must remain whole and unbroken. The best Teochew muay places throw away their pot of porridge when the rice grains are broken.

My idea of a perfect Teochew porridge lunch is porridge with dishes like chye poh (preserved radish) omelette, braised pork belly, sliced lup cheong (waxed Chinese sausages) and braised peanuts. But over time, I have realised that such choices only qualify me to be an entry level Teochew Ah Hia! The true blue, hard core, fair dinkum, no play play Teochew Ah Hia will order dishes like steamed peh dou her (rabbit fish), steamed mullet, and steamed squid in tau cheo (fermented bean sauce) and chilli. In addition, the epitomy of steamed fishes – white pomfret – is another favourite classic dish. It doesn't get any more classic than steaming white pomfret with sour plums. Teochew Ah Hias like myself have learnt from a young age that for some reason, the Teochews seem to "own" this fish much more than other dialect groups. We were taught as young boys that the pomfret should only be steamed as it preserves the tender smooth flesh. Doing it any other way is sacrilegious. White pomfret is one fish I actually liked when I was young because it never tasted or smelled fishy, like mullet. When steamed right, the sour plum lends a tang to the smooth flesh which makes you salivate and want to eat more.

By the way, while we are on the topic of pomfrets, there is a world of difference between a white pomfret *(pampus agenteus)* and a black pomfret *(parastromateus niger)*. For a start, they are from different genuses, so it is like comparing a sheep with a goat. No self-respecting Teochew would ever serve steamed black pomfret to an honoured guest. Of course, if you feel the guest has overstayed his welcome, then an oversteamed black pomfret might be just the thing to serve, provided of course that your guest is also Teochew and gets the subtle hint! For those that are really in the know, there is one type of pomfret that is even more prized than the white pomfret –

it is what we call "dao chior", or Chinese silver pomfret *(pampus chinensis)*. This is the type of pomfret you should serve if you are trying to impress your prospective mother-in-law who happens to be Teochew. The Chinese silver pomfret is more expensive and less readily available than the white pomfret. The flesh is even more delicate compared to the white pomfret. The easiest way to recognise this fish is to look at the ventral (bottom) fin – the white pomfret has a sharp tipped fin while the Chinese silver pomfret has a blunt fin. The latter tends to be more round in shape and more speckly grey as compared to the white pomfret.

· · · · ·

One of the best places to enjoy Teochew porridge is **Xu Jun Sheng Teochew Cuisine** at Joo Chiat. In addition, it is one of the very few places where you can select from readily prepared dishes and also order a la carte dishes. The taste of the white pomfret here is as good as it gets. I also like the lor bak (braised pork belly) here, which is not overly spiced with five spice powder and has a very balanced flavour. One of the best braising sauces I have come across. The fish cakes here are another gem which you must try. There is one ingredient which they add to the fish cake that you do not readily get elsewhere – dang cai (preserved vegetable). I usually do not like dang cai, but the combination of dang cai and fish cake is fantastic. This is easily the tastiest fish cake I have come across. Finally, there is something in the prawn rolls that makes them very tasty. You may not get big pieces of prawns to give you that visual satisfaction, but put it in your mouth, and you'll find yourself closing your eyes, trying to analyse why the taste is so perfect. One of the secrets, the Teochew Ah Chik here revealed, is that they use pork mesentery to wrap their prawn rolls.

Xu Jun Sheng is my gold standard by which I compare all other Teochew muay stalls to.

LIM JOO HIN EATING HOUSE

Photos of Chow Yuen Fatt adorn the walls of **Lim Joo Hin Eating House**. One of the dishes I can recommend here is the lor bak (braised pork belly). Tender and savoury, it is not the best I have eaten, but I would be happy to order it when I come back again. Another outstanding dish is peanuts with ikan bilis (dried anchovies). This dish had some really addictive crunchy bits, which I found out later was a mixture of chilli with sugar crystals. The other dishes, like the hae bee hiam (prawn paste) and the gu lou yoke (sweet and sour pork) were all quite good.

· · · · ·

If you are looking for a good deal on Teochew porridge, head down to **Teochew Muay** at Mohammed Sultan, run by my makankaki SCS Butter. This restaurant serves up a Teochew muay buffet for lunch and dinner, in air-conditioned comfort, with the dinner buffet including a free flow of bak kut teh. My personal favourite was the minced meat chye poh (preserved radish) omelette, a special order item. Just tell them you want to try the *"ieat* omelette", which comprises a freshly fried omelette topped with very shiok minced meat, chye poh and chilli sauce. I also enjoyed the minced meat with pickled radish – the tangy, savoury and sweet dish went really well with the hot porridge. I was pleasantly surprised to find da chang luo mi (glutinous rice sausage), a Teochew classic that is not easily found nowadays, on the buffet menu. The glutinous rice was very flavourful and packed with dried shrimp, mushrooms and peanuts. The tofu with pork floss was also very good – although usually served cold, SCS Butter steams the tofu before topping it with soya sauce and pork floss. It is very good and available only during the dinner buffet. They also have steamed fish and mei cai kou rou (preserved vegetables with pork belly slices), the latter of which desperately needed a makeover.

One thing about this restaurant is that it will appeal to the health conscious – the food here is not overly oily, so you can go back to the office after lunch without having to take some Eno.

· · · · ·

Ask a handful of people where to eat the best Teochew porridge in Singapore and most of them will point you to **Teo Heng Porridge Stall**. Indeed, you cannot really discuss Teochew porridge if you have not eaten the porridge here. Mr Liew has been dishing out hawker food for 60 years – he started selling food at the age of 17 and still looks remarkably fit and has a keen mind. If you think that Japanese Rutan (seasoned eggs) with watery yolks is new to the Singapore food scene, think again. This stall has been selling such eggs for over a generation! This may very well be the only Teochew porridge stall that sells its lou nerng (seasoned eggs) this way. (The more common hard-boiled version often has that ugly green grey ring around it because it has been overcooked. Most of the hawkers will buy their eggs hard-boiled and then put them into the braising sauce.) Mr Liew also serves up a perfectly balanced and fragrant braising sauce with various porcine parts stewing in its goodness. I am also told that his steamed fish dishes are die-die-must-try dishes, though they were sold out when I was there.

· · · · ·

At **Xin Jia Po He Pan Teochew Rice and Porridge**, the dishes I ordered – steamed squid, homemade fish cake and braised pork belly – were all very good, but the one that really caught my attention was the sambal shark meat. I was pleasantly surprised at just how tasty shark's meat can be. It was the kind of dish that goes really well with plain porridge because it coats the mouth with all the tasty goodness that just begs to be washed down with piping hot porridge.

· · · · ·

Did you know that Hougang is one of the Teochew enclaves in Singapore? Specifically, Hougang ngou kor kior (5 miles). So if you are trying to look for Teochew porridge, then this must be the place to find it right? If you ask any Hougang resident where to eat Teochew porridge, he or she will point you to **Ah Seah Eating House** – this place is very established and is synonymous with Hougang.

I loved the homemade fish cake and meatballs at this stall. The texture of the fish cakes and the contrast between the cool and smooth fish cake and the hot porridge was excellent. I also tried the braised peanuts here, but they were not soft or flavourful enough for my liking.

· · · · ·

It was makankaki Fashionfoodie who organised an outing for the makan kakis to eat at **Bukit Merah View Economic Teochew Porridge**. Here, my makankakis raved over the peh dou her (rabbit fish) and the steamed squid. Peh dou her is especially prized during the Chinese New Year period when they are about half the normal size and full of roe. Teochew Ah Hias like makankaki Fashionfoodie tell me that the stomach is bitter and when taken with the roe, it is supposed to bring you to heavenly Swatow!

However, try as I might, I really could not bring myself to appreciate peh dou her (rabbit fish), because of the fishiness of the fish. Even as my makankakis were attacking the fish with gusto, I was only able to finish a few mouthfuls. Similarly with the steamed squid, my first bite was nothing spectacular, and nothing I would rave about. Alas, what kind of Teochew Ah Hia can I claim to be if I don't like these dishes?

· · · · ·

LESLIE'S TOP PICKS FOR TEOCHEW PORRIDGE

Xu Jun Sheng Teochew Cuisine
4.75/5 for prawn rolls
4.5/5 for lor bak (braised pork belly) and fish cake
4.25/5 for white pomfret
Xu Jun Sheng is my gold standard by which I compare all other Teochew muay stalls to.

59 Joo Chiat Place S427783, 11am to 9pm from Mondays to Saturdays, 10.30am to 3pm on Sundays, closed on Wednesdays

Lim Joo Hin Eating House
4.5/5 for peanuts with ikan bilis (dried anchovies)
4.25/5 for lor bak (braised pork belly)
Their peanuts and ikan bilis (dried anchovies) have some really addictive crunchy bits.

715/717 Havelock Road S169643, 11am to 5am, open everyday

Teochew Muay
4.5/5 for *"ieat* omelette"
4.25/5 for minced meat with pickled radish, da chang luo mi (glutinous rice sausage) and tofu with pork floss
3/5 for mei cai kou rou (preserved vegetables with pork belly slices)
Try the *"ieat* omelette", which comprises a freshly fried omelette topped with very shiok minced meat, chye poh (preserved radish) and chilli sauce.

5 Mohammed Sultan S239014, 12pm to 3pm and 6pm to 10pm, open everyday

Teo Heng Porridge Stall
4.25/5 for seasoned eggs and braising sauce
Mr Liew serves up a perfectly balanced and fragrant braising sauce with various porcine parts stewing in its goodness.

Hong Lim Complex Temporary Market and Food Centre, 10 Upper Pickering Street #01-28 S058285, 7am to 2pm, closed on Sundays

Xin Jia Po He Pan Teochew Rice and Porridge
4.25/5
I was pleasantly surprised at just how tasty their sambal shark's meat was.

Maxwell Road Food Centre, 1 Kadayanallur Street #01-98 S069184, 10.30am to 8.30pm, open everyday

Ah Seah Teochew Porridge
4.5/5 for homemade fish cake
3.5/5 for braised peanuts
The texture of the fish cakes and the contrast between the cool and smooth fish cake and the hot porridge was excellent.

Ah Seah Eating House, Kovan Centre, 9 Yio Chu Kang Road S545523, 11am till late at night, open everyday

Bukit Merah View Economic Teochew Porridge
3/5 for steamed squid (Makankakis' rating 4.5/5)
2.5/5 for peh dou her (rabbit fish) (Makankakis' rating 4.5/5)
Here, my makankakis raved over the peh dou her (rabbit fish) and the steamed squid.

Bukit Merah View Food Centre, 115 Bukit Merah View #01-377/379 S151115, 10am to 7pm, closed on Sundays

WANTON
MEE

372 | The End of Char Kway Teow

Preparing noodles is a lost art which I am glad is being revived. Perhaps we are being influenced by the growing number of la mian, soba, ramen and pasta stalls popping up. Why shouldn't we celebrate our humble mee kia and give it its rightful place alongside these other noodles?

When it comes to wanton mee, there are two groups of people. Those who consider the dish as a whole, and those who focus solely on the noodles. For the former group, the sauce, char siew (barbecued meat), wanton and noodles all have to be good. For the latter group, they don't really care if the char siew and wantons are quite ordinary. They just go for the noodles and chilli. When I was younger, I belonged to the former group – the char siew was the main thing for me. But as I got older, I began to appreciate the quality of noodles in wanton mee more. I love my noodles QQ (al dente) with lovely bite and good, springy texture. But, I still have a preference for juicy, succulent char siew, crispy fried wantons, also known as keow, dark sauce and crispy pork lard.

Wanton mee is the quintessential street food, yet I have had much difficulty finding one that I can truly call "the best". I really cannot understand why it is so difficult to make a great wanton mee. The way I see it, you need (1) great noodles, (2) great sauce, (3) great char siew and (4) great wantons.

Regarding noodles, hawkers used to make them from scratch in the past. Then, we went through a time when everything started to be outsourced, like those horrible factory-made pau. But of late, there have been more hawkers who are bucking the trend and trying to differentiate themselves by going back to the good old ways. Preparing noodles is a lost art which I am glad is being revived. Perhaps we are being influenced by the growing number of la mian, soba, ramen and pasta stalls popping up. Why shouldn't we celebrate our humble mee kia and give it its rightful place alongside these other noodles? While the majority still procures standard noodles from suppliers, the better noodle hawkers these days custom-order their noodles from factories that follow a specific recipe given by the hawkers themselves. I am told the difference in cost may be as much as five times, but it is certainly worth it. So, there are great noodles to be found out there, and great sauces too – be it the Hong Kong style dark sauce or the Singapore style chilli and tomato sauces, which though simple, has a fierce loyal following.

I reckon that the stumbling blocks for most wanton mee sellers must be the char siew and the wantons. Unless you are able to chargrill your own char siew, it is difficult and expensive to procure char siew that is really good.

Most hawkers end up serving dry, thin slivers of excuses for char siew. And as for wantons, I was talking to some passionate Hong Kong foodies the other day and they summed up the sad state of our wantons well, "Pfffff! You call this wanton mee? Yao mo gao chor ah? (You gotta be kidding right?)" You see, unlike the wanton mee in Hong Kong where you get big juicy wantons with the noodles, our wantons are pathetically anorexic, with more skin than filling. To call the dish wanton mee is a misnomer. Gon lou (dry tossed) mee would be a more accurate name to better differentiate our version from the Hong Kong version. Can any enterprising hawker please dish out a truly good version of wanton mee, with ping pong-sized wantons? That will surely get the attention of the foodie community!

· · · · ·

It was makankaki SCS Butter who first brought me to **Da Jie Famous Wanton Mee** at Jalan Besar, and it turned out to be quite a find. The noodles and sauce really hit the U-spot (umami spot). The texture of the noodles was perfect, coming alive when you slurped and chewed on them. One of the secrets to the texture of the noodles, aside from the fact that they use a specially ordered egg noodle, is Da Jie's practice of loosening all the noodles and allowing them to rest in a big box. The sauce has that extra something that makes the difference between great and eye opening. Phwaa, shiok! (Yes, I tasted lard in there!) Now, if this wanton mee had big, juicy wantons and char siew that had a little more fatty burnt bits, then I would have found perfection.

By the way, makankaki SCS Butter raves about the chicken feet at Da Jie. They are stewed till super soft and gelatinised, so you really get to slurp up the sticky gooey juices and it is literally finger-lickin' good! A bit more kick with the sauce, perhaps by adding a little cut chilli and fermented black beans, might just make it more enjoyable.

. . . . .

Madam Leong of **Nam Seng Wanton Mee** has been dishing out wanton mee since 1959. At 80 years of age, I think she is the oldest working hawker I have met. Amazingly, she still comes to the stall at six in the morning to prepare the ingredients for the day. This stall is the famous wanton mee stall that was located at the old National Library, where Senior Minister (SM) Goh Chok Tong recounted eating these noodles during his early dating days at the National Library. According to Madam Leong, SM Goh also went there to get his foodie fix back in the days when he was the Minister for Trade and Industry, and she also rattled off a few other Ministers and VIPs who frequented her stall. I guess she is quite a living legend in the hawker scene!

This wanton mee is one where the noodles take centre stage. You will not be impressed by the appearance of the dish because the noodles look quite plain and the fluorescent red char siew, dry and unappetising. But when you take your first mouthful of the noodles, you will be rewarded with a great-tasting noodle and a secret sauce that will make you stop and wonder. I tried very hard to find out more about her secret sauce, but only managed to guess correctly that there are dried scallops in it. The noodles and sauce alone deserve top marks. Unfortunately, the char siew is not the juicy charred type I like, and the wantons though very good, are not the best I have tasted.

. . . . .

If you are the type that laments that the char siew that accompanies wanton mee is often an afterthought rather than the main event, then **Wanton Noodle** stall at Tiong Bahru Market is one place you'll want to visit on your next wanton mee outing. Both the sauce and the noodles are good, but they are backup singers for the char siew, which is perfectly caramelised with the fat just wanting to dissolve the instant it comes into contact with your tongue. If you are willing to brave the long queues, you will be rewarded with a very nice plate of wanton mee where you can really savour the char siew. Just be forewarned that the pig's armpit cut, which is the best cut of char siew, sells out earlier than the normal cuts, so you might want to get there early to avoid disappointment.

· · · · ·

Fei Fei Wanton Mee is probably one of the best known wanton mees in Singapore. The first time I tried Fei Fei was when I stumbled upon it in 2007, driving past the newly renovated corner coffeeshop in Joo Chiat, with the Fei Fei name and the "open 24 hours" sign. I was not too impressed with the noodles at the time, and so did not write about it. Then I discovered there was another Fei Fei Wanton Mee just down the road, in an "original" condition coffeeshop. The story goes that there was once a grandfather, Chan Ah Yean, who gave his wanton mee stall to his two grandsons. They shared the stall by taking turns to run it on alternate weeks. After a few years, the elder brother decided to go the franchising route and opened a brand new corner coffeeshop selling Fei Fei Wanton Mee 24 hours daily. He also kept his rights to the old stall which he continued manning on alternate weeks. The younger brother later decided to give up his rights to the old stall and opened his own stall in Bedok. He then moved twice and settled in a 24-hour coffeeshop in Ubi, right opposite the automotive Megamart. Although he owns the whole coffeeshop, the actual Fei Fei Wanton Mee is but an inconspicuous stall, sharing a single shop space with another stallholder.

That aside, the wanton mee still tastes the same as it did when I tried it at the original coffeeshop in Joo Chiat. The focus of Fei Fei has always

been on the noodles, which is best enjoyed plain with a slice of pickled green chilli. I had the chance to try the chilli sauce version, the black sauce version and the chicken feet sauce version, but the one which really brought out the flavour of the noodles was the plain version, with just a dash of light soya sauce and fragrant oil. If you have not tried eating plain noodles with pickled green chillies, give it a try – it's a trick I learnt from the noodle maker himself, Vincent. The char siew is still the same red poster coloured char siew, whose primary function is to add colour to the bowl of noodles. The wantons have actually grown bigger since the last time I had them, and are still as flavourful. Now, they have also added deep-fried wantons which give you a crunchy contrast to the chewy noodles. Overall, a satisfying bowl of noodles for those who place top priority on the quality of the noodles.

By the way, Vincent also told me that he and his elder brother have reconciled and he has even helped his brother improve on the quality of his noodles. So now you have two 24-hour Fei Fei stalls. One in Joo Chiat, the other in Ubi, and one big happy family.

· · · · ·

Foong Kee Coffee Shop has only been in operation for six years, but has quickly risen to the top of the wanton mee rankings. You could wait up to an hour during peak periods to get your food! The strength of this stall lies in the fact that they roast their own char siew and they use a very good cut of pork, so the char siew is tender and juicy. The noodles are custom-made from a factory so they do have a quality taste and texture. The sauce was good, but just a little too bland for me. The wantons and shui gao (prawn dumplings) were also very good, but not outstanding.

· · · · ·

Quite a few people regard **Hong Mao Wanton Mee** as the best in Singapore. Its most famous supporter is Gerard Ee, the ex-President of the Automobile Association of Singapore and also Singapore's most well-known philanthropist. Apparently, he comes here every Saturday to have his wanton mee fix. The other not-quite-as-famous supporter who frequents this stall is Aston of Astons Specialties. When Aston is not eating steak, he is here eating what he considers to be the best wanton mee in Singapore.

However, I feel this wanton mee, though very good, is not exceptional. The char siew is the stumbling block. The texture and taste of the noodles are very good, as are the wantons. And the soup is full of anchovy flavour. But the char siew just "cannot make it".

· · · · ·

The **Yi Shi Jia Wanton Mee** stall prides itself in selling wanton mee that is hot, sour, sweet and salty. They want the world to know that they are still using the same Sin Sin brand of tomato ketchup which their father used when he started the shop some 30 to 40 years ago. This wanton mee is very old school. You still get a generous helping of crispy pork lard as well as the traditionally thin slivers of tasty char siew. The noodles are of quite good quality and I am told by the Lao Ban Niang that they spend a little more money to procure a better quality egg noodle. Undoubtedly, the star of the show for me was the wantons. They were very tasty and some of the best I have ever tasted. However, I would have loved a juicier and thicker char siew to go with it.

· · · · ·

There is only one wanton mee stall in East Coast Lagoon Food Village and it is **Hwa Kee BBQ Pork Noodles**, famous for dousing its noodles with sweet char siew sauce. I found it nice, but was not crazy about it. The char siew was

good, but not stellar, even though it was charcoal roasted on the premises. They have a special machine to slice the char siew and it came out a little ragged. When I tasted it, it was a tad dry. The wantons were good but not remarkable. Still, if you are hankering for wanton mee late at night, this is a famous stall where you can satisfy your craving.

. . . . .

The good thing about the wanton mee at **Hong Ji Mian Shi Jia** stall in Telok Blangah is the noodles, which are really thin, transluscent and flat (rather than round). The flatness of the noodles gives them more of a lively bite and more curl. However, the wantons here are a waste of calories – full of wanton skin with very little meat, they were really very disappointing for such a famous stall. However, I am pleased to say that the char siew was excellent – the stall still makes its own char siew with a charcoal oven hidden in the corner. Sweet and succulent, with just enough crunchy burnt bits. The only problem might be that you have to ask them to pile it on in order to get some real satisfaction.

. . . . .

I thought I would also include **Koung's Wanton Mee** since it is so established. The noodles were good, while the char siew and the chilli sauce were competent, but unremarkable. The one good thing about the dish was the liberal use of crispy pork lard. Overall, a good plate of wanton mee but not something I would make another trip down to eat.

. . . . .

If you are after some controversy, check out **Kok Kee Wanton Mee** at Lavender Food Square – some of the forum members on my blog loved it, while others did not think much of it. When I arrived to check it out for myself, there was a long queue of about eight people despite the fact that it was 2.30pm in the afternoon! One man in the queue was from Taiwan and he told me he came all the way from Taiwan to eat this wanton mee! I was definitely getting curious, though the char siew looked like the "boiled in a pot with red dye" type and the noodles were bought from a supplier.

Still, I must admit, I quite liked the dish. While the char siew and the wantons were pretty lousy, the sauce was a real winner. I deduced that it is their boiling cauldron of gong tau (addictive substance) which combines so well with the noodles that keeps customers coming back again and again.

· · · · ·

LESLIE'S TOP PICKS FOR WANTON MEE

Da Jie Famous Wanton Mee
4.6/5 for wanton mee
4.25/5 for chicken feet
The noodles and sauce really hit the U-spot (umami spot).

209 Jalan Besar S208895, 7am to 2pm, closed on Sundays and public holidays

Nam Seng Wanton Mee
4.6/5 for noodles and sauce alone
4.5/5 for overall dish
Senior Minister Goh Chok Tong recounted eating these noodles during his early dating days at the National Library.

Far East Square, 25 China Street #01-01 S049567, 8am to 8pm, closed on Sundays

Wanton Noodle
4.5/5
The char siew is perfectly caramelised, the fat waiting to dissolve as it meets your tongue.

Tiong Bahru Market and Food Centre, 30 Seng Poh Road #02-30 S168898, 10.30am to 3pm, closed on Fridays

Fei Fei Wanton Mee
4.25/5
The focus is on the noodles, best enjoyed plain with a slice of pickled green chilli.

302 Ubi Avenue 1 #01-09 S400302, open 24 hours everyday

Foong Kee Coffee Shop
4.25/5
They roast their own char siew and they use a very good cut of pork, so it is tender and juicy.

6 Keong Saik Road S089114, 11am to 8pm, closed on Sundays and public holidays

Hong Mao Wanton Mee
4.25/5
The noodles and wantons are very good. But the char siew just "cannot make it".

128 Eating Corner, 128 Tembeling Road S423638, 7am to 4pm, closed on Mondays

Yi Shi Jia Wanton Mee
4.25/5
The wantons are very tasty and some of the best I have ever tasted.

Kovan Food Centre, 209 Hougang Street 21, Stall 57 S530209, 7.30am to 8pm, closed on Sundays

Hwa Kee BBQ Pork Noodles
4/5
This stall is famous for dousing its noodles with sweet char siew sauce.

East Coast Lagoon Food Village, 1220 East Coast Parkway, Stall 45 S468960, 7.30pm to 12.30pm, closed on Wednesdays

Hong Ji Mian Shi Jia
4/5
The char siew here is sweet and succulent, with just enough crunchy burnt bits.

Telok Blangah Drive Food Centre, 79 Telok Blangah Drive #01-05 S100079, 7am to 7pm, closed on Fridays

Koung's Wanton Mee
3.75/5
The one good thing about the dish was the liberal use of crispy pork lard.

1 Geylang Lorong 13 S388639, 7.30am to 8.30pm, open everyday

Kok Kee Wanton Mee
3.75/5
While the char siew and the wantons are pretty lousy, the sauce is a real winner.

Lavender Food Square, 380 Jalan Besar #01-06 S209000, 12pm to 2am, closed every three weeks on Wednesdays and Thursdays

YONG
TAU
FOO

The End of Char Kway Teow

Although I like yong tau foo, I used to find it hard to rave about something as simple as beancurd with fish paste. This was until I tried it the way it should be served.

Ever wondered why yong tau foo is called yong tau foo? "Tau foo", we all know, means beancurd. But what does "yong" mean? Well, as it turns out, the word "yong" is actually a simplification of the Hakka word "ngiong", which means "to stuff". So, "yong tau foo" simply means "stuffed beancurd".

Of course, these days, yong tau foo stalls serve much more than just stuffed beancurd. The same minced meat or fish paste is used to stuff everything, from bittergourd to eggplant. I guess someone must have thought that we should eat more vegetables.

So, what is the difference between yong tau foo and Hakka yong tau foo? Even though the dish is Hakka in origin, over time, the Hakka practice of using meat stuffing was replaced by fish paste stuffing. When I asked how this came about, some people said that it might have been due to the fact that our ancestors wanted to make the dish suitable for Muslims, who do not eat pork. Over time, fish paste yong tau foo became so common that the stalls selling the original Hakka version, with meat stuffing, began to distinguish themselves from others by calling their dish Hakka yong tau foo.

I tend to eat yong tau foo when I want something reasonably tasty yet healthy, with less cholesterol. Although I like yong tau foo, I used to find it hard to rave about something as simple as beancurd with fish paste. This was until I tried it the way it should be served. I learnt that the way to really appreciate yong tau foo is to have it piping hot after blanching, with a drizzle of fragrant oil. The main ingredients in yong tau foo, like the vegetables and beancurd, must be fresh, and it is the quality of the sweet sauce and the fish/meat paste that will distinguish a great yong tau foo from a so-so version. Here are my picks for the best stalls in Singapore.

· · · · ·

At **Hong Hakka Yong Tau Foo** stall in Tampines Round Market, you will be spoilt for choice. This stall boasts 60 yong tau foo items, which means you can come every day of the week and still eat something different. The boss proudly declared to me that there are 16 items on his menu that are not found anywhere else in the world! True enough, many of the items did not even have a name, but were just described by the ingredients.

Uncle has a giant, fried item that looks like a sui gao (prawn dumpling), which he calls a popiah. It might look like an XXL fried sui gao, but when you bite into it, you find that the ingredients are quite complex. I could make out black fungus, carrots, vermicelli and maybe meat and fish paste. It was very yummy and had a very unique texture that can really only be described as spongy. The filling was like a spongy matrix which traps all the juices within. Very difficult to describe. But very easy to eat.

The paste here is made from a combination of meat, fish and salted fish, and it is very good. The paste is found in many of the items here, including pig's skin, fish paste roll, seaweed fish paste roll and even, an interesting item with no name, made of long beans which have been weaved into a circle and filled with fish paste in the middle!

Still more items managed to get me excited – one being ngoh hiang (fried pork rolls) with very different ingredients from the norm, fried yam with meat paste, as well as several types of homemade meatballs which were very addictive. The one that I liked best was the pig's tendon ball, which had texture and taste that was a cross between a siew mai (steamed meat dumpling) and a normal pork ball. If normal yong tau foo were a sightseeing tour, this stall would be an expedition! A definite must-try for yong tau foo lovers!

· · · · ·

If you are craving for something healthy, then the yong tau foo at **Fu Lin Tou Fu Yuen** is not the stall to go to. At this stall, they do not blanch the items in water, but actually deep-fry everything before serving them in a soya-based minced pork sauce. So, even the healthy stuff like fresh tofu and lady's fingers get deep-fried in oil. This is what makes this yong tau foo so shiok! If you are the type that finds yong tau foo a bit bland, this one will tingle your taste buds and change your mind! It is yong tau foo with oomph! Even though they do not use any pork in their filling, their ngoh hiang (fried pork rolls) and wantons are all very savoury and yummy!

Another unique thing about this yong tau foo is that it is served with thick bee hoon in a meat sauce made from minced chicken. According to the stall owner, this style of yong tau foo was introduced by him 10 years ago. The stall became so popular, it moved out of a coffeeshop in Siglap to become a standalone restaurant.

Another not-so-healthy yong tau foo can be found at **Hup Chong Hakka Niang Dou Foo** in Toa Payoh. The trays of deep-fried wantons, meatballs and ngoh hiang (fried pork rolls) are simply irresistible. The Hakka style minced meat stuffing used here was shiokadelicious and very addictive. It was great in the tofu, but when simply deep-fried as a meatball and dipped into the sweet sauce, phwaa sayah! Why does something that tastes so good have to be bad for you?

· · · · ·

Xi Xiang Feng Yong Tau Foo at Ang Mo Kio Central is reputed to have a perpetual queue throughout the day. I went down and sure enough, there was a queue outside the stall of more than 10 persons very obediently picking their yong tau foo and waiting patiently in line for their lunch to be cooked. Lao Ban Niang tells me that they have been at the Ang Mo Kio Ave 6 Market and Food Centre since it first opened more than 30 years ago. There are two things that are seriously good about this stall. That's not to say the rest are mediocre, but the two things that are really outstanding are the bee hoon and the sweet sauce. Both are very different from the ones you get from your run-of-the-mill yong tau foo stall and are the most memorable bits for me. The fresh bee hoon has a wonderfully chewy texture and excellent fragrance. The sweet sauce here is spiked with lots of sesame seeds and is very addictive.

· · · · ·

For a nice yong tau foo in the Central Business District, head to **Rong Xing Cooked Food**. The 40 or so items offered here are all made on the premises. The owners take a lot of pride in the fact that they make their own fish and meat paste, as well as all the other items on the menu. I especially liked their handmade pork balls, which were very savoury and tasty. The soup had a strong taste of ikan bilis (dried anchovies) and the silken tofu used for some of the items was really soft and silky.

· · · · ·

Another shiok yong tau foo can be found at **Simpang Yong Tau Foo** stall in Bedok which serves up a unique version of yong tau foo. This is our very own Simpang yong tau foo, not Ampang yong tau foo, mind you. Ampang yong tau foo originated in a suburb called Ampang in Kuala Lumpur. Like Ampang yong tau foo, the ingredients used in this stall are fried first, and then doused in a soya-based sauce. But that's where the similarity ends. The sauce here is quite unique. It is sweet, a little tangy and mildly spicy. Perhaps the right adjective is "piquant". Quite shiok and definitely unique.

· · · · ·

Tucked away in People's Park Complex Food Centre is a yong tau foo stall with a perpetual long queue. It was, in fact, the longest queue I had ever seen! At the **Yong Xiang Xing Yong Tau Foo** stall, everyone gets a standard bowl of yong tau foo, with no options for noodles or bee hoon, and no questions asked. (Sounds like the hawker is a bit of a Food Nazi!) How did I find this stall's version of the dish? The fried beancurd roll with the fish paste was definitely the star of the bowl. It was freshly fried and I have never tasted anything so good from any other yong tau foo stall. The handmade fish balls were also very good, but the rest of the tofu items were nothing to rave about, though still good. The reason this stall opens at 1pm is because all the preparation is done in the morning – from the beating of the fish balls, to the wrapping of the ngoh hiang (fried pork rolls), to the frying. I suppose this is why it is so popular – because everything is freshly prepared!

· · · · ·

If, however, you do not feel like queuing up behind 30 people, head over to the other end of People's Park Complex Food Centre where you can find **Poy Kee Yong Tau Foo** stall. The soup is very different from the previously mentioned stall, but the ngoh hiang (fried pork rolls) and tofu items are all pretty good. At least over here, you get to choose what you want to include in your bowl of yong tau foo and you don't have to queue that long!

· · · · ·

Goldhill Hakka Restaurant along Changi Road is the only stand alone yong tau foo restaurant I have blogged about. The beancurd served here was excellent – the silken tofu was smooth as silk. Every day, fresh ikan parang (wolf herring) is cut into fillets and beaten to a paste by hand. It is then used to stuff chilli, bittergourd, tau pok (fried beancurd) and ngoh hiang (fried pork rolls). Those who like their food sweet will really appreciate the sweet sauce – this is one of the best sweet sauces I have ever tasted! It is really thick, sweet and substantial. Their sauce does not come out of a bottle. Secret ingredients are used and it is stewed for two hours. Definitely worth a try!

· · · · ·

LESLIE'S TOP PICKS FOR YONG TAU FOO

Hong Hakka Yong Tau Foo
4.6/5

You will be spoilt for choice as this stall boasts 60 yong tau foo items and 16 of them are not found anywhere else in the world!

Tampines Round Market and Food Centre, 137 Tampines Street 11 #01-01 S521137, 7am to 1pm (when food is usually sold out), open everyday

Fu Lin Tou Fu Yuen
4.5/5

They actually deep-fry everything before serving them in a soya-based minced pork sauce.

721 East Coast Road S459070, 8.30am to 8.30pm, open everyday

Hup Chong Hakka Niang Dou Foo
4.5/5

The Hakka style minced meat stuffing used here was shiokadelicious and very addictive.

116 Toa Payoh Lorong 2 S310116, 6.30am to 3pm and 5pm to 8.30pm, closed on Tuesdays

Xi Xiang Feng Yong Tau Foo
4.5/5

The two things that are really outstanding here are the bee hoon and the sweet sauce.

724 Ang Mo Kio Avenue 6 #01-23 S560724, 7am to 7pm, closed on Sundays

Rong Xing Cooked Food
4.25/5

The 40 or so items offered here are all made on the premises – the owners take a lot of pride in the fact that they make their own fish and meat paste.

Tanjong Pagar Market and Food Centre, 6 Tanjong Pagar Road #02-04 S810006, 7am to 2.30pm, closed on Thursdays, Sundays and public holidays

Simpang Yong Tau Foo
4.25/5

This is our very own Simpang yong tau foo, not Ampang yong tau foo from KL!

Bedok Market Place, 348 Bedok Road #02-05/06 S469560, 9.30am to 7pm, open everyday

Yong Xiang Xing Yong Tau Foo
4/5

Everyone gets a standard bowl of yong tau foo, with no options for noodles or bee hoon, and no questions asked.

People's Park Cooked Food Centre, 32 New Market Road #01-1084A S050032, 1pm till sold out (4pm latest)

Poy Kee Yong Tau Foo
4/5

The tofu items and ngoh hiang (fried pork rolls) are quite good and you don't have to queue that long.

People's Park Cooked Food Centre, 32 Market Road #01-1066 S050032, 11am to 7pm, open everyday

Goldhill Hakka Restaurant
4/5

They serve one of the best sweet sauces I have ever tasted! It is really thick, sweet and substantial.

299A Changi Road (after SPC Station) S419777, 11.30am to 4pm, open everyday

MUST-TRY STALLS BY LOCATION

NORTH
Hougang, Jalan Kayu, Kovan, Sembawang, Serangoon, Upper Thomson, Yio Chu Kang

Casuarina Road
Casuarina Curry (for prata)
126 Casuarina Road (off Upper Thomson) S579514, 7am to 11.30pm on weekdays, 7am to midnight on weekends and eve of public holidays

Chomp Chomp Food Centre
Ah Hock Fried Hokkien Noodles
20 Kensington Park Road, Stall 27 S557269, 5.30pm to midnight, closed once a fortnight

Carrot Cake
20 Kensington Park Road, Stall 36 S557269, 5.30pm to midnight, closed on alternate Tuesdays

Che Jian Fried Hokkien Mee
20 Kensington Park Road, Stall 11 S557269 (left hand side towards the back), 5.30pm to 1am, open everyday

Defu Lane
Riyadh Muslim Food (for prata)
Soon Soon Lai Eating House, 32 Defu Lane 10, Stall 12 S539213, 6.30am to 7pm, closed every last Wednesdays of the month

Hougang
Man Ji Handmade Pau
327 Hougang Avenue 5 S530327, 6am to 1pm, open everyday

Jalan Kayu
Thasevi Famous Jalan Kayu Prata Restaurant
237/239 Jalan Kayu S799461, open 24 hours everyday

Thohirah Restaurant (for biryani)
258 Jalan Kayu (next to the car park) S799487, open 24 hours everyday

Kovan Centre
Ah Seah Teochew Porridge
Ah Seah Eating House, 9 Yio Chu Kang Road S545523, 11am till late at night, open everyday

Kovan Food Centre
Yi Shi Jia Wanton Mee
209 Hougang Street 21, Stall 57 S530209, 7.30am to 8pm, closed on Mondays

Serangoon Garden Market and Food Centre
Ah Seng Braised Duck Rice
49A Serangoon Garden Way, Stall 44 S555945, 11am to 9pm, open Mondays to Saturdays

Garden Street Kway Chap
49A Serangoon Garden Way, Stall 21 S555945, 8am to 3pm, closed on Mondays

Tan Soon Mui Beancurd
49A Serangoon Garden Way, Stall 41 S555945, 8am to 8pm, closed on Mondays

Thong Soon Avenue
The Prata Place
1 Thong Soon Avenue (Springleaf Estate) S787431, 7.30am to midnight, open everyday

Upper Serangoon Road
Oyster Omelette
Nam Heng Restaurant, 949 Upper Serangoon Road (at junction with Simon Road) S534713, evening till 10pm, open everyday

Upper Thomson Road
The Prata House
246 Upper Thomson Road S574370, open 24 hours everyday

EAST
Aljunied, Bedok, Changi Road, Changi Village, East Coast Parkway, East Coast Road, Elias Road, Eunos, Geylang, Geylang Serai, Jalan Besar, Joo Chiat, Katong, Macpherson, Marine Parade, Old Airport Road, Paya Lebar, Siglap, Tampines, Telok Kurau, Ubi

Aljunied Market and Food Centre
Ah Xiao Teochew Braised Duck
117 Aljunied Avenue 2 #01-18 S380117, 11.30am to 7.30pm, closed on Mondays

Ng Soon Kee Fish & Duck Porridge
117 Aljunied Avenue 2 #01-11 S380117, 12pm to 9pm, closed on Sundays

Bedok Food Centre (Bedok Corner)
No Name Stall (for oyster omelette)
1 Bedok Road S469572, open everyday

Bedok Interchange Food Centre (New Upper Changi Road Food Centre)
Bedok Chwee Kueh
207 New Upper Changi Road #01-53 S460207, 7am to 11pm, open everyday

Bedok Market Place
Simpang Yong Tau Foo
348 Bedok Road #02-05/06 S469560, 9.30am to 7pm, open everyday

Bedok North Street
Changi Lorong 108 Fei Lao Seafood (for hor fun)
86 Bedok North Street 4 #01-165 S460086, 11am to 2pm and 5pm to 10pm, closed on alternate Tuesdays

Bedok Road (Simpang Bedok)
Syed Restaurant (for prata)
326 Bedok Road S469496, open 24 hours everyday

Bedok South Market and Food Centre

Hill Street Char Kway Teow
16 Bedok South Road #01-187 S460016, lunch till 4pm, then 6pm onwards till Uncle runs out of food, closed on Mondays

Changi Road

Goldhill Hakka Restaurant
(for yong tau foo)
299A Changi Road (after SPC Station) S419777, 11.30am to 4pm, open everyday

Seng Kee Mushroom Minced Pork Noodles
316 Changi Road S419792, 8am to 4.30pm, open everyday

Changi Village Market and Food Centre

Changi Beef Kway Teow Noodle
2 Changi Village Road #01-19 S500002, 11am to 11pm, open everyday

Guan Kee (for carrot cake)
2 Changi Village Road #01-02 S500002, 11am to 11pm, closed on Mondays

International Nasi Lemak
2 Changi Village Road #01-57 S500002, 9.30am to 3.30pm, 6pm to 12am from Mondays to Fridays, 9.30am to 7.30pm on Saturdays and 9.30am to 12am on Sundays

Mizzy's Corner (for nasi lemak)
2 Changi Village Road #01-55 S500002, 7am to 4pm, open everyday

Sri Sujana (for nasi lemak)
2 Changi Village Road #01-54 S500002, 7am to midnight, closed on Mondays and Tuesdays

Wing Kee Ipoh Hor Fun
2 Changi Village Road #01-04 S500002, 10.30am to 11pm from Mondays to Fridays, 8am to midnight on Saturdays and Sundays

Circuit Road Food Centre

Yong Lai Fa Ji Cooked Food
(for fish soup)
79A Circuit Road #01-648 S370079, 5am to 9pm, closed on Sundays and public holidays

Circuit Road Market and Food Centre

Chye Kee Chwee Kueh
89 Circuit Road #01-129 S370089, 6.30am to 3pm, open everyday

Crane Road

Joo Chiat Prawn Noodle
Xin Hua Ji Food House, 15 Crane Road S429812, 7am to 3pm, closed on Tuesdays

Dunman Road Food Centre

Lau Hong Ser Rojak
271 Onan Road #02-14 S424768, 4.38pm to 1.38am, closed on Sundays

East Coast Lagoon Food Village

Cheok Kee Duck Rice
1220 East Coast Parkway, Stall 29 S468960, 11am to 10pm, open everyday

Hwa Kee BBQ Pork Noodles
1220 East Coast Parkway, Stall 45 S468960, 7.30pm to 12.30pm, closed on Wednesdays

Kampong Rojak
1220 East Coast Parkway, Stall 9 S468960, dinner till 11pm, open everyday

Musa Ikan Bakar BBQ
1220 East Coast Parkway, Stall 51 S468960, 4pm to past midnight, closed on Mondays

Sheng Hokkien Mee
1220 East Coast Parkway, Stall 12 S468960, 12pm to midnight, open everyday

East Coast Road

328 Katong Laksa
216 East Coast Road S428914, 8am to 10pm, open everyday

Astons Specialties (for western food)
119/121 East Coast Road S428806, 11.30am to 10pm from Sunday to Thursday, 11.30am to 11pm on Fridays, Saturdays and public holidays

Beach Road Prawn Noodle House
370 East Coast Road S428981, 8am to 4pm, closed on Tuesdays

Boon Tong Kee (Katong)
(for chicken rice)
199 East Coast Road (opposite Holy Family Church) S428902, 11am to 10pm, open everyday

Chin Mee Chin Coffee Shop
(for kopi and toast)
204 East Coast Road S428903, 8.30am to 4pm, closed on Mondays

Five Stars Kampung Chicken Rice
191/193 East Coast Road S428897, 9am to 3am, open everyday

Fu Lin Tou Fu Yuen (for yong tau foo)
721 East Coast Road S459070, 8.30am to 8.30pm, open everyday

Geylang Lorong 29 Fried Hokkien Mee
396 East Coast Road S428994, 11.30am to 9.30pm, closed on Mondays

Glory Catering (for popiah)
139 East Coast Road, S428829, 8.30am to 8.30pm, closed on Mondays except public holidays

Elias Road

Godzilla Handmade Tim Sum & Da Pau
Orient Success Coffee House, 623 Elias Road, Stall 5 S510623, 6.30am to 8pm, open everyday, but only till 1pm on Tuesdays

Eunos Crescent Market and Food Centre
Epok Epok Central (for curry puff and nasi lemak)
4A Eunos Crescent #01-09 S402004,
7am to 7pm, closed on Mondays

Fengshan Food Centre
Seng Hiang Food Stall (outer stall)
(for bak chor mee)
85 Bedok North Street 4, Stall 8 S460085,
5pm to 12.30am, open everyday

Xing Ji Rou Cuo Mian (inner stall)
(for bak chor mee)
85 Bedok North Street 4, Stall 7 S460085,
5pm to 1am, closed on Mondays

Geylang
Bali Nasi Lemak
2 Geylang Lorong 15 (Geylang side)
S388596, 6pm to 4am, open everyday

Koung's Wanton Mee
1 Geylang Lorong 13 S388639,
7.30am to 8.30pm, open everyday

Kwong Satay (original stall)
Sing Lian Eating House, 549 Geylang
Lorong 29 S389504, 5pm to 11pm,
closed on alternate Wednesdays

Lorong 9 Beef Kway Teow
237 Geylang Lorong 9 S388756,
4.30pm to 2.30am, open everyday

Sin Huat Seafood Restaurant
(for crabs)
659/661 Geylang Road (junction of
Geylang Lorong 35) S389589,
6pm to midnight

Geylang Serai Market and Food Centre
Geylang (Hamid's) Briyani Stall
1 Geylang Serai #02-146 S402001,
9am to 5pm, closed on Mondays

Hajjah Mona Nasi Padang
1 Geylang Serai #02-166 S402001,
8am to 7pm, closed on Wednesdays

Sinar Pagi Nasi Padang
1 Geylang Serai #02-137 S402001,
9am to 10.30pm, closed every fortnight
on Mondays and Thursdays

Haig Road Cooked Food Centre
Warong Sudi Mampir (for satay)
14 Haig Road #01-19 S430014,
10.30am to 7pm on weekdays,
10.30am to 5pm on weekends,
closed on Wednesdays and Thursdays

Yong Li Cooked Food
(for kway chap)
14 Haig Road #01-33 S430014,
7am to 2pm, open everyday

Jalan Ayer
Jalan Sultan Prawn Mee
2 Jalan Ayer (off Geylang Lorong 1,
opposite Kallang MRT station) S347859,
8am to 3.30pm, closed on Tuesdays

Jalan Batu
Tanjong Rhu Pau & Confectionery
7 Jalan Batu #01-113 S431007,
12.30pm to 8pm, closed on Sundays

Jalan Eunos
Kim's Hokkien Mee
62B Jalan Eunos S419510,
11am to 1am, open everyday

Joo Chiat
D'Bun
358 Joo Chiat Road (junction of
Marshall and Joo Chiat Road) S427603,
8am to 10pm, open everyday

Eng Seng Restaurant (for crabs)
247 Joo Chiat Road (junction of Joo
Chiat Place and Still Road) S427502,
4.30pm to 8pm, open everyday

Kway Guan Huat Joo Chiat Original Popiah and Kueh Pie Tie
95 Joo Chiat Road S427389,
10am to 8pm, closed on Mondays
(but takeaway is available on Mondays)

Sin Heng Claypot Bak Koot Teh
439 Joo Chiat Road S427652, open
24 hours, closed on Mondays

Tian Tian Hainanese Chicken Rice
(Other stall at Maxwell Road Food Centre)
443 Joo Chiat Road S427656,
10.30am to 10.30pm, open everyday

Xu Jun Sheng Teochew Cuisine
59 Joo Chiat Place S427783,
11am to 9pm from Mondays to
Saturdays, 10.30am to 3pm on Sundays,
closed on Wednesdays

Macpherson Road
Chuan Lai Guo Zhi Wang
(for kway chap)
560 Macpherson Road S368233,
8am to 12.30am, open everyday

Marine Parade Central
Roland Restaurant (for crabs)
89 Marine Parade Central #06-750
S440089, 11.30am to 2.30pm and
6pm to 10.30pm, open everyday

Marine Parade Central Market and Food Centre
Hilmi Sarabat Stall (for teh tarik)
84 Marine Parade Central #01-146
S440084, 5.30am to 11pm (Presidential
teh tarik is available only till 12.30pm)

Katong Chicken Curry Puff
84 Marine Parade Central
#01-132 S440084, 8am to 6pm,
closed on Mondays

Mr Wong's Seremban Beef Noodle
84 Marine Parade Central
#01-184 S440084, 11am to 8.30pm,
open everyday

Marine Terrace
132 Mee Poh Kway Teow Mee
MP 59 Food House, 59 Marine Terrace
#01-05 S440059, 7am to 3.30pm, closed
on Mondays and 1st and 3rd Sundays of
the month

Old Airport Road Food Centre
Chuan Kee Satay
51 Old Airport Road #01-85 S390051,
6pm till sold out, open at 1pm
on Sundays, closed on Mondays
and Thursdays

Dong Ji Fried Kway Teow
51 Old Airport Road #01-138 S390051,
8am to 2pm, open everyday

Nam Sing Hokkien Fried Mee
51 Old Airport Road #01-32 S390051,
11am to about 8pm when everything is
sold out, closed as and when Uncle
feels tired

Toa Payoh Rojak
51 Old Airport Road #01-108 S390051,
12pm to 8pm, closed on Sundays

To-Ricos Guo Shi (for kway chap)
51 Old Airport Road #01-135/36 S390051,
11.30am to 4.30pm, closed on Mondays

Western Barbeque
51 Old Airport Road #01-53 S390051,
11am to 8pm, open everyday

Xin Mei Xiang (for lor mee)
51 Old Airport Road #01-116 S390051,
7am to 2.30pm, closed on Thursdays

Sims Avenue
Hong Qin Fish and Duck Porridge
Yue Yuan Coffee Shop, 302 Sims Avenue
Lorong 27 S387516, 8am to around 2pm,
closed on 1st and 15th of the month

Yue Yuan Coffeeshop
(for kopi and toast)
302 Sims Avenue Lorong 27 S387516,
8am to 10pm, open everyday

Syed Alwi Road
Ah Guan Mee Pok (for bak chor mee)
69 Syed Alwi Road S207648,
7am to 9pm, open everyday

The Beef House (for beef kway teow)
Gar Lok Eating House,
217 Syed Alwi Road S207776,
9am to 6pm, closed on Fridays

Tai Thong Crescent
Lao Zhong Zhong Five Spice Stall
Lao Zhong Zhong Eating House,
29 Tai Thong Crescent (corner of Tai
Thong Crescent and Siang Kiang
Avenue) S347858, 11.30am to 11.30pm,
closed on alternate Mondays

River South (Hoe Nam) Prawn
Noodles Eating House
31 Tai Thong Crescent (facing Jackson
Centre) S347859, 6.30am to 4.30pm,
closed once a month on Mondays

Tampines Round Market and
Food Centre
Hong Hakka Yong Tau Foo
137 Tampines Street 11 #01-01 S521137,
7am to 1pm (when food is usually sold
out), open everyday

Tanjong Katong Road
Lian Kee Duck Rice
Hin Hollywood Canteen,
57 Tanjong Katong Road S436952,
10am to 8.30pm, open everyday

Telok Kurau Road
Hong Ho Phang Hong Kong Pau
5 Telok Kurau Road S423758, 7.30am to
around 4pm, closed on Mondays

Katong Laksa
1 Telok Kurau Road (opposite SPC Petrol
Station) S423756, 8am to 3.30pm,
open everyday

Tembeling Road
Hong Mao Wanton Mee
128 Eating Corner,
128 Tembeling Road S423638,
7am to 4pm, closed on Mondays

Ubi
Fei Fei Wanton Mee
302 Ubi Avenue 1 #01-09 S400302,
open 24 hours everyday

Upper Paya Lebar Road
Kay Lee Roast Meat Joint
125 Upper Paya Lebar Road S534838,
10am to 7pm, closed on Tuesdays

WEST

Boon Lay, Bukit Merah, Buona
Vista, Clementi, Dover, Ghim Moh,
Lengkok Bahru, Pasir Panjang,
Queenstown, Redhill, Telok
Blangah, Upper Bukit Timah

ABC Brickworks Food Centre
Fatty Cheong (for roasted meats)
6 Jalan Bukit Merah #01-120 S150006,
11am to 8.30pm, closed on Thursdays

Guang Ji Bao Zai (for pau)
6 Jalan Bukit Merah #01-135 S150006,
10am to 10pm, closed on Thursdays

Wow Wow West
6 Jalan Bukit Merah #01-133 S150006,
10.30am to 9pm, closed on Sundays

Boon Lay Place Market and
Food Centre
Boon Lay Power Nasi Lemak
221 Boon Lay Place #01-06 S641221,
5pm to 2am, open everyday

Bukit Merah Lane 1
Hong Kong Street Chun Kee
(for fish soup)
125 Bukit Merah Lane 1 #01-190
S150125, 11am to 2.30pm and
5pm to 11pm

Bukit Merah View
Tian Tian Hainanese Curry Rice
116 Bukit Merah View #01-253
S151116, 9am to 9pm, closed on
alternate Tuesdays

Bukit Merah View Food Centre
Bukit Merah View Carrot Cake
115 Bukit Merah View #01-279 S151115,
7am to 2pm and 6pm to 1am,
open everyday

Bukit Merah View Economic
Teochew Porridge
115 Bukit Merah View #01-377/379
S151115, 10am to 7pm,
closed on Sundays

Bukit Purmei Avenue
Bukit Purmei Lor Mee
109 Bukit Purmei Avenue #01-157
S090109, 7.30am to 3.30pm,
closed on Mondays

Clementi
Chin Huat Live Seafood Restaurant
(for crabs)
105 Clementi Street 12 (Sunset Way)
#01-30 S120105, 11.30am to 2.30pm and
5.30pm to 11pm, open everyday

Commonwealth Avenue
Food Centre (Margaret Drive
Food Centre)
Queenstown Poh Pia Stall
40A Commonwealth Avenue #01-484
S140040, 10am to 10pm, open everyday

Dover Crescent
Holland Village XO Fish Head
Bee Hoon
Jumbo Coffee Hub, 19A Dover Crescent
S131019, 11.30am to 2pm and
5pm to 11pm, open everyday

Ghim Moh Market and
Food Centre
Ghim Moh Chwee Kueh
20 Ghim Moh Road #01-31 S270020,
6.15am to 7pm, open everyday

Guan Kee Char Kway Teow
20 Ghim Moh Road #01-12 S270020,
9.30am to 2.30pm, closed on Mondays
and Fridays

Jiu Jiang Shao La (for roasted meats)
20 Ghim Moh Road #01-45 S270020,
10.30am to 2pm, closed on Wednesdays

Teck Hin Fried Hor Fun
20 Ghim Moh Road #01-44 S270020,
10am to 3pm, closed on Mondays

Tong Fong Fatt (Ghim Moh)
(for chicken rice)
20 Ghim Moh Road #01-49 S270020,
10am to 9pm, open everyday

Henderson Road
**Soon Soon Huat 1A Crispy
Curry Puff**
94 Henderson Road #01-276 S150094,
8am till sold out, closed on Mondays

Lengkok Bahru
Seng Hong Coffeeshop
(for kopi and toast)
58 Lengkok Bahru S150058, 6am to 6pm,
closed on alternate Sundays

Mei Chin Food Centre
Shi Hui Yuan Hor Fun Specialty
159 Mei Chin Road #02-33 S140159,
7.30am to 2pm, closed on Mondays
and Tuesdays

Sin Kee/Xin Ji Famous Chicken Rice
159 Mei Chin Road #02-22 S140159,
11am to 8pm, closed on Mondays

Pasir Panjang Food Centre
Heng Huat Fried Kway Teow
121 Pasir Panjang Road #01-36
S118543, 11am to 9.30pm, closed on
Sundays and public holidays

Pasir Panjang Road
Tong Lok Kway Chap
114 Pasir Panjang Road S118539,
7am to 2pm, closed on Sundays,
Mondays and public holidays

Redhill Food Centre
Redhill Curry Rice
85 Redhill Lane #01-95 (facing main
road) S150085, 10.30am to 9.30pm,
closed on Sundays

South Buona Vista Road
Lim Seng Lee Duck Rice
38 South Buona Vista Road
S118164, 10.30am to 8.30pm,
closed on Sundays

Telok Blangah Crescent Market
and Food Centre
Hai Kee Teochew Char Kway Teow
11 Telok Blangah Crescent
#01-102 S090011, 5pm to 10pm,
closed on Sundays

Telok Blangah Drive Food Centre
Hong Ji Mian Shi Jia
79 Telok Blangah Drive #01-05 S100079,
7am to 7pm, closed on Fridays

CENTRAL
Adam Road, Ang Mo Kio, Balestier,
Newton, Novena, Sin Ming,
Toa Payoh, Whampoa

Adam Road Food Centre
**Noo Cheng Adam Road
Prawn Noodle**
2 Adam Road #01-27 S289876,
9.15am to 4pm and 6.30pm to 2am,
open everyday

Selera Rasa Nasi Lemak
2 Adam Road #01-02 S289876,
7am to 10pm, open everyday

Taj Mahal (for teh tarik)
2 Adam Road #01-15 S289876,
open 24 hours everyday

Ang Mo Kio
Xi Xiang Feng Yong Tau Foo
724 Ang Mo Kio Avenue 6 #01-23
S560724, 7am to 7pm, closed on Sundays

Ang Mo Kio Market and
Food Centre
**Joo Heng Mushroom Minced
Pork Mee**
628 Ang Mo Kio Avenue 4 Street 61
#01-86 S569163, 7am to 2pm

Balestier Road
Founder Bak Kut Teh Restaurant
347 Balestier Road (New Orchid Hotel)
S329777, 12pm to 2pm, and 6pm to 2am,
closed on Tuesdays

Bukit Timah Food Centre
and Market
Seng Kee Carrot Cake
116 Upper Bukit Timah Road
#02-182 S588172, 7.30am to 11pm,
closed on Thursdays

Coronation Shopping Plaza
Prince Coffee House (for hor fun)
587 Bukit Timah Road #02-15 S269707,
11am to 9pm, open everyday

Jalan Datoh
Tiong Bee Bah Kut Teh
588F Jalan Datoh (off Balestier Road)
S329899, 7am to 3pm, closed on
alternate Mondays

Kim Keat Palm Market and
Food Centre
Ah Chuan Oyster Omelette
22 Toa Payoh Lorong 7
#01-25 S310022, 3pm to 9pm,
closed on Tuesdays

Hai Nan Xing Zhou Beef Noodles
22 Toa Payoh Lorong 7
#01-06 S310022, 8am to 7pm,
closed on Mondays

Old Long House Popiah
22 Toa Payoh Lorong 7 #01-03
S310022, 6am to 5pm, closed on
Mondays and Tuesdays

Newton Food Centre
Heng Carrot Cake
500 Clemenceau Avenue North
#01-28 S229495, open in the
evenings everyday

Novena Ville
**Wee Nam Kee Hainanese
Chicken Rice**
275 Thomson Road #01-05 S307645,
10am to 2am, open everyday

Sin Ming Road
Rong Chen Bak Kut Teh
Eng Ho Hup Coffeeshop,
22 Sin Ming Road S570022,
7am to 4pm

Sin Ming Roti Prata
24 Sin Ming Road #01-51 S570024,
6am to 7pm, open everyday

Toa Payoh

Fong Kee Roast Duck
(Fong Kee has two branches)
*116 Toa Payoh Lorong 2 #01-140 S310116,
8am to 8pm, open everyday;
128 Toa Payoh Lorong 1 #01-811
S310128, 8am to 8pm, closed
on Thursdays*

Hup Chong Hakka Niang Dou Foo
*116 Toa Payoh Lorong 2 S310116,
6.30am to 3pm and 5pm to 8.30pm,
closed on Tuesdays*

Toa Payoh HDB Hub
Soon Heng Silver Stream Rojak
*480 Toa Payoh Lorong 6 #B1-23,
S310480, 11am to 8pm, open everyday*

Toa Payoh Lorong 4
Hawker Centre
93 Wu Xiang Xia Bing
(for ngoh hiang)
*93 Toa Payoh Lorong 4 #01-33 S310093,
12pm to 9pm, closed on Thursdays*

Toa Payoh West Market and
Food Court
Chey Sua Carrot Cake
*127 Toa Payoh Lorong 1 #02-30 S310127,
6am to 1pm, closed on Mondays*

Teochew Handmade Pau
*127 Toa Payoh Lorong 1 #02-02 S310127,
6am to 2pm from Mondays to
Saturdays, 6am to 12pm on Sundays*

**Tian Tian Lai (Come Daily) Fried
Hokkien Prawn Mee**
*127 Toa Payoh Lorong 1
#02-27 S310127, 9.30am to 9pm,
closed on Mondays*

Whampoa Drive Makan Place
(Whampoa Food Centre)
Ah Hock Fried Oyster Hougang
*90 Whampoa Drive #01-54
S320090, 11am to midnight,
closed on Wednesdays*

Hoover Rojak
*90 Whampoa Drive #01-06 S320090,
10.30am to 9.30pm on Mondays and
Wednesdays to Sundays, and 10.30am
to 6pm on Tuesdays*

Nan Xiang Chicken Rice
*90 Whampoa Drive #01-21 S320090,
11am to 10pm, open everyday*

No Name Tau Huay
*90 Whampoa Drive #01-57 S320090,
6.30am to 4.30pm, closed on Mondays*

Rubiah Muslim Food Nasi Melayu
(for nasi padang)
*90 Whampoa Drive #01-34 S320090,
10am to 6pm, closed on Sundays*

Ruby Poh Piah
*90 Whampoa Drive #01-53 S320090,
12pm to 8pm, closed on Wednesdays
and Thursdays*

Singapore Fried Hokkien Mee
*90 Whampoa Drive #01-32 S320090,
4pm to 1.30am, open everyday*

DOWNTOWN/CITY

Beach Road, Central Business
District, Chinatown, Esplanade,
Lavender, Little India,
Mohammed Sultan, North Bridge
Road, River Valley, Rochor,
Tanjong Pagar, Tiong Bahru

Amoy Street Food Centre
Han Kee Fish Porridge (for fish soup)
*7 Maxwell Road #02-129 S069111,
10am to 3pm, closed on Sundays*

Piao Ji Fish Porridge (for fish soup)
*7 Maxwell Road #02-100/103 S069111,
10.30am to 3pm, closed on Thursdays*

Rafee's Corner (for teh tarik)
*7 Maxwell Road #02-85 S069111,
6.30am to 6pm from Mondays to Fridays
and 6.30am to 2pm on Saturdays
and Sundays*

Yuan Chun Famous Lor Mee
*7 Maxwell Road #02-79/80 S069111,
8.30am till around 4pm when sold out,
closed on Mondays and Tuesdays*

Baghdad Street
No Name Sarabat Stall (for teh tarik)
*21 Baghdad Street S199660,
6.30am to midnight, open everyday*

Beach Road
Alex Eating House (for roasted meats)
*Chye Sing Building, 87 Beach Road
#01-01 S189695, 9am to 6pm,
open everyday*

Leong Kee (Klang) Bak Kut Teh
*321 Beach Road (Jalan Sultan Gate and
Beach Road) S199557, 11am to 9pm,
closed on Wednesdays*

Bencoolen Street
Delicious Muffins (for curry puff)
*Sunshine Plaza, 91 Bencoolen Street
#01-51 S189652, 11.30am to 8pm,
closed on 8th, 18th and 28th of
every month*

Beo Crescent
No Name Hainanese Curry Rice
*40 Beo Crescent S160040,
6.30am to 3pm, closed on Wednesdays*

Berseh Food Centre
Coffee Hut
*166 Jalan Besar #02-43 S208877,
7am to 4pm, closed on alternate
Saturdays or Sundays*

Mei Xiang Fish Soup
*166 Jalan Besar #02-44 S208877,
10.12am to 3.16pm, closed on Saturdays,
Sundays and public holidays*

Chinatown Complex Market
Heng Ji Chicken Rice
*335 Smith Street #02-131 S050335,
3pm to 9pm, open everyday*

**Teochew Street Mushroom Minced
Meat Noodle**
*335 Smith Street #02-23 S050335,
12.30pm to 9pm, closed on Mondays
and Tuesdays*

Chinatown Point
Good Morning Nanyang Café
*133 New Bridge Road #03-01
S059413, 8am to 8.30pm from
Mondays to Fridays and 10.30am to
8.30pm on Saturdays, Sundays and
public holidays*

Crawford Lane
Happy Chef Western Food
*Tai Hwa Eating House,
466 Crawford Lane #01-12 S190466,
11am to 10pm, open everyday*

Esplanade
Hup Kee (Orchard) Oyster Omelette
*Esplanade Mall, Makansutra Gluttons
Bay, 8 Raffles Avenue #01-15,
Stall K S039802, 6pm to 3am,
open everyday*

Hill Street Tai Hwa Pork Noodle
Tai Hwa Eating House,
466 Crawford Lane #01-12 S190466,
9.30am to 9pm, closed on 1st and 3rd
Mondays of the month

Dunlop Street
Bismillah Biryani Restaurant
50 Dunlop Street S209379,
11am to 10.30pm, open everyday

Eng Hoon Street
Loo's Hainanese Curry Rice
57 Eng Hoon Street #01-88 S160057,
7.45am to 2.30pm, closed on
alternate Tuesdays

Far East Square
Hock Lam Street Beef Kway Teow
22 China Street #01-01 S048761,
9.30am to 8pm from Mondays to Fridays
and 10.30am to 5pm on Saturdays,
Sundays and public holidays

Nam Seng Wanton Mee
(for wanton mee and vension hor fun)
25 China Street #01-01 S049567,
8am to 8pm, closed on Sundays

Mr Teh Tarik Cartel
135 Amoy Street #01-01 S049964,
7am to 9.30pm, open everyday

Golden Mile Food Centre
Bugis (Longhouse) Lim Kee
Beef Noodles
505 Beach Road #B1-27 S199583,
11am to 9pm, open everyday

Hainan Fried Hokkien Prawn Mee
505 Beach Road #B1-34 S199583,
11am to 2pm, and 3pm to 9pm, closed
on Wednesdays

Rosraihanna Soto and Satay
505 Beach Road #B1-19 S199583,
12pm to 10pm, closed on Sundays

Havelock Road
Lim Joo Hin Eating House
(for Teochew porridge)
715/717 Havelock Road S169643,
11am to 5pm, open everyday

Meng Kee Char Kway Teow
22 Havelock Road #01-669 S160022,
10.30am to 7pm from Mondays to
Saturdays, 10.30am to 4pm on Sundays

Hong Lim Complex Temporary
Market and Food Centre
Ah Kow Mushroom Minced
Pork Mee
10 Upper Pickering Street #01-17
S058285, 9am to 7pm

Old Stall Hokkien Street Famous
Hokkien Mee
10 Upper Pickering Street #01-11
S058285, 9am to 7pm, closed
on Thursdays

Teo Heng Porridge Stall
10 Upper Pickering Street
#01-28 S058285, 7am to 2pm,
closed on Sundays

Hong Lim Food Centre
(under renovation)
Famous Sungei Road Trishaw Laksa
(Closed till Q1 2011)
531A Upper Cross Street #02-67 S510531,
10.30am to 6.30pm, closed on Sundays

Jalan Berseh
Sungei Road Laksa
Jalan Shui Kopitiam, 27 Jalan Berseh
#01-100 S200027, 9am to 6pm, closed on
first Wednesdays of every month

Jalan Besar
Beach Road Scissor Cut Curry Rice
Lao Di Fang Restaurant,
229 Jalan Besar S208905,
11am to 3.30am, open everyday

Beancurd City
133 Jalan Besar (after Desker Road)
S208851, 11.30am to midnight,
open everyday

Da Jie Famous Wanton Mee
209 Jalan Besar S208895, 7am to 2pm,
closed on Sundays and public holidays

Keong Saik Road
Foong Kee Coffee Shop
6 Keong Saik Road S089114,
11am to 8pm, closed on Sundays and
public holidays

Tong Ya Coffeeshop
36 Keong Saik Road S089143,
11am to 2.30pm and 5.30pm to 10.30pm
from Mondays to Fridays,
11am to 2.30pm and 5.30pm to 11pm
on Saturdays and Sundays,
closed on alternate Wednesdays

Killiney Road
Killiney Curry Puff
93 Killiney Road S239536,
7am to 7.30pm

Killiney Kopitiam
67 Killiney Road S239525,
6am to 11pm on Mondays and
Wednesdays to Saturdays,
6am to 6pm on Tuesdays, Sundays
and public holidays

Lavender Food Square
Kok Kee Wanton Mee
380 Jalan Besar #01-06 S209000,
12pm to 2am, closed every three weeks
on Wednesdays and Thursdays

Miow Sin Popiah and Carrot Cake
380 Jalan Besar #01-04 S209000,
open till midnight, closed on
alternate Wednesdays

Market Street Food Centre
(Golden Shoe Food Centre)
Wei Nan Wang Hock Kian Lor Mee
50 Market Street #03-03 S048940,
9.30am to 3.30pm

Jason's Fish Soup
50 Market Street #03-25 S048940,
10am to 3pm

Maxwell Road
Funan Weng Ipoh Hor Fun
32 Maxwell Road #01-07 S069115,
11am to 9pm, closed on Sundays

Maxwell Road Food Centre
Hup Kee Wu Siang Guan Chang
(also known as China Street Fritters)
1 Kadayanallur Street #01-64 S069184,
12pm to 8pm, closed on Mondays

Jing Hua Sliced Fish Bee Hoon
1 Kadayanallur Street #01-77 S069184,
11am to 8.30pm, closed on Thursdays

Tian Tian Hainanese Chicken Rice
(Other stall at Joo Chiat)
1 Kadayanallur Street #01-10 S069184,
11am to 8pm, closed on Mondays

Xin Jia Po He Pan Teochew Rice
and Porridge
1 Kadayanallur Street #01-98 S069184,
10.30am to 8.30pm, open everyday

Mohammed Sultan

Teochew Muay
5 Mohammed Sultan S239014, 12pm to 3pm and 6pm to 10pm, open everyday

North Bridge Road

Briyani Bistro (formerly known as House of Biryani)
742 North Bridge Road (corner of North Bridge Road and Kandahar Street) S198710, 11am to 7pm, closed on Sundays, Mondays and public holidays

Famous Islamic Beryani Shop
754 North Bridge Road (corner of North Bridge Road and Klapa Road) S198772, 10.30am to 9.30pm, closed 1pm to 2pm on Fridays

Nasi Padang Sabar Menanti II
747 North Bridge Road (at the junction of Jalan Kledek) S198715, 6am to 5pm, closed on Sundays and public holidays

Seng Huat Eating House
(for bak chor mee)
492 North Bridge Road (opposite Parco Bugis Junction) S188737, open 24 hours everyday

Singapore Zam Zam Restaurant
(for murtabak)
697 North Bridge Road S198675, 8am to 11pm, open everyday

Warong Nasi Pariaman
(for nasi padang)
738 North Bridge Road S198706, 7.30am to 3pm, closed on Sundays and public holidays

Pek Kio Market and Food Centre
Tong Siew Fried Rice
(for oyster omelette)
41A Cambridge Road #01-23 S211041, 11am to 12am, closed on Wednesdays

Wah Kee Prawn Noodles
41A Cambridge Road #01-15 S211041, 7.30am to 2pm, closed on Mondays

People's Park Cooked Food Centre
Lee Kheong Roasted Delicacy
32 New Market Road #01-1040 S050032, 10am to 4pm, closed on Tuesdays

Poy Kee Yong Tau Foo
32 New Market Road #01-1066 S050032, 11am to 7pm, open everyday

Toh Kee (for roasted meats)
32 New Market Road #01-1014 S050032, 10.30am to 7pm, closed on Mondays

Yong Xiang Xing Yong Tau Foo
32 New Market Road #01-1084A S050032, 1pm till sold out (4pm latest), closed on Mondays

Queen Street
New Rong Ge Liang Hong Kong Roast
269B Queen Street #01-235 S182269, 9am to 8pm, closed on 1st Wednesdays of every month

Rangoon Road
Ng Ah Sio Pork Ribs Soup Eating House
208 Rangoon Road S218453, 6am to 2pm, closed on Mondays

Selegie Road
Sri Vijaya Restaurant (for teh tarik)
229 Selegie Road S188344, 6am to 10pm, open everyday

Short Street
Eryimin (for beancurd)
4 Short Street S188212, noon to midnight, open everyday

Rochor Original Beancurd
2 Short Street S188211, noon to midnight, open everyday

Shaw Towers
Qi Ji Poh Piah
100 Beach Road #01-01 S189702, 7.30am to 8pm, open everyday

South Bridge Road
Lee Tong Kee Ipoh Sar Hor Fun
278 South Bridge Road S058827, 10am to 9pm, open everyday

Tanjong Pagar Complex (PSA)
Outram Park Ya Hua Rou Gu Char
7 Keppel Road #01-05/07 S089053, 7am to 3pm, closed on Mondays

Tanjong Pagar Market and Food Centre
Rong Xing Cooked Food
(for yong tau foo)
6 Tanjong Pagar Road #02-04 S810006, 7am to 2.30pm, closed on Thursdays, Sundays and public holidays

Tanjong Pagar Road
Cumi Bali Indonesian Restaurant
(for nasi padang)
66 Tanjong Pagar Road S088487, 11am to 2.30pm and 6pm to 9.30pm, closed on Sundays

Tekka Market and Food Centre
Allauddin's Briyani
665 Buffalo Road #01-297 S210665, 8am to 3pm, open everyday

Tiong Bahru Market and Food Centre
Jian Bo Shui Kweh (for chwee kueh)
30 Seng Poh Road #02-05 S168898, 6.30am to 11pm, open everyday

Lor Mee 178
30 Seng Poh Road #02-58 S168898, 6am to 9.30pm, closed on Wednesdays

Tiong Bahru Pau
30 Seng Poh Road #02-18/19 S168898, 7.30am to 9pm, closed on Mondays

Wanton Noodle
30 Seng Poh Road #02-30 S168898, 10.30am to 3pm, closed on Fridays

Zion Road
Five Spice Prawn Fritter
56 Zion Road S247781, 11am to 1pm, open everyday

Zion Riverside Food Centre
Clementi Brothers Rojak (branch)
70 Zion Road, Stall 21 S247792, 12pm to 10pm, closed on Mondays

No. 18 Zion Road Fried Kway Teow
70 Zion Road, Stall 17 S247792, 12pm to 3pm and 6pm to 11pm, open everyday

Noo Cheng Adam Road Prawn Mee
70 Zion Road, Stall 4 S247792, 11am to 11pm, open everyday

Others
Merpati Putih (for curry puff)
Operates from home
To order, call 91653577

ACKNOWLEDGEMENTS

This book was made possible by the grace of God who has provided all the resources
to make the blog a success and turn it into a book. He has done exceedingly and abundantly,
above all that I could have ever asked for or even think of asking.

I would also like to thank:
My wife, Lisa, for being my constant source of encouragement and support.

Our children, James and Megan, who wait patiently,
albeit hungrily, while I take my photographs.

All my makankakis who have been the backbone of our community:
Cactuskit, Soundman, Smart, Mien, Liverpool, PowerAunty, SCS Butter, Fashionfoodie,
Champagne, Holydrummer, Holybro, Joao, Drazarael, Jems, ijeff and many more.
This book would not have been possible without their support.

Peter A Knipp, the gourmet guru, for taking time off his busy schedule
to write the foreword of the book. He firmly believes that passion makes food good.

My publisher Epigram, especially Edmund Wee and Ruth Wan for their vision of
transforming my blog into a book, Beh Kay Yi for designing the book, as well as
Lo Sok Wan and Nikhil Charan for helping to bring the book to print.

Finally, I would also like to thank the following sponsors for their generous support:
Canon
MHC Asia
Nuffnang
Astons
Killiney Kopitiam
Karri Family Clinic
Fonterra Food Services
Prima
Core Concepts
Pek Sin Choon